CONSUMING ANGELS

CONSUMING ANGELS

*Advertising and
Victorian Women*

Lori Anne Loeb

New York   Oxford
OXFORD UNIVERSITY PRESS
1994

Oxford University Press

Oxford   New York   Toronto
Delhi   Bombay   Calcutta   Madras   Karachi
Kuala Lumpur   Singapore   Hong Kong   Tokyo
Nairobi   Dar es Salaam   Cape Town
Melbourne   Auckland   Madrid

and associated companies in
Berlin   Ibadan

Published by Oxford University Press, Inc.
200 Madison Avenue, New York, New York 10016

Library of Congress Cataloging-in-Publication Data
Loeb, Lori Anne.
Consuming angels : advertising and Victorian women / Lori Anne Loeb.
p. cm.   Includes bibliographical references and index.
ISBN 0-19-508596-5
1. Advertising—Social aspects—Great Britain—History—
19th century. 2. Social values—Great Britain—History—19th century.
3. Great Britain—Social conditions—19th century. 4. Women
consumers—Great Britain—History—19th century. I. Title.
HF5813.G7L63   1994
659.1'042'094109034—dc20   93-46094

1 3 5 7 9 8 6 4 2

Printed in the United States of America
on acid-free paper

In memory of my grandmother
Vera E. Sparfel (1898–1985)
who taught me
by her love
and
by her example

Preface

The Victorian advertisement exposes materialistic fantasies. It tells of goods that excited the imagination and of mundane realities of everyday life. It is concerned with concrete embodiments of existence, and also with chimerical images of prosperity and progress. It captivates, alarms, and amuses. Yet its potential as an historical document is unrealized. Within the pages of innumerable magazines, the advertisement seems hidden. A once lively and provocative instrument, it is ready to be uncovered, to reveal the rise of consumerism, the emergence of a materially defined cultural ideal and the transformation of a society.

In the late nineteenth century, I will argue, many middle-class Victorians gradually turned away from the puritanical focus that has been so strongly identified with the Victorian period in general. They moved toward a new and surprisingly more hedonistic emphasis that glorified democracy; the access of all not simply to political participation, but to consumer participation; the access of all to a good life, increasingly defined in material terms. The Victorian advertisement provides an iconography of this new emphasis in cultural orientation.[1]

The material redefinition of the late Victorian middle-class ideal is more than tangentially linked to an intriguing paradox illuminated by historians of the Victorian family. The Victorian home has been seen as a "walled garden," a refuge from sordid industry that both nurtured family virtue and prepared family members for confrontation with the outside world.[2] But the maintenance of the "sanctuary," argues Patricia Branca, contributed to the early demise of many a frail, unassisted "angel in the house." Moreover, even when well equipped with a retinue of experienced servants, the angel became a shrewd chancellor of the exchequer of the family purse.[3] Domestic economy literature analyzed by J. A. Banks in *Prosperity and Parenthood* suggests that middle-class angels were voracious consumers, who sustained a keen interest in household management.[4] These two views of the Victorian home, as temple of virtue and center of consumption, seem irreconcilable, and yet they underpin most interpretations of Victorian culture.

Curiously, the simple material abundance of the Victorian middle-class world has received little historical attention. Material culture studies have focused on the realities of everyday life of the working class.[5] Studies of objects owned by the prosperous have been preoccupied with aesthetics and style rather than the object as embodiment of culture. Studies of Victorian interiors have stressed opulence.[6] Historians of the industrial revolution have concentrated on mass production rather than mass consumption.[7] All the major studies of British advertising[8] focus on the emergence of advertising as a business. None deals more than marginally with the advertisement itself as a carrier of culture.

In this book I will use Victorian advertisements as historical documents in order to explore late Victorian cultural ideals. But I do not argue that the Victorian advertisement provides a simple reflection of Victorian reality. Recognizing that consumers often do not want to see life as it really is, advertisers depict fantasy, ideals, life as it ought to be. Advertisers, further, are driven inexorably by the desire to sell goods. Finally, the class and social characteristics of advertising agents influences their depiction of social reality.

T. R. Nevett, the leading historian of the Victorian advertising agency, identifies London's early advertising agents as male black-coated workers.[9] Since the late 1700s the function of the British advertising agents had been mostly administrative: they provided information about newspapers and they negotiated the price and insertion of advertisements. Only a few wrote copy. Then, during the last quarter of the nineteenth century, as lavishly illustrated advertisements became more common, advertising agencies installed art departments. The advertising agent assumed creative control. Male agents paid attention to the demonstrable characteristics of a predominantly female market, but, unconsciously or not, they inevitably incorporated their masculine biases and preconceptions into their advertisements. The Victorian advertisement may reflect three determining factors: the consumer, the agent, and the product. But as it becomes part of a visual and verbal vocabulary, it may even indirectly and unconsciously shape as well as reflect popular perceptions.[10]

Each of these factors is considered in an analysis based on a qualitative and quantitative examination of over 250,000 advertisements. Many are from the John Johnson Collection of Printed Ephemera, a collection, held at the Bodleian Library, which contains hundreds of advertisements, yet has never been explored by an historian of advertising. Other advertisements are drawn from a range of women's magazines, home journals, general interest magazines, sporting magazines and the religious press— *Queen, The Lady, Lady's Pictorial, Home Chat, Illustrated London News, Sphere, Illustrated Sporting and Dramatic News, Christian Age, Family Circle, Hand and Heart*. I have concentrated on print advertisements that appeared mainly between 1880–1914. Advertisements during this period were usually illustrated and relatively unencumbered by editorial conventions, developments that made them richer cultural artifacts than early unillustrated advertisements. Further, it may be argued that there is a cultural coherence to the period between 1880–1914, which in most schemes of periodization sets it apart from the mid-Victorian years. I refer to the period between 1880–1914 loosely as late Victorian, although clearly it encompasses the Edwardian years as well.

In the absence of historical conventions for evaluating advertisements, all advertisements were subjected first to a frequency content analysis that grouped advertisements according to product type, setting, sex roles, age depiction, and marketing strategies. This preliminary quantitative survey provided a foundation for the more substantive qualitative analysis that is the focus of this book. Painterly images; pictorial conventions; artistic, literary, and religious symbolism; historical allusions; repetitive poses, dress, settings, or actions; and social themes were all considered. Analysis of these patterns was informed by an appreciation of marketing strategy, the limitations of technology, the interaction of text and illustration, cognitive and affective response, and the demands of commercial convention. This sort of cultural reading does not depend on a doctrinaire commitment to a particular interpretation of one or even of several advertisements.

Ultimately the Victorian advertisement emerges as a graphic depiction of the deepest materialistic desires of the Victorian middle class. While it illuminates the material reality of Victorian middle-class existence, it reveals Victorian hopes, fears, and aspirations. It helps to dictate the Victorian paraphernalia of gentility. In doing so, it charts the cultivation of a commercial and hedonistic definition of late Victorian middle-class ideals, an orientation relevant to our understanding of Victorian culture.

I WOULD LIKE to thank Richard J. Helmstadter, who, as my supervisor at the University of Toronto, led me to study advertisements. Without his advice, discerning judgment, and support this book would not have been possible. Trevor Lloyd read critically an earlier draft. R. K. Webb has provided thoughtful commentary and encouragement; he has inspired me in ways I cannot express. I have been privileged to work with wonderful collections of Victorian periodicals at Robarts Library at the University of Toronto and at the British Library at Colindale. The staff of the John Johnson Collection at the Bodleian Library, especially its curator, Julie Anne Lambert, provided incomparable professionalism and warmth. Gordon Phillips of the History of Advertising Trust offered invaluable assistance. Funding from the Social Sciences and Humanities Research Council of Canada helped support some of the research. Nancy Lane at Oxford University Press has been a wonderful editor. Finally, I should also like to thank my parents, for their love and for their endurance.

Columbia, S.C.   L.A.L.
December 1993

Contents

CONSUMING ANGELS

1

Victorian Consumer Culture

By the late nineteenth century, Victorian optimism, bred by industrial accomplishment, was tempered with anxiety. Labor troubles, poverty, foreign competition, and the agricultural depression were grim realities. And yet, for all the dislocation and anomie wrought by industrialism and the sobering developments of the last decades of the century, the middle class especially welcomed an improvement in its standard of living. However mythical or psychological the Great Depression may have been, the middle class, with careful planning and budgeting, seemed determined to perpetuate an invigorating sense of material possibility.

Accordingly, the English middle-class family selected an astounding paraphernalia of gentility. Room upon room in the Victorian home became cluttered with heavily carved furniture; pottery, paintings, and photographs competed for space on every wall and table surface; flocked and floral wallpapers, luxurious Oriental carpets and intricate lace curtains provided a visual assault of pattern and texture.[1] Amid so many things, human figures must have sometimes seemed insignificant, dwarfed by the commanding presence of their material surroundings. This very material emphasis of the Victorians reflected the assimilation by the middle class of a hedonistic ethos.

To be middle class[2] implied a moderately affluent income (generally £150 to £1,000 per annum), freedom from manual labor outside and inside the home, and the employment of domestic servant(s).[3] But for much of the Victorian period, middle-class status also connoted particular habits and virtues. At mid-century, most of all, the Victorian middle class,

while scarcely homogenous,[4] was associated with high standards of morality, education, and refinement, "gentleness and [a] desire to be thought
different from the common herd,"[5] with a puritanical focus on thrift, self-
help, and diligence. But in the late nineteenth century the middle class,
whom advertisers explicitly targeted, shed this puritanical focus for a more
hedonistic emphasis.

The new cultural direction approached hedonism, seemingly a strange
term to apply to any part of the Victorian period, not in the sense of moral
abandon (which hedonism sometimes but not always connotes), but rather in its pursuit of pleasure and especially the satisfactions gained through
material objects. Colin Campbell describes this unexpected feature of the
nineteenth century as "self-illusory hedonism" and has linked it to the
Romantic ethic. He claims that a Romantic ethic evolved in the eighteenth
century from the pietistic strain of Puritanism. It involved sensitivity to
pleasure, intensity of emotion, an estrangement from utilitarian rational
society, an aching sense of pleasure lost. This Romantic ethic supported a
restless pattern of consumption in the nineteenth century.[6] Modern consumerism became characterized by consumption of luxuries, either superfluous goods or sensuous pleasures. Consumption of these luxuries, says
Campbell, is motivated by a Romantic "self-illusory hedonism" in which
the consumer desires a novel rather than a familiar product. This enables
him to project an idealized pleasure. Each purchase leaves the consumer
disillusioned and determined to satisfy the longings generated by daydreams and fantasies. I will draw on Campbell's characterization of self-
illusory hedonism throughout. The cultural pattern it embodies, I suggest,
may hinge on concrete historical realities.

For much of the century, puritanical energies had often been directed
toward achieving political and religious equality. The repeal of the Test and
Corporation Acts, the abolition of compulsory church rates, the reform of
marriage laws, the provision of civil registration of births, marriages, and
deaths, and the abolition of religious tests at Oxford and Cambridge
removed major Nonconformist civil disabilities. Gladstonian Liberalism
provided the middle class and Nonconformists with a powerful political
voice. The First, Second, and Third Reform Acts broadly extended the
franchise. Middle-class interests, of course, were not always democratiz-
ing. Substantial Nonconformist support for the repeal of the Corn Laws,
for example, clearly reveals the political force of middle-class economic
self-interest. Despite the middle-class defence of class-specific goals in
particular instances, the first three quarters of the nineteenth century reveal a considerable middle-class absorption in the drive toward religious
and political equality. When political democracy seemed virtually a *fait
accompli*, the middle-class passion for self-help and self-improvement began
to be channelled away from political ends. With new and unprecedented
fervor, the middle class embraced material goals. A sense of unease about
material acquisitiveness remained, but it was cushioned by contextualizing

consumerism within radical democratic traditions of shared wealth and utopian splendor.

Mass consumption, and especially the acquisition of goods that conferred status, was not necessarily behavior that legitimized and stabilized the hierarchial order. The lure of material things that could define class was most profitable in an open social and political structure; the product with snobbish appeal that connoted the taste and affluence of its purchaser could find a market much broader than the aristocracy once democracy assumed a material as well as a political dimension. Status and the luxury goods associated with status were potentially available to all in a democratic society. One of the pleasures, a fantasy dangled before the consumer was the fulfilment of the democratic dream, at first politically and now materially. Luxury goods were not so much a reflection of hardened class lines as the ultimate, even if illusory, pleasure of an increasingly democratized society.

As the department store was born and the multiple shop sprang into existence, the advertisement also became an increasingly visible feature of Victorian consumer culture. Between 1850 and 1880 a combination of factors—new techniques of illustration, the recognition of an expansive middle-class market, the rise of the press, the abolition of the advertising duty, and the professionalization of technical and creative assistance—produced an unparalleled advertising craze.[7] At first, according to Virginia Berridge, advertisements were uncommon in the middle-class press mainly because they seemed to lack respectability.[8] Advertisements were thought to advance fraudulent claims; to promote products of poor quality; to disrupt the aesthetic tone of a refined publication. The advertisement was a necessary evil associated with inexpensive papers. Accordingly, floridly illustrated and boldly captioned advertisements became accessible first to thousands of working-class people. In working-class periodicals advertisements marketed a wide variety of products—condiments, furniture, an array of patent medicines. In doing so, they provided fledgling working-class newspapers with essential financial assistance. But gradually, the middle-class press, confronted with pressure from advertisers, the promise of financial gain, and the attraction of political independence,[9] succumbed to the display advertisement.

In the periodical press women, the clear audience for most nineteenth-century advertisements, encountered all the puffery and paraphernalia that a Victorian consumer society could supply. They found advertisements for the latest fashions, for companies that could furnish a house "of any magnitude" in less than a week,[10] for cocoas, beef extracts, and lemonades. They read advertisements that promised to lessen household labor with sewing machines, manglers, and knife cleaners. They found illustrations for trusses, respirators, and artificial limbs; advertisements for myriad pills, tonics, and syrups. They were tempted by advertisements for lavender colognes, almond skin creams, and walnut hair dyes; by Swiss clocks,

Figure 1-1. Keating's Powder, *Pick-Me-Up,* 1894. (Robarts Library.)

Brussels carpets, and Venetian blinds. Children pored over illustrations of dolls, trains, model engines, "conjuring tricks," and dissolving views; adults studied advertisements for cruises to the land of the midnight sun or railway excursions to the "sunshine and bracing air" of Bournemouth.[11] The print advertisement reflected the diversity of the Victorian material world. But it also inspired Victorian material fantasies.

It employed evocative illustrations. Keating's Powder featured cameos of sleeping children; Scott's Emulsion pictured hysterical women fainting before distressed husbands; images of consumptive war veterans alternated with illustrations of mythical figures wielding shields in the battle against disease.[12] Cocoa companies portrayed impressive factories or exotic plantations. Biscuit manufacturers favored illustrations of tea parties or children's schoolroom antics. Soap companies attracted consumers with nostalgic images of Elizabethan courtiers or pictures of provocatively disheveled women. Soldiers sold everything from paint to cigarettes. The late nineteenth-century magazine advertisement possessed an unprecedented visual potency that made it almost as important to nineteenth-century culture as the television commercial is to our own time.

Visual interest was often matched by verbal excess. Hyperbole caused many observers to denounce the print advertisement as "puffery." Pulvermacher's Galvanic Chain-Bands, Belts, and Pocket Batteries suggested that by making "electricity perfectly self-applicable" they contained "the embryo of a universal remedy."[13] Phosferine advertised

its world wide reputation as the only safe reliable phosphoric remedy for permanent cure of Brain Wreckage, Paralysis, Sleeplessness, Harassing Dreams, Premature Decay of Vital Power and all Functional and Diseased Conditions of the System . . . It cures dyspepsia, lung and heart disease. Cures kidney and liver complaints. Cures consumption.[14]

Advertisements that tested credulity alternated with sensational headlines such as "Baby on the Battlefield" or "Do Not Let Your Baby Die." The Victorian consumer, so recently confronted with the print advertisement on a wide scale, must have felt inundated by visual and verbal exaggeration. There were few legal constraints.[15]

Before mid-century, advertisements were small, confined to the back pages, and carried by only a few Victorian periodicals. Mostly unillustrated, they were almost always simple announcements that relied on repetition, bold headlines, and small logos. They advertised a small range of products by a few well-publicized producers. By 1880 advertisements employed stunning illustrations reproduced with meticulous care and artistry. Text was inventively persuasive, even sensational, no longer bound by the tiresome printing conventions that had dictated justified columns and uniform type. The range of advertised products expanded to reflect extensive brand-name differentiation and an increasing interest in innovation, novelty, and luxury. Between 1850–1914, as middle-class interest shifted from political democracy toward material democracy, the advertisement gradually changed from being a creature of need to being a creature of fantasy.

For many, the print advertisement was a dramatic introduction to the products of the industrial age. Here readers learned about the latest invention in waterproofing. They welcomed desiccated soups and prepared baby food. They encountered linoleum and disinfectants. They read that machines could replace "the antiquated, absurd and destructive method of washing by rubbing, brushing and boiling . . . with a nice, easy process."[16] Within the advertising sections of magazines, the increasing material acquisitiveness of the Victorian middle class is revealed.

Advertising agents explicitly stated that they were trying to reach the middle class. One trade journal explains,

> The buyers of the world are the great MIDDLE CLASS PEOPLE—the man and woman in good or fairly well-to-do circumstances. These people are the backbone of every city and every country. These are the men who have built the houses and the shops, the women and men who fill the churches and make life worth living and upon whose children rest the future of every nation under the sun. These people have ready cash, because they are continually making it and these are the people who can be reached by advertising.[17]

This perception reflected statistical fact.[18] The rise in the middle-class standard of living was conspicuous. Between 1850 and 1870 incomes for middle-class people rose as much as £100 per head. Prices during this period rose only 16%, well below the rise in incomes. The effect of rising middle-class incomes was compounded by the growth of the lower middle class (people within the income level of £100 to £200) attributed to the rise of white collar and professional employment. As middle-class incomes rose and the lower middle class expanded, there was a dramatic change in middle-class expectations of comfort. The range of satisfactions considered appropriate for civilized existence accelerated at an alarming rate. Contemporaries noted increasing consumption of servants, carriages, foreign food, dress, travel, washing, all the paraphernalia of gentility.[19]

But especially after 1870 the rise in the middle-class standard of living must be qualified. While historians have attempted to debunk the contention that a Great Depression occurred between 1873 and 1896, it may be argued that as the rate of market growth slackened and competition developed overseas in the third quarter of the nineteenth century, business did suffer a decine in confidence and expectations.[20] Amid the erosion of this confidence, prices increased for some key items that were the focus of middle-class weekly expenditure such as dairy products and meat (even though prices in general declined). At the same time, a perception at least of rising rents contributed to the middle-class belief that the cost of living was increasing. This in turn, according to J. A. Banks' well-known hypothesis, encouraged the middle class to pay special attention to the budgeting practices recommended in domestic economy manuals and to exercise family planning. But as the middle class bemoaned the high cost of living, the very popularity of the domestic economy manuals evidences their desire nonetheless to achieve middle-class standards of material affluence. It is not surprising, then, that the Victorian advertiser fervently wished to reach this segment of the market.

Moreover, advertisers accepted the adage that "the hand that rocks the cradle, is the hand that buys the boots." Because the "woman at home [represents] the power of the purse in household affairs," advertisers considered that they must attempt to reach her "at home—that is either in her domestic citadel itself or in such a surrounding area as she covers in her daily walks abroad." The woman was perceived as a careful critic. She

> reads more thoroughly than the average man; also she takes a far greater interest in advertisements than most men. Her function as chancelloress of the family exchequer makes them of practical importance to her.[21]

By 1913 one trade journal[22] speculated that

> a full 90% of advertisers have found it or are finding it, advisable to leave the man practically out of account altogether when designing their announcements.[23]

Advertisers perceived middle-class women as the agents of material acquisition.[24]

Reaching the middle-class market often necessitated a considerable capital investment. As early as 1842 Holloway's Pills, an extensively advertised remedy, spent £5,000 on advertising.[25] By the 1880s, Pears' Soap, renowned for its "Bubbles" portrait and a number of memorable slogans, allocated £30,000 to £40,000 per annum for advertising.[26] By 1914 a Royal Commission Report estimated that over £2,000,000 was invested annually in patent medicine advertising alone.[27] Ironically, Victorian advertisements emphasized economy. They attempted to cushion the expense of material acquisitiveness with promises of "Great Savings," "Special Bargains," and "Values Unobtainable Elsewhere."[28] Certain types of products—silver, clothes, tea, and wine—featured price lists as a conventional and integral part of their advertisements. If the price itself was not attractive, an advertisement might focus on economy nonetheless by listing the special services included in the price of the merchandise. Firms offered "goods, carriages paid to any part of the U.K."[29] and free sketches or catalogues by post. Under the guise of saving money, the consumer was being tempted to spend.

Extensive stock displayed in spacious showrooms offered the consumer new variety and selection. Furniture and clothing manufacturers were especially likely to emphasize the availability of a large quantity of goods. Atkinson's Furniture promised the "largest stock in the U.K.,"[30] while Christian and Rathbone Mercers suggested that their stock was both "extensive and recherché."[31] Jewelers emphasized variety by picturing a large assortment of goods in crowded, illustrated advertisements. Retailers stressed the size of their shops and the magnitude of their displays. Smiths Furniture, for example, advertised "premises containing twenty-five shops and warehouses which are the largest and most complete in the U.K."[32] Alternately, the focus on quantity in the Victorian advertisement shifted to large yearly sales. Colman's Mustard purported to be "the staple food of more than 300 million people"[33]; Beecham's boasted "over 6 million boxes [of pills] sold annually."[34] At every turn, the advertisement seemed to emphasize the vast scale of industrial mass production: it seemed to tempt the consumer with promises of endless material wealth.

By the 1880s advertisers emphasized a "special appointment to the principal sovereigns of Europe,"[35] the opinions of leading medical men, or the favor of renowned beauties, opera singers, or actresses. Adelina Patti endorsed Pears' Soap; the *Lancet* lent its favor to Savory and Moore Baby Food and Cavé Corsets[36]; and editors of religious magazines supported St. Jacob's Oil. Even laundry starch seemed more intriguing if it was "used in the Royal Laundry."[37] Lists of medals and awards won at international fairs and exhibits similarly attested to the positive judgment of experts. Testimonials from the famous or highly esteemed were mirrored by a plethora of testimonials from happy consumers. The same product could be used by the famous as well as the most humble householder. The acquisition of consumer goods by rich and poor alike became a significant agent of democratization.

Innovation was an important selling mechanism. Corsets were suddenly "prepared by a new and scientific process,"[38] hair lotions became "the latest triumph of chromatic chemistry,"[39] and even Bovril advertised that it retained a "consulting chemist."[40] Domestic machines began to promise not just simplicity and durability, but the "newest improvement."[41] While established products emphasized their improvement through "scientific process," new products stressed their scientific origin. Aertex underwear was warmer because "cellular cloth is composed of small cells in which air is enclosed and warmed by the heat of the body.[42] Formamint Medicine was effective because it benefited from "remarkable experiments by leading scientists."[43] Material plenty made the fruits of science broadly accessible.

The advertisement became both a mirror and instrument of the social ideal. The advertisement suggested that with the acquisition of creams to whiten the complexion, fringes to improve the coiffure, and corsets to mold the female figure it was possible to create the illusion of the "perfect lady," a beacon of Victorian affluence. The acquisition of domestic machines would facilitate the characteristic middle-class pursuit of leisure. The acquisition of the accoutrements of class from biscuits to baby food, from carpets to crystal, from pianos to pottery would foster the appearance of the middle-class domestic environment. By the late nineteenth century, the attainment of the social ideal was determined not only by the cultivation of culturally desirable habits; attitudes or virtues, but by the acquisition of material things as well. Gentility came to be expressed in the Victorian print advertisement almost exclusively in material terms.

The "perfect lady" was commercially apotheosized through her identification with distant, historical ideals. Swathed in robes, barefoot, and crowned with laurel wreaths, the advertised Victorian woman bore little resemblance to the real-life version. The Grecian figures who wielded shields in battles against disease or played Justice in the interests of Aspinall's Enamel presented an aggrandized portrait of feminine power that was notably more aggressive and sexual than the Victorian "angel in the

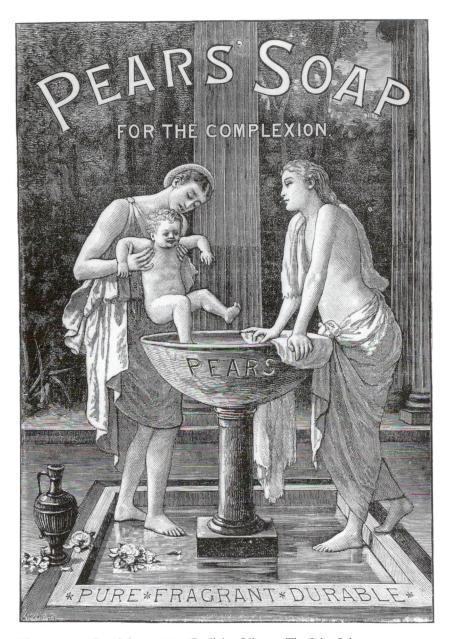

Figure 1-2. Pears' Soap, 1884. (Bodleian Library: The John Johnson Collection; Soap 4. Reprinted by permission.)

house." In contrast, the advertisement presented a somewhat one-dimensional ideal of "robust manhood."[44] Men were depicted riding bicycles, playing tennis, scaling mountains. Most of all, they were likely to be soldiers, riding toward the front, on the battlefield, or stoically braving primitive camp conditions. Yet the male voice was rarely an important

feature of the Victorian advertisement. Acquiring the goods for consumption, it seems, was socially perceived as a feminine task.

Babies sold wholesome products from soap to cocoa. Whether floating in a basket amid the bulrushes or staring wide-eyed at a kitten, the commercial view of the baby praised redemptive innocence. Even older chil-

dren were a source of joy. Brooke's Soap hoped to "brighten the home like
a child's laughter"[45] and Peek Frean capitalized on the appeal of little girls
in schoolroom settings. Stern Victorian discipline is scarcely ever evidenced in the commercial view of the child. The older child is above all a
lively and impish troublemaker. He hides from his exasperated Nanny at
bath time, so disfigures the floor that his parents must cover it with Treloar
Carpeting, and races into the sea in a carefully tailored sailor suit.

For all of its members, the Victorian home provided cosiness, a pure
atmosphere, "cheerful and inviting warmth."[46] It was a center of "attraction"[47] "after the toil and turmoil of the day."[48] Domestic economy literature suggests that this atmosphere could be fostered by daughters like
sunbeams and mothers like angels. But advertisements argue for more
direct means of attainment. Simply by buying a piano, a gramophone, or a
stove, the home was instantly transformed into a hub of warmth and
familial entertainment. No moral redemption was required. However, the
advertised view of the family sometimes suggested that the home was far
from an oasis of tranquillity. The parent, especially the mother, constantly
fretted about her child's ability to confront a competitive world.

> Two babies are born on the same day. They are both beautiful, bright-eyed
> boys and yet whereas one is always the centre of an admiring crowd, the other
> is hardly noticed. This is a source of grief and surprise to the mother; but has
> she ever thought whether she herself is entirely free from blame? Are her
> baby's clothes as spotless as they might be?[49]

As much as a mother worried about her sons, raising a daughter seemed
even more problematic. One advertisement asked, "What to do with our
Daughters?" It suggested that

> if daughters would learn to make their own clothes instead of paying dress-
> makers' bills which often far exceed the cost of the material dealt with, and if
> they would become more domesticated, they might be a help rather than a
> hindrance to their parents.[50]

The home was rife with anxiety.

Advertisements preyed on consumer fears such as disease or infant death.
Bovril promised to be "Liquid Life,"[51] while Cadbury's Cocoa could
give "staying power and [impart] new life and vigour to growing children
and those of delicate constitution."[52] Hudson's Soap enabled "Sanitary
Washing at Home." Through its use "All risk of contagion with infected
clothes at laundries or where washing is put out is entirely avoided."[53]
Pears', on the other hand, offered a "Caution to Parents" about soap
"commonly adulterated with the most pernicious ingredients."[54] Keating's
Medicine used the caption "No fear now" over the picture of a sleeping
child. Fear of premature infant death was especially apt to be sensationalized. Mellin's Food featured gruesome pictures of children in various

stages of starvation. Children were described as "wasting fast," and dramatic testimonials predicted that a child without Mellin's Food "will not last long."[55] "Raw Milk" was portrayed as "one of the Most Dangerous Foods . . . Milk that has been improperly sterilized is such a dangerous food that those who allow it to be served to their families take a great responsibility."[56]

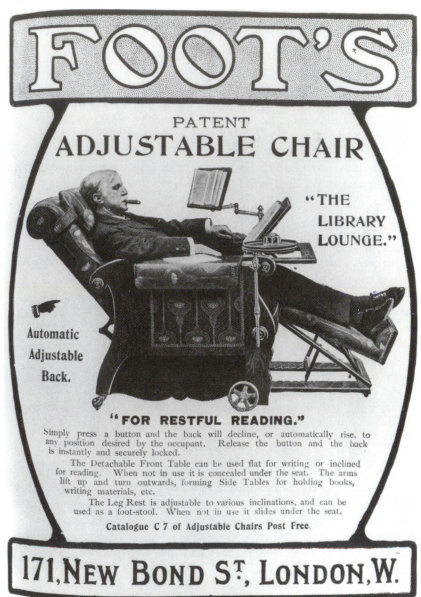

Figure 1-4. Foot's Adjustable Chair, *Illustrated London News*, 1910. (Robarts Library.)

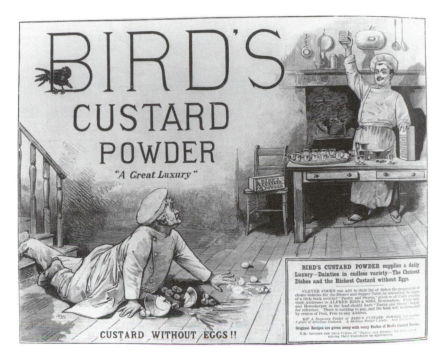

Figure 1-5. Bird's Custard Powder, *Illustrated London News*, 1889. (Robarts Library.)

Progress was equated with the reduction of toil. The ultimate ideal of prosperity was portrayed in an advertisement for Foot's Adjustable Chairs. "The Library Lounge" pictured an older gentleman, smoking a cigar, feet up, reading a book.[57] The image embodied leisure, freedom from care and from the necessity of labor. Any number of products could be advanced by their ability to reduce toil. Liebig Extract asked, "If your kitchen drudgery/You'd greatly lighten, come to me—/And when you've found your toil made light,/ You'll be like me, a Liebigite."[58] Bird's Custard Powder was "a great luxury" because it reduced toil by making "custard without eggs."[59] Freedom from toil would be the "stepping stone to happiness,"[60] to a life of leisure in a literary chair, clustered around a piano, sipping lemonade by the tennis courts.

Political democratization had an important material concomitant which, like political emancipation, extended benefits beyond the narrow confines of aristocracy. "The main idea of [the late nineteenth-century advertisement] is . . . making life easier. This ought to be a great recommendation in this nineteenth century when we all want to save ourselves from toil and use our energies in pleasure."[61] The "use [of] our energies in pleasure" became the commercially defined middle-class ideal.

2

Commercial Interpretations of the Domestic Ideology

A woman, eyes shielded from the sun by her bonnet, sleeves rolled up past her elbows, and dress carefully protected by a pristine white apron, does her laundry. Her arms look strong and capable as she wrings a garment into a sturdy wooden bucket. Her attention is diverted toward two young children, a boy and a girl, who peer over the sides of the laundry tub to blow at a toy boat floating alongside the laundry. The woman smiles benignly at the children at play. Another woman emerges in the foreground. With a broad back, one arm bent and the other carrying a bucket, she presents a stereotypical image of the washerwoman. Behind them, a basket of laundry lies carefully folded. A Chinese man draws water from the well. The garden is bordered by a white picket fence. A single sunflower rises above it. Two doves circle a church tower in the background. Overhead, dark clouds have opened up to reveal a piercing ray of light and a winged angel. Incongruously, an oversized box of Sinclair's Cold Water Soap is slashed across the scene. The caption reads, "Saves Money, Saves Labour, Saves Time, Saves Fuel . . . the Family Wash without the Misery of a Steamy House."

This advertisement, widely reprinted in the middle-class press in 1885,[1] draws on a heavily romanticized view of domestic toil. Clearly, the manufacturer intended the consumer to imagine that washing would be an easy, indeed a relaxing and pleasurable task with Sinclair's Soap. He hoped to associate his product with positive imagery—angelic children, the wholesome outdoors, peaceful doves, even heavenly angels.

But this advertisement also conveys, along with other suggestive

Figure 2-1. Sinclair's Cold Water Soap, *Family Circle of the Christian World,* 1885. (British Library.)

themes, a distinctive view of Victorian domestic life. It is not intended to
provide a realistic portrayal of an average garden. Few gardens are presided
over by angels and circling doves. But the advertisement does communicate significant cultural values and their implications for the family. The
Romantic picturesque setting, accented with Victorian chinoiserie, hark-
ens back to a golden age before smokestacks darkened the Victorian horizon. The family is physically contained within a walled garden (here in the
form of a picket fence), far removed from the sordid world of industry. The
wholesome purity associated with the English rural tradition is suggested
by a few stray chickens. Family life, as portrayed here, is dominated by
feminine solicitude and protective competence. Note the muscular arms of
the two washerwomen. Above all, the family endeavors to pursue leisure.
The product will "save time . . . save labour." It will free the family from
drudgery, liberate its members for the enjoyment of innocent pleasure,
exemplified by the children at play.

The view of family life forwarded by this and by other advertisements
may contribute to our understanding of the complex dynamics of Victorian home life. Historical studies of the Victorian family have increased
markedly since 1975 when Anthony Wohl observed that "the attention so
far devoted by family historians to the Victorian family is in inverse ratio
to the importance and esteem in which the Victorians themselves held it."[2]
Since then many historians have advanced a middle-class domestic ideology derived from the opinions of Victorian social critics, prominent literary
figures, and evangelicals and from a wealth of prescriptive domestic economy literature that flourished especially after 1850.

The Domestic Ideology

Catherine Hall and Leonore Davidoff have argued persuasively that from
the 1820s the evangelical belief in the universality of sin and the need for
constant struggle against it contributed to a redefinition of the function of
the home and the role of women in middle-class Victorian society. The
home increasingly was regarded as a forum in which members daily bat-
tled sin and prepared to confront the dangerous temptations of the competitive marketplace.[3] Industrial capitalism heightened the separation of
economic and social functions. The family became the center for nurturing
virtue and emotion. According to Edward Shorter, the egotism of the
marketplace, transferred to family life, encouraged the family to look inward.[4] Moreover, the swiftness of change in industrial society increased
the social value of a stable home life.

Confronted with the pressures of evangelicalism, market capitalism, and
rapid social change, the home was practically deified. It became a sanctuary, a temple of virtue, "a divine institution."[5] As much as it was an inner
world unsullied by contact with worldly vice, it was also a springboard to
the world outside. Within its haven (Houghton's "walled garden"), the
individual prepared to enter and to influence society. Ruskin, whom histo-

rians have widely regarded as a principal ideologue of the late Victorian domestic ideology, wrote in *Sesame and Lilies,*

> [Home] is the place of peace; the shelter, not only from all injury, but from all terror, doubt and division. In so far as it is not this, it is not home; so far as the anxieties of the outer life penetrate into it and the inconsistency-minded, unknown, unloved or hostile society of the outer world is allowed by either husband or wife to cross the threshold, it ceases to be home: it is then only a part of that outer world which you have roofed over and lighted a fire in. But so far as it is a sacred place, a vestal temple, a temple of the hearth watched over by household Gods, before whose faces none may come but those for whom they can receive with love—so far as it is this and the roof and fire are types only of a nobler shade and light—shade as of the rock in a weary land and light as of the Pharaohs in the stormy sea—so far it vindicates the name and fulfils the praise of home.[6]

The "temple of the hearth," "the vestibule of heaven"[7] depended on the redemptive presence of a "household God," an "angel in the house"—immortalized by Coventry Patmore's famous poem. The woman was expected to act as a moral regenerator. Closeted within the sanctuary, this angel could nurture purity and dependence; she could retain her asexuality and child-like simplicity. Her cheery prettiness and lady-like accomplishments would make her a dutiful companion. Her innocence and helplessness would touch the heart of the most wayward. Her self-sacrifice and deference would assist the needy. Her example and soft reproach would be an enduring moral guide.

> She must be endearingly, incorruptibly good: instinctively, infallibly wise—wise, not for self-development, but for self-renunciation: wise not that she might set herself above her husband, but that she may never fall from his side; wise, not with that narrowness of insolent and loveless pride, but with the passionate gentleness of an infinitely valuable but infinitely applicable modesty of service.[8]

The woman was the focus of family life.

The apotheosis of the angel in the house was partly an expression of a gendered definition of separate spheres. A woman being more delicate, fragile, reserved, yet virtuous, loving, and pretty was properly confined to the household sphere where her gentleness and nurturing were best employed. Domestic economy literature explicitly condoned this opinion. *Cassell's Household Guide* advises, "It is there [the household] that the fruits of man's labour are ultimately enjoyed, there that woman finds her chief sphere of duty, as the helpmate of man."[9] Man being grand, forceful, aggressive, pursued the sphere of business. With the growth of suburbs, travel to and from work gave physical expression to the social distance between the public male world and the private sphere of the household. While the principal duties of the woman within the domestic sphere—

looking after her family and setting a good example—were socially valued, indeed denoted moral superiority, her ostensible ineptitude in the economically rewarding male sphere of action made her, in Mrs. Ellis' phrase, "a relative creature."

By 1850 the rising middle-class standard of living made it increasingly difficult to shield the domestic temple from the "commercial chariot"[10] of market capitalism. New prosperity for the first time gave many "angels" money to spend on things that were not necessities. They turned for advice to an expansive range of domestic economy manuals.[11] Such books usually purported that the modern woman had lost the art of housekeeping and servant management. They advocated rational planning and the maintenance of daily accounts. Such manuals probably assuaged some anxieties and fed others. J. A. Banks in *Prosperity and Parenthood* (1954) argues that the increasing standard of living meant an increase in incomes, but also an expansion of the range of satisfactions considered appropriate for civilized existence. He quotes a correspondent to *The Times* in 1858 who debated whether or not it was possible to live a genteel life on £300 per year:

> A young man must plunge into married life at full gallop; begin where his father ended. He must have a house replete with elegancies, with plate, pier glasses, pictures and all the paraphernalia of a drawing room of fashion and he must be prepared to give an extensive entertainment once or twice a year to all with whom he is on speaking terms; or if he will not do this, if he will not be bound by such conventionalism, he must submit to sink his status in society and be considered a plebian and a boor by his former associates.[12]

After 1850, Banks argues, the middle class complained about the rising cost of living. Rents were rising, but especially an expansion in standards, evidenced by contemporary testimony and the recommendations of prescriptive literature, required additional expenditure. Proportionately more money was needed to rise in the social scale of domestic consumption. The drive for social esteem, according to Banks, was expressed through the display of "a paraphernalia of gentility"—servants, special clothing, more frequent washing, fine food, imported wine, tasteful decoration, and above all by the maintenance of feminine leisure.

The transformation of the perfect wife into the perfect lady by mid-century was a crucial mark of middle-class status. At the beginning of the nineteenth century, Martha Vicinus describes the perfect wife as an active participant in the family who fulfilled a number of vital tasks, especially related to child-rearing.[13] Through caring for children, purchasing and preparing food, making clothes, the woman indirectly provided economic support. In contrast, the perfect lady of the mid and late nineteenth century appeared ornamental, leisured, and expensive. She cultivated a refined appearance and superficial accomplishments; servants and nannies relieved her of her economic functions. Her life of leisure was punctuated by social occasions rather than family responsibilities. The very existence of the middle-class lady was evidence of prosperity. Her maintenance was the ultimate form of conspicuous consumption.

The perfect lady stereotype, though, may distort reality. Patricia Branca argues in *Silent Sisterhood* that in order to create the appearance of leisure most middle-class women who struggled within the £150 to £300 range needed to be functional and responsible.[14] If the manly economic ideal was the effective direction of production: the womanly ideal was the beneficent ordering of consumption.[15] The woman became a prudent financial manager and often an employer of servants, whose varying levels of experience and ability might necessitate training and supervision. The woman, in effect, exchanged the physical drain of child care and cleaning for the mental anguish of managing a household in a manner that would convey family standards and values to the outside world. Victorian ladies quoted the dictum "the eye of the mistress will do more work than both her hands."[16] Domestic economy manuals urged, "Money is of small worth without the brains to know what to do with it and the knowledge of housekeeping is the training of a queen."[17] A husband, after all, would recognize "the value of the angel in the house who is not too angelic to know what goes on in the kitchen, down to the very drains."[18] "The wife's incompetent management and irritability" would bring "misery . . . upon the married state" and "ill-health is sure to follow."[19] To "retain [her] husband's love with a deeper affection than when in its youthful freshness," the Victorian woman was instructed to "cultivate every winning charm of mind and manner—every grace of proper attire," but she was also warned to "let [her] household management be such as shall ensure comfort, pleasure and recreation."[20]

The historical interpretation of the Victorian domestic ideology delineates several themes—the home as refuge and walled garden; the home as a separate sphere; the home as a central arena for the display of paraphernalia of gentility; the home as a prime expression of a dualistic, but defining role for the woman as redemptive angel and prudent household manager. In the commercial forum these themes acquire altered nuances and sometimes even radically deviate from conventional interpretations.

Commercial Interpretations

The Walled Garden

The commercial interpretation suggests that the home was indeed a refuge and a separate sphere. Within this sphere men were increasingly marginalized and women assumed a role of protective competence and solicitude.

The contrast between depictions of families in the mid-nineteenth-century and late nineteenth-century advertisements throws the characteristics of the late nineteenth-century advertisement into sharp relief. In 1865 an illustration for Serjeant & Co. Tea features a rustic gathering outside a simple cottage.[21] Attention is directed toward the father who playfully

SERJEANT & COMPY.,
Tea, Coffee & Colonial Merchants,
29, GRAFTON STREET,
CORNER OF MOOR STREET, SOHO,
And at 31, CLERKENWELL CLOSE.

Figure **2-2.** Serjeant & Co. Tea, 1865. (Bodleian Library: The John Johnson Collection, Tea & Grocery Papers I. Reprinted by permission.)

hoists a young child above his head. The casual warmth of the domestic scene is suggested by the father's hat strewn on the ground and the family dog leaping at his heels. The mother stands before the door of the family home, arms outstretched in welcome. A small girl, tentatively extends a posy, as a nurse hovers protectively behind her. The young boy looks away, but his identification with his father is indicated by their close proximity. A large shovel is poised on his shoulder and his small back is bent by the weight of the sack he carries. Both his posture and his action foreshadow the future burdens of his male role. He may well have carried his father's tools back from work. The door to the cottage beckons. A wooden fence and a clinging vine trailing over the doorway suggest the protective atmosphere of the family home. This advertisement portrays the centrality of the paterfamilias to the mid-Victorian home and, through its representation of family roles, suggests the polarity of male responsibility and female nurturing.

The working-class characteristics of the Serjeant advertisement—the humble cottage, the sack of tools, the simple dress of the protagonists—do not diminish its broad appeal. The rural idyll was inextricably linked with the Victorian domestic ideology. Mrs. Ellis, whose books helped to prescribe the domestic behavior of that "interesting and influential class . . . the middle rank of society in Great Britain,"[22] openly commends the rural life. She writes in the *Mothers of England*,

> If I were asked to point out the happiest situation on earth, I believe I should say—that in which children enjoy a free life in the country shared with affectionate brothers and sisters and watched over by kind and judicious parents.[23]

The ideals of countryside and home seemed complementary. The rural life promised happiness. The village evoked timeless virtues—unity, tradition, solidity, the myth of Old England. Both became essential constructs of the English national identity,[24] which persisted long after the popularity of Mrs. Ellis, as Martin Wiener has demonstrated.[25] The image of the dependable worker and his devoted wife fused concepts of home and country. Like paintings of this genre (e.g., *The Sinews of Old England*), the Serjeant advertisement enshrines a timeless simplicity and virtue that transcends class. Family virtues, like material goods, were accessible to everyone.

Specific aspects of the Victorian domestic ideology found clear commercial expression. Advertisers were anxious, for example, to promote the separation of the spheres. "The mothers of England" should endeavor to "diminish [the] burdens [of the family] and [to] increase their own happiness by adding immeasurably to that of their little ones." "Harmony in every home,"[26] though, would ultimately be achieved when the children are "the companions of the [father's] pastimes" and "the time of relaxation [can pass] merrily by."[27] The role of "every Father" was to "banish crying from [the] house, [to] turn tears into smiles and [to] make . . . home the seat of jocund mirth." Advertisers, from the mid-Victorian period, saw the home as a center of the cultivation of virtue, diligence, and self-help, but their increasing interest in "jocund mirth" gradually shaped the commercial interpretation of late Victorian middle-class values.

In contrast to the mid-Victorian commercial image, late Victorian commercial depictions of the family rarely include a paternal figure. For exam-

Figure 2-3. Cadbury's Cocoa, *Illustrated London News*, 1900. (Robarts Library.)

ple, an advertisement for Cadbury's Cocoa features a mother as the dominant focus in a triangular composition.[28] The largest figure in the scene, she patiently helps her child drink from a cup. An old woman sits hunched at a table holding her own cocoa, part of the family, yet removed from the central action. The triangular configuration causes our eyes to move constantly from figure to figure, enhancing an impression of the tightness of

Figure 2-4.   Bile Beans for Biliousness, 1902. (Bodleian Library: The John Johnson Collection, Patent Medicine 5. Reprinted by permission.)

the relationship. A window provides a glimpse of lilies, symbols of the innocence of the family and the regenerative link of the three generations. The father is absent. The women on their own form a self-contained and curiously complete unit. An advertisement for a patent medicine in 1902 echoes the suggestion of maternal dominance and paternal absence.[29] A woman concentrates on needlework. Seated at her feet, a daughter, work basket in her lap, is similarly occupied. A toddler attends to her dolls, a suggestion of the maternal role she will one day assume. But the father is obscured. Only his legs are visible as he reads the newspaper. Behind them, as in the Cadbury's advertisement, a window reveals a garden; potted plants on the window sill suggest the hothouse atmosphere of the family. Such vignettes imply that by 1900 the separation of the spheres had reached its fullest expression. The father's importance in the sphere of action physically distanced him from the gentleness of the domestic sphere. His commanding presence, amplified in mid-Victorian advertisements, was ultimately replaced by an image of feminine competence.

Advertisements throughout the late Victorian period stressed the importance of the womb-like protection of the home. Defensively, the family, as prescriptive literature suggests, turned inward, and its reluctance to confront the frequent ugliness of the outside world is even given physical manifestation. McCaw, Stevenson & Orr Glacier Window Decoration advertised that it could add "all the beauty of stained glass to ordinary windows," but also the ability to "shut out disagreeable views."[30] Advertisements focused on the temptations of the outside world. A piano would make "home more attractive and save more expensive and dangerous amusements . . . No investment . . . [could] be made in a family [which could] bring greater or more lasting returns."[31] By 1910 "autopianos" could bring "a new attraction to the home . . . after the toil and turmoil of the day" with "never a false note, never a jarring chord."[32]

The home as portrayed in the Victorian advertisement was a protective but attractive enclave, which was shaped by feminine hands and shielded its members from ugliness, but strengthened them to confront the world outside. This was an appealing vision. It constituted a significant backdrop for the elaboration of hedonistic themes, especially a commercial focus on superfluous variety.

The Paraphernalia of Gentility

Advertisements for all sorts of products meant to be enjoyed at home—clothing, food, decorative art, "domestic machines"—increasingly forwarded variety, selection, even superfluity as a commercial ideal. Advertisers urged consumers to pursue material acquisition for the intrinsic pleasure of the objects themselves, for the pleasure of the status the objects connoted, and for the anticipatory delight of pursuing each of these goals.

Nowhere is the quest for superfluous variety more apparent than in the Victorian fashion advertisement. The emergent grandeur of the fashion

Get rid of all Disagreeable Views from your Windows

by using M'Caw, Stevenson & Orr's Patent Glacier Window Decoration

Figure 2-5. McCaw, Stevenson & Orr Window Decoration, 1890. (Bodleian Library. Reprinted by permission.)

advertisement partly reflects improved technology. At mid-century advertisements were small and print dense. Fashion advertisements often resembled little more than a price list or itemized inventory. Later, though, they became large and superbly illustrated, more like Parisian fashion plates than price lists. By 1890 fashion advertisements were clearly among the most visually arresting in the Victorian periodical press. The increasingly glamorous fashion advertisement suggests a heightened consumer interest in the pleasures of personal ornament and in the pleasures of the social use of the middle-class figure, especially the female figure, for display and status enhancement. It also offers a stilted, but stylish view of the angel of the house, one that emphasizes leisure and conspicuous affluence rather than redemptive purity.

Inevitably, fashion advertisements helped to dictate refined feminine appearance as an essential aspect of the Victorian "paraphernalia of gentility." Advertisements were informative and unambiguous. The Victorian woman had only to consult the advertisement section of prestigious society magazines like the _Court Journal_ to discover the sorts of goods and the retail establishments that were popularly identified with Victorian taste and wealth. In 1850 a middle-class woman might desire "rich, plain and brocaded glace silks . . . Fancy dresses, bareges . . . bellonas, French-printed jaconets and organdies, printed Swiss cambrics . . . chintzes and brillianteens . . . rich silk [or] lace and muslin mantles"[33] from Cameron and Viall or White and Finley. For mourning costumes, she was likely to consult Nicholas Jay & Co, purveyor of mourning wear to the "nobility, gentry and the public"[34] or Peter Robinson of Oxford Street. By 1870 she might buy "plain, striped, checked or fancy silks" from Baker & Crisp or W. W. Sheath or "black real lace shawls, half shawls, mantles and flouncings" from Haywards,[35] poplin from Atkinson or from Inglis & Tinkler. She might have shoes made to measure from Holland & Co. or Major Howe in satin or with bows and could purchase the "best French kid gloves at Paris prices at Ganterie Francaise."[36] Dressing gowns could be had in "flannel . . . cashmere . . . satin, silk and foulard." By 1890 she might require "artistic, antique, elegant" fans from J. Duvelleroy[37] and "the luxury of the age," "undyed hand-woven combinations, vests and slip bodices."[38] For "high class dressmaking" she would consult seamstresses in preferred locations—Grosvenor Square, Cavendish Square, Hanover Square.[39] Her gown might be further embellished by "dress sprays" from Wills & Segar, Royal Exotic Nursery, South Kensington.[40] In 1910 a corset was advertised as being essential for a woman's "social success."[41]

Commercially idealized feminine appearance was also characterized by exquisitely coiffed hair, delicate scent, and a pale complexion. The Victorian press advertised hair dyes, oils, balsams, lotions, combs, nets, pins, and curlers and a range of sensational hair restorers. Once the Victorian lady had achieved luxurious hair, gentility required that it be styled at a London salon. The beautifully attired and coiffed Victorian lady attempted to envelop herself in a floral scent—lavender, lily of the valley or violet. Even toothpastes—Floriline or Floral Bell—were "fragrant," "sweet as rosebuds bursting forth," "sweet as the ambrosial air."[42] A variety of skin creams would foster the "soft white" complexion and "youthful freshness" that was the ideal of genteel society. Although makeup was rarely advertised (except for occasional, but not increasing advertisements for rouge and for face powder), its use must have been more widespread than the number of advertisements suggest. One well-known complexion brush advertised that its primary purpose was the elimination of residues left by "poisonous cosmetics."[43] Brushes, skin creams, hair lotions, and perfumes could all be stored in fashionable dressing cases. Such cases, advertised with increasing frequency after 1870 in "polished morocco . . . lined with silk; completely fitted [in] sterling silver with beautiful hand-engraved design" equipped with as many as thirty bottles,[44] suggest that the Victorian purchaser would require many toiletries to perpetuate genteel appearance.

The commercial ideal of feminine appearance was distinctively elaborate and complex. It required a wardrobe fashioned from a wide assortment of beautiful and imported fabrics, one that included "les dernières nouveautés"[45] from Paris, "the most recherché colours,"[46] and was purchased from shops with fashionable addresses—mostly Regent Street or Oxford Street. It could only be created by an income that enabled a lady to purchase extensive variety. Moreover, it required a leisured existence conducive to its simple maintenance and perpetuation. These were the requisites of the Victorian woman as leisured ornament rather than humble angel.

Non-ornamental consumables were similarly marketed through a consumerist promotion of superfluity and variety. Food and beverage advertisements shifted away from mid-Victorian staples—tea, coffee, flour (which had constituted as much as 30% of all food and beverage advertisements before 1880)—and toward luxurious prepared foods—biscuits, confectionery, alcohol. Wedding cake or "bridecake" manufacturers (e.g., William Buszard, Richard Gunter, R. Bolland) and confectioners (e.g., Charbonnell & Walker, John Searcy, Bainbridge's) featured full-page advertisements with elaborate illustrations. The modest household might bake its own cakes and sweets, but only an extensive retinue of kitchen servants could rival the elaborately decorated confections of firms like W. Buszard or John Searcy. For those able to afford the expense, "nougat de Montelimart aux Pistaches . . . chocolate and coffee walnuts . . . French fondants . . . fancy chocolates, bons-bons, preserved fruits, dragées, fruit pastilles, burnt almonds . . . [and] dundee cakes"[47] could all be delivered.

Advertisements helped to prescribe virtually every element of a genteel domestic environment. Victorian consumers found advertisements for a wide assortment of products for the home—furniture, bedding, silver, curtains, blinds, carpets, parquet, linoleum, china, clocks, barometers, glassware, and lighting. Even paperhangers, upholsterers, tinned paints and stains, garden decorations (trellises, arches, marquises, or shelters), greenhouses (for ferns and domestic potted plants), and florists (for table decorations and exotic flowers) were extensively advertised.

Particular decorative objects from 1850 were identified with refinement. At mid-century iron French bedsteads japanned in any color, enameled and polished bedsteads or Brussels carpets seemed distinctive. By the late Victorian period the array of desirable decorative items is even more elaborate, varied, and complex. Carter's Literary Chairs would allow the gentleman of the house to enjoy a book and a cigar at the end of a busy day. "Gentlemen about to decorate their mansions" might choose "paperhanging" by Piltz & Lee, "a great want of the age," available "in every variety of colour and design and decorated by first class art-workmen."[48] Prestige dinnerware was Minton, Dresden, or Wedgwood, purchased from Henry James Allen of Jermyn Street or Phillips China. "Artistic accessories" were advertised as being especially important because "placed in harmonious juxtaposition about the table," they were the "embodiment of art and refinement." The Victorian was to imagine

> sitting at a grand banquet, the table groaning with the good things of the earth and made beautiful by the more massive of these treasures; or descending a little in the scale . . . imagine the homelier but not less enjoyable— perhaps rather more enjoyable—repast, whose table decoration of equally dainty design, if less ample in their proportions, throw light and colour and artistic effect upon the family circle. The conversation "across the walnuts and wine" must be all the brighter for these accessories.[49]

"Mirrors made beautiful for reflecting the beautiful . . . lamps of imposing design, candelabra of dainty construction and articles of table decoration of the most récherché character" would afford a "feast for the eye,"[50] the pinnacle of middle-class taste and refinement.

The pursuit of gentility through material acquisition was definitely an adult preoccupation. Victorian advertisements rarely identified a children's market. Advertisements for toys occurred frequently in adult magazines, usually in December. Advertisements for Hamley's, for example, featured several illustrations of toys—dolls, printers, trains—with text designed for adult readers. Such advertisements seemed to be directed toward adults in search of a Christmas gift rather than toward the manipulation of children. In mid-Victorian children's publications, similarly, advertisements more often than not displayed consumer goods of interest to parents rather than children—stoves, glassware, sewing machines. By the turn of the century, advertisements in children's magazines forwarded an increasing assortment of child-oriented products—a bewildering array of stamps, bicycles, cameras, sporting equipment, and even a nest of live ants. But such products almost invariably have an educational or at least a wholesome aspect, which contrasts decidedly with the increasingly hedonistic orientation of adult-oriented advertising.

The favored commercial image of children, similarly, is consistently

THE BEST BEVERAGE FOR CHILDREN

Absolutely Pure.

CADBURY'S COCOA is closely allied to milk in the large proportion of flesh-forming & strength-sustaining elements that it contains. It is prepared on the principle of excluding the superabundance of fatty indigestible matter with which Cocoa abounds —supplying a refined thin infusion of absolutely pure cocoa, exhilarating and refreshing for Breakfast, Luncheon, Tea or Supper —giving staying power and imparting new life and vigour to growing Children, and those of delicate constitutions.

CADBURY'S COCOA

Figure 2-6. Cadbury's Cocoa, *Graphic*, 1889. (Robarts Library.)

cheerful and redeeming. Boys, stereotypically, are portrayed as mischievous adventurers, an image consistent with their conventional portrayal in Victorian children's literature. Pears' Soap, for example, featured a long-running advertisement in which an old woman, holding a protesting boy by the ear, attempted to wash him as she exclaims, "Oh, you dirty boy." In contrast, the female child was typically sweet and helpful. An advertisement for Cadbury's depicted a female toddler, dressed in white, head framed by an almost wimple-like headdress, gazing wide-eyed at a kitten. The commercial image of children mimics the Victorian prescriptive ideal; but the children's market remains relatively undefined and unexploited. In contrast, the adult market with growing fervor pursues a hedonistic vision of the good life, perceived in material terms.

For adults Victorian advertisements did more than simply advance a wide variety of products as facilitators of status and genteel appearance. Acquisitiveness was encouraged by brand-name differentiation resulting from increasing numbers of competitive manufacturers. Brand competition characterized advertisements for products as diverse as fabric, corsets, cocoa, soap, and furniture in the 1880s, 1890s, and 1900s. For example, although there had been rising competition among advertised mercers, drapers, and lace makers since mid-century, brand-name differentiation rose markedly with the emergence of new materials in the 1880s. A large variety of waterproofed fabrics, serge, and especially velveteen began to compete in the Victorian press. One brand might feature romantic illustrations of dashing soldiers courting swooning damsels dressed alluringly in velveteen. Another might use long print columns to attest to practicality, durability, and economy. The ubiquitous corset advertisement was also characterized by considerable brand name differentiation. While as late as 1880 several Victorian magazines carried few corset advertisements (e.g., *Family Circle*, *Hand and Heart*, *Illustrated London News*, *Illustrated Sporting and Dramatic News*), by 1900 advertisements for over forty different brands of corsets dominated as much as 25% of clothing advertisements in ladies' and even general readership Victorian magazines. Similarly, whereas at mid-century the five brands of advertised soap were mostly all-purpose, by 1900 there were thirty advertised brands. There were toilet soaps such as Lux and Pears', children's soaps such as Dixon or Price's, washing soaps such as Sinclair's Cold Water Soap and Watson's Compressed Laundry Soap, as well as carbolic soaps and arsenical soaps. Increasing brand name differentiation ensured that the same product by different manufacturers was presented repeatedly to the consumer with a variety of persuasive appeals. If one of these arguments did not convince the consumer to buy at least one version of the product, the frequency of the product's advertised appearance might suggest to the consumer that the product was popular, fashionable, or essential. Brand-name differentiation endeavored to convince the consumer to buy more goods than ever before and reinforced the late Victorian quest for superfluous variety.

The pursuit of superfluous variety defined a very particular view of the goal of consumption. Material acquisition should not simply fulfil needs; it should create wants. Consumers sought to satisfy their basic needs, but also to surpass simple comfort. Pleasure might be achieved by simple or repeated acts of consumption and by the anticipatory delight encouraged by endless product variations and brand name versions. The pleasure focus of these advertisements reveals a self-illusory form of hedonism, in which consumption cannot approximate imagined pleasures.

The Angel in the House

The commercial ideal with its pursuit of superfluity and "pleasing variety" seems pleasure centered, leisure oriented, hedonistic, far removed from puritanical visions of the home as temple. In keeping with this context, the female presence in Victorian advertisements is frequently commanding and controlling, rather than demure and unassuming. The commercial woman offers a portrait of feminine power, which contradicts a prevalent myth—that the ideal Victorian woman was passive, submissive, and sexually anaesthetic.

In the public economic sphere it is clear enough that Victorian women possessed few rights. Most occupations outside the home were closed to her; even amid the widening sphere of employment in the late nineteenth century as, for example, nursing, teaching, and clerical positions became more plentiful for women, her earning potential and opportunities remained relatively limited. Perceptions of gender designated her natural qualities of gentleness and nurturing as inappropriate for the masculine world of business. Her property rights as a married woman and her right to divorce, at first practically denied in law, were only gradually expanded in the late nineteenth century. She was deprived the franchise. Business, law, and politics effectively excluded her from the public exercise of power. But whether business, law, and politics were the only avenues through which power was accessible to women is open to debate.

Historical discussions of the feminine ideal have coalesced around two very different concepts of power[51] described by Mill on one hand in *On The Subjection of Women* (1869) and by Ruskin on the other in *Sesame and Lilies* (1865). Mill's characterization of the woman enslaved focuses on the Victorian woman's absence of political and legal rights; Ruskin focuses on her hidden influence, especially moral suasion. In recent years Mill's interpretation has been married with contemporary theories of patriarchy: the absence of legal and political rights for women in the nineteenth century has been seen as evidence of male domination. Because the chief institution of patriarchy is the family, Ruskin's glowing description of the household god is accordingly dismissed as a "gossamer of literary idealization"[52] contrived to placate the Victorian woman, to keep her in her place. This popular evaluation, though, includes two assumptions. It assumes that the real measure of a person's importance in society is his or her relationship to the means of production—in a society that is increasingly consumer oriented rather than production oriented this may be problematic. But even more difficult for feminists it assumes, as Kathy Davis has argued, that all women of varying ability and intelligence were helpless victims at the hands of male oppressors.[53]

The victim may not be as victimized as she appears. Even with limited or unequal resources, Victorian women wielded some control. As society moved from an ethic of production to an ethic of consumption, the role of women as household purchasers acquired new social significance. In the commercial forum the woman exercised a considerable degree of free choice. It is probable that, especially for expensive items such as furniture or appliances, husbands contributed to the decision to purchase, either by indicating a preference for one product over another or by dictating the level of expenditure. Even on a weekly basis for some women a household allowance may have limited purchasing latitude. But within these constraints each woman had freedom of action. She could select the products from which her husband would make a final decision and she could influence the direction of that decision. She could, for example, emphasize her superior understanding of taste, status, or utility as applied to the domestic sphere, appeal to the flexibility within the family budget (often carefully crafted from her own reading of domestic economy manuals), or she could suggest that a particular purchase would bring her special pleasure. The latter ploy should not be discounted: few advertisements, even for luxuries, overtly target the man of the house and when they do they invariably promise to please his wife. Although she did not earn the money, the woman of the house could significantly control the way that it was spent. Advertisers could attempt to manipulate, husbands could limit the funds available, but the ultimate decision (to buy or not to buy) was usually hers.[54] As a consumer ideology of choice and of pleasure proliferated, women were empowered. They gained a new form and degree of economic control and they became arbiters of new social values including gender. Advertisements trace the shifting contours of the feminine ideal.

Classicizing imagery aggrandized the feminine image in advertisements. Draped in timeless Grecian costume, hair loosely knotted and frequently adorned with flowers or a laurel wreath, feet bare or in sandals, the classical commercial goddess contrasted dramatically with the elaborate reality of late Victorian and Edwardian feminine appearance.[55] The commercial goddess seems spare, her beauty somehow heightened because it is unadorned. Within the context of innumerable fashion advertisements that attest to the seemingly endless variety and artifice of Victorian fashion, her simplicity is more dramatic. Paradoxically, since advertisers themselves promoted the complexities of Victorian feminine appearance, in advertisements mostly for soap and medicine, the appearance of the classical goddess is cleansed of accoutrements of style. She seems above the vagaries of fashion.

Classical subjects in Victorian advertisements allowed the admirer to reveal an appreciation of higher ideals. The classical image seemed elevating. Its images were borrowed from fine art; its themes were scholarly; its appearance was dignified. Hellenic society had achieved the grandeur to which the Victorians aspired and had approximated the Victorian democratic ideal. For Victorians Athens was the state that had approached political perfection.[56] And yet the classical motif was scarcely patrician. Richard Jenkyns in *Dignity and Decadence: Victorian Art and the Classical Inheritance*[57] rejects the association of the classical with mandarin taste. Although some Victorian classicism is refined, he contends that much of the Victorian enjoyment of the classical is loud, vigorous, even vulgar.[58]

Figure 2-7. Beecham's Pills, *Illustrated London News*, 1890. (Robarts Library.)

The classical goddess suggests only a pretense of purity. In style and in subject advertisers copy the painterly conventions established by Frederic Leighton (1830–1896) and popularized by Alma-Tadema (1836–1892), artists who intended to construct a view of the antique world in which the aspiring middle class could see themselves reflected. The Alma-Tadema school especially favoured sleepy, sexy beauties. Advertisers provided their own variations. Breasts partially exposed, arms and feet bared, the goddess seems half-dressed in a costume that is often unashamedly diaphanous.[59]

Figure 2-8. Osler China and Glass, *Illustrated Sporting and Dramatic News*, 1890. (British Library.)

Arms immodestly bared, breasts emphasized by the bodice of her costume, she appears lost in reverie, languid, even indolent. She plucks idly at a few stray grapes, resting on a silver tray, while behind her urns, a classical statue, and a basket of fruit reinforce the classicism of the image.[60] She explicitly portrays the erotic potential suppressed in the angel in the house ideal. Yet she is no passive sexual object. Like the sleeping beauties explored by Adeline Tinter and Susan Casteras in Victorian art,[61] her veiled eyes and supine posture betray a sensuality about to be awakened. In advertisements she is fanned as she lies upon a bed of roses, a creature of pleasure who commands the most slavish devotion.[62]

Figure 2-9. Pears' Soap, 1887. (Bodleian Library: The John Johnson Collection, Soap 5. Reprinted by permission.)

Classical allure is overlaid with suggestions of domination. Nina Auerbach speculates that images of the mermaid, the queen, the angel, the demon, the old maid, and the fallen woman actually exalted feminine power.[63] In advertisements the commercial goddess assumes alternating postures of queen-like dignity and warrior-like aggression. Seated regally on a platform dais[64] or enthroned, petitioning subjects prostrate at her feet,[65] the classical goddess attains a capricious, but commanding control. In art stereotypical feminine qualities such as gentleness and purity constitute a woman's strength. Guillaume Geefs' *The Lion in Love* and John Bell's *Una and the Lion*, for example, both depicted lions tamed with gentle innocence. In the advertisement, in contrast, she wins through unmitigated aggression. She wears a warrior's helmet.[66] As an apparent gladiator before a crowd of spectators, she slays her enemies. A slogan proclaims "opposition is useless . . . Progress proves power . . . This is where we Shine."[67] The use of such imagery for marketing products with a predominantly female market—household cleaners, toilet soap, patent medicines—suggests the advertisers' recognition of a latent female power (at least in the commercial sphere) and the potential appeal to a female audience of a commercial image dramatically more aggressive, controlling, and certainly more sexual than the gentle piety of Una and the virtuous passivity of the angel in the house.

The female figure seems venerable and austere. Feminine depictions of Justice, for example, are a frequent commercial gambit. Aspinall's Enamel places a stunning full-page advertisement in which a Grecian woman, posing as Justice, weighs Aspinall's against spurious imitations. The purpose is "to test real value."[68] The choice to depict women as judges is dictated partly by the desire to create dramatic effect, partly to suggest that women are reasonable judges of household consumables. But it is also motivated by a confidence in the cultural resonance of the image. The ancient Greeks identified justice as a blindfolded woman with scales. The classical identification was very familiar to Victorians, widely reproduced in the form of statues on courthouses and jails on both sides of the Atlantic (e.g., The Old Bailey). For Victorians the identification of justice as a woman seemed doubly appropriate. Although women in Victorian society held no positions within the formal judicial system, they were at "the altar of family love" the chief evaluators of moral character.

Even the image of the fairy in advertisements functions as a whimsical reminder of feminine power. Advertisers borrowed a pictorial form popularized by a school of fairy painters (Paton, Fitzgerald, Doyle) that flourished at mid-century. For Floriline toothpaste, "Fair Flora, the Goddess of Flowers" appears as a fairy.[69] Amid ferns, lilacs, lilies, and sunflowers, a waterfall, and swirling rapids, she mixes her potion. She is assisted by two cherubic assistants and illuminated by a stark ray of light. In the foreground, roses in full bloom, the largest flowers represented in the garden, push toward a poetic text. Only the thorns of the rose bush intrude. The commercial fairy is a delicate, diminutive almost child-like presence. She

Figure 2-10. Matchless Metal Polish, n.d. (Bodleian Library: The John Johnson Collection, Oil and Candles I. Reprinted by permission.)

Figure 2-11. Aspinall's Enamel, *Illustrated London News*, 1889. (Robarts Library.)

Figure 2-12. Floriline, *Illustrated London News*, 1910. (Robarts Library.)

plays and teases. Unlike the classical goddess, she does not threaten. She is conventionally sweet and demure, but she is magical. She transcends human limitations.

These recurrent motifs, and especially repeated and sustained interest in the woman as classical goddess, provide a commercial feminine ideal that contrasts markedly with the conventional image celebrated in Victorian prescriptive literature. The commercial goddess is neither passive nor submissive. In recline or eyes veiled, she reveals not her weakness, but her potent temptation. She is a controlling and commanding force, an agent of super-human strength, of mythical power. Superficially, at least, her appearance associates her with purity and moral elevation, but her thinly disguised sensuality suggests a hedonistic interest in gratification.

A Life of Leisure

In the advertisement, far from embodying evangelical piety, the family, especially the commercial woman, sought leisure. Alone, she seemed absorbed in her own beautification. As mother, servants relieved her of onerous or unattractive burdens. As wife, she enjoyed companionable leisure, as well as romance. As household manager, domestic machines reduced her household labor. At every turn, advertisements directed the family and women in particular toward the pursuit of leisure.

The commercial woman had a focus on pleasure that necessarily required leisure. The recurrent motif of the woman looking into her mirror amplifies this commercial ideal. It draws on an artistic convention that identifies the woman with Venus. In fine art, Anne Hollander suggests that the ordinary woman who looks in a mirror may be thwarted by the inadequacy of her perceived image. Alternately, she may through vanity magnify her own beauty, become dangerously self-absorbed.[70] In advertisements, the beautifying effects of Erasmic Soap and Beecham's Glycerine and Cucumber Powder,[71] for example, facilitate a satisfying reflection. They seem to create beauty or at least they improve the viewer's perception of her reflected image. These advertisements suggest that the ideal woman was self-absorbed and pleasure-oriented enough to delight in her own reflection. But the woman in the mirror motif also reinforced a commercial ideal of the Victorian woman as an ornament. Moreover, it confirmed the expectation that a middle-class woman should possess sufficient leisure and affluence to invest considerable time, effort, and money in her quest for beauty.

But even in her more responsible roles commercial depictions emphasize the Victorian woman's access to leisure. By the turn of the century as advertisers increasingly focus on the mother-child relationship, servants appear in family-oriented advertisements with alarming frequency. In real life by 1900 the servant crisis and a renewed impetus toward familial privacy encouraged middle-income families to forsake domestic help. In contrast, in the advertisement servants are depicted three times as often in 1910 as in 1890, and with altered functional emphasis—servants stop cleaning and begin attending to infants. Amid a real-life servant shortage, the commercial linking of the mother-infant bond with domestic labor reinforces not only the primacy of the infant, but a general commercial tone of leisured affluence.

As wife, the commercial woman increasingly is joined with her husband in a shared pursuit of leisure. In 1890 the commercial depiction of the couple was painterly and sentimental, replete with allusions to the Victorian artistic convention of the courting wall and damsels reclining in hammocks. Such images emphasized sexual interest. But by 1910 the commercial image emphasizes the couple's social function, especially their shared enjoyment of affluent leisure. The prosperous couple is inevitably leaving a party[72] or dining by candlelight for Berncasteler wines, Lea and Perrins Worcestershire Sauce, Lemco, Caffeta, and Montserrat Lime Juice. The commercial ideal relieves the couple of occupational or familial duties. It focuses their attention on the pursuit of pleasure.

Access to convenience and attendant leisure emerged as a prominent aspect of the Victorian commercial ideal. Firms like Maple & Co. established a reputation for being "the most convenient furnishing establishment in the world" by promising to furnish a house "of any magnitude" in three days, a service that was regarded as "an immense advantage to country purchasers."[73] They advertised "estimates free of charge for painting and all kinds of interior decoration, structural alterations, sanitary work, electrical lighting etc."[74] Such services meant that the home decorating process required minimal attention from the householder; it seemed effortless. Access to convenient home services helped to define gentility.

Prepared foods similarly celebrated convenience. Desiccated soups, patented by Edwards in 1840 and Symington in 1847, became small, but steady advertisers.[75] Prepared baby foods seemed to attract an increased market. In 1880 there were only six brands, but by 1900 there were twelve brands of food advertised for "infants, growing children, invalids and the aged."[76] Even prepared dog food was frequently featured in advertisement sections of Victorian magazines. Moreover, illustrated advertisements explicitly linked prepared foods with leisure. Biscuit manufacturers, for example, depicted ladies' tea parties. One company even produced a "cycle biscuit."[77] Prepared foods, like home decorating services, promoted convenience and attendant leisure. They reflected an increasingly hedonistic interest in the pursuit of pleasure.

The commercial ideal promoted "domestic machines" to alleviate the pressures of household work and to maintain the appearance of gentility. Between 1860 and 1880 sewing machine advertising constituted as much as 80% of domestic machine advertisements. As many as fourteen brands—Singer, Wheeler & Wilson, W. F. Thomas, Willcox & Gibbs, J. Wood, Atlas, T. Weir, and the British & Foreign Sewing Machine Co.—rivaled each other for the "simplest shuttle, shortest needle, best stitch adjustment, most perfect tension . . . prettiest stitch."[78] "The right sewing machine" would be "a perpetual source of satisfaction, comfort, leisure and benefit to the whole family."[79] One telling advertisement described a member of

> . . . that numerous middle class of Englishwomen, whose comfort depends on economy and good management. [Her] family sewing had . . . outgrown [her] capabilities long before, and help had become more and more frequently indispensable. [She] could not add another costly servant to [her] already large household, and the occasional service of a seamstress had proved expensive and besides did not altogether answer [her] purpose. A sewing machine might lighten [her] work . . . [80]

A sewing machine would provide such a family with "the comfort of having a quiet evening with [the] family"[81] and thereby foster the appearance of gentility. It would provide the key for "how to be happy all the year round."[82] It could make home "a haven of peace on earth."[83] All of this was possible because it could facilitate the *"elegant leisure* without which a lady's infinitely more to be pitied than the hardest working serving maid."[84] Sewing machines and other mechanical contrivances—washers, wringers, manglers, knife cleaners, irons, carpet sweepers, vacuums—were invaluable as a part of the paraphernalia of gentility because they (interestingly not servants) liberated the lady of the house from "drudgery." Branca's overwhelmed lady of the house needed not the stimulants of patent medicine, but merely the acquisition of domestic machines to transform her drudgery into leisure.

Similarly, the right soap could eliminate the "misery of a steamy house." For

> if home is to be the very dearest spot on earth it can only be such if the mother or wife brightens it with the sunlight of her cheerful smile. This radiance must be natural, and the genuine fruit of peace, kindness and serenity. When things go right in the kitchen, the laundry and the bath, the good housewife's face is lit up with a loving, smiling calm. This brightness always follows the use of [the right soap.][85]

It was not so much that a particular brand of soap was part of the paraphernalia of gentility; rather the use of the proper soap would, by saving labor, facilitate the necessary appearance of leisured comfort.

The commercial ideal of family life in the late nineteenth century embraced increasing leisure and affluence. "Pleasing variety," indeed superfluity, was encouraged by mounting brand-name differentiation. A complex feminine and domestic appearance was commercially prescribed. Only children seemed untouched by commercial greed. Amid the acquisitive thrust of late Victorian commercial culture, the angel in the house was usurped by a commanding and controlling commercial goddess, who seemed elevating, but who ultimately advanced a hedonistic pursuit of pleasure. Convenience products liberated the family from drudgery. Mothers were increasingly assisted by servants; couples were linked by their

shared enjoyment of leisure. The late Victorian home in the eyes of advertisers became not a temple of virtue, but a hall of material goods, one that
elevated acquisition with classical motifs, which attempted to free the
Victorian family from evangelical moral constraints, and which increasingly defined the middle-class ideal in material terms.

3

Progress in the Victorian Advertisement: Productive Engines and Consuming Conflagrations

The Victorian attitude toward progress was characteristically ambivalent. Victorians welcomed unprecedented material accomplishment. But by the end of the century there was a pervasive unease especially about the country's moral condition. This concern with moral progress found a number of well-known expressive avenues such as the aesthetic movement. I will argue in this chapter that advertisements, too, reflect the conflicted temper of the popular mood. Advertisements celebrate material progress; they praise its miraculous potential with grandiose images of smokestacks and production lines. But the springs of guilt that ran beyond consumerism are brought to a focus in advertisements in a surprising stress on feminine sexuality. With very particular images of sexy women, advertisers, probably unconsciously, remind consumers of the Fall, a message that apparently contradicts the advertiser's commercial intentions. Such contradictions characterize the advertisement's portrait of the material and the moral side of progress.

The Idea of Progress

J. B. Bury, the great historian of the idea of progress, has suggested that a belief in progress did not really arrive in western thought until the Enlightenment of the eighteenth century.[1] Progress was built on the Enlightenment's celebration of scientific and technological advances and on the political values of liberty and equality espoused during the French and American Revolutions. For the first time instead of looking back to a

golden age or the Garden of Eden, people looked forward to the regenera-
tion of society, to the creation through human reason of an earthly uto-
pia.[2] But the Enlightenment view of progress met little acceptance outside
the cloistered salon of the philosophes. The idea of progress did not gain
prominence until the industrial revolution.

Progress then came to mean the material, moral, and spiritual transformation of the world through industrialization, the betterment of conditions not just for the few but for the many. Before the nineteenth century,
most people had seen earthly life as a trial en route to eternal bliss or
eternal damnation. By the early Victorian period, it became popular to
believe that the world could be bettered through sustained human effort
and intelligence.[3] The nineteenth century became an "Age of Improvement." The very word "future" acquired a freshly positive connotation.
The *OED* offers an 1852 definition of the future as "a condition in time to
come different (especially in a favourable sense) from the present,"[4] a view
of the future as a better and brighter time to come. Victorians assumed
that if the present was good, the future would be even better. Tennyson's
hero of "Locksley Hall" circa 1841 imagined that the future would reveal
marvels that would surpass Victorian steam and rail. Smiles praised

> a number of machines and inventive men without apparent relation to each
> other . . . [who] in various parts of the kingdom . . . succeeded in giving an
> immense impulse to all the branches of national industry . . .

"The result" he declared, "has been a harvest of wealth and prosperity."[5]
Society was, according to Prince Albert, "in transition," caught between
the old disappearing world and the new emerging world. The transition
was characterized by "wonder," "choice," and "confidence." Macaulay,
probably the most vigorous exponent of the Victorian idea of progress,
wrote that

> We are on the side of progress. From the great advances which European
> society has made during the last four centuries, in every species of knowledge,
> we infer, not that there is no room for improvement, but that in every science
> which deserves the name, immense improvements may be confidently ex-
> pected. The history of England is emphatically the history of progress.[6]

For the Victorian, material change was particularly remarkable. Frederic
Harrison wrote that "the merely material, physical, mechanical change in
human life in the hundred years from the days of Watt and Arkwright to
our own, is greater than occurred in the thousand years that preceded."[7]
Inventions—steamships, railways, telegraphs, telephones, typewriters, and
automobiles—transformed everyday life. Rapid communications and
transport made far corners of the globe seem less remote. The factory
system irrevocably altered the experience of work. These changes were
abundantly visible. Mass production was, by definition, a large-scale en-

deavor, producing vast quantities of consumer goods. Industrial machines were big. The railway encompassed vast territories. Such mammoth changes must have seemed exhilarating, but also bewildering. While the Victorian understanding of progress was not simply material, the material component of the definition was clearly immediate and imposing.

Indeed, in 1851 the famous Great Exhibition of the Arts and Industry of All Nations seemed to celebrate a peculiarly material form of progress. Contemporaries were unreserved in their admiration for the accomplishments that the exhibit represented. Tennyson wrote,

> . . . lo! the giant aisles
> Rich in model and design;
> Harvest-tool and husbandry,
> Loom and wheel and engineering,
> Secrets of the sullen mine,
> Steel and gold, and coal and wine,
> Fabric rough or fairy-fine . . .
> And shapes and hues of Art divine!
> All of beauty, all of use,
> That one fair planet can produce.

Seven thousand objects were displayed in a gallery 1,848 feet long by 408 feet wide. Over six million visitors came, many more than once.[8] Queen Victoria wrote that as she stood in the middle of the building, she was "filled with devotion."[9] Devotion was inspired by a sincere and widely felt wonderment at Britain's industrial accomplishment. The Great Exhibition had achieved its goal: "to present a true test and living picture of the point of development at which the whole of mankind has arrived . . . and a new starting point, from which all nations will be able to direct their further exertions."[10]

This is not to say that the Victorians perceived progress from a wholly material perspective. The Victorians also esteemed the considerable political, social, and economic advances of their own age. Three successive Reform Acts had widened the base of democracy. The Repeal of the Test and Corporation Acts and Catholic Emancipation had ushered in a more tolerant religious climate. The revision of the criminal code, the reform of the prisons, and the advent of child protection laws had revealed an active moral impulse. The worst horrors of the factory system had been gradually mitigated or removed by legislation. Education had become more accessible. Economic prosperity had seemed unstoppable, at least in the third quarter of the nineteenth century. Such accomplishments seemed to suggest that progress was more than material; it seemed to justify Macaulay's assertion that "immense improvements may be confidently expected."[11] Frederic Harrison declared:

> The cause of progress is bound up with every principle worth having; and material progress is an indispensable step in general progress . . . We all feel

a-tiptoe with hope and confidence . . . It is *not* the age of money-bags and cant, soot, humbug and ugliness. It is the age of great expectation and unwearied striving after better things.[12]

Despite prevalent optimism, there were nineteenth-century critics who opposed an ethos that seemed to thrive on Carlyle's "cash nexus." Ruskin and Morris perceived a sort of "Whig frame of mind" among "modern prosperous middle class men," a complacency about "their plentiful style," which opposed socialist objectives.[13] The good life seemed to them to be that which progress was destroying—order, tranquillity, harmony.[14] Ruskin, for example, questioned industrial values—the worship of machinery, efficiency, and material wealth. Was it not better

to watch the corn grow, and the blossoms set; to draw hard breath over ploughshare or spade; to read, to think, to have, to hope, to pray . . . [than to depend] upon iron or glass, or electricity, or steam . . . [15]

He echoes Mill's earlier caution in *On Liberty* (1859) that the ingenuity of man could not be replaced by "automatons in human form," "starved specimens of what nature can and will produce."[16] William Morris' "passion for . . . the past," his medievalism, his socialism, sprang from the same "hatred of modern civilization." In "the Earthly Paradise" (1870) he exhorts readers to

> Forget six counties overhung with smoke,
> Forget the snorting steam and piston stroke,
> Forget the spreading of the hideous town;
> Think rather of the pack-horse on the down,
> And dream of London, small, and white, and clean.[17]

Railways and steamships disturbed aesthetic sensibilities, but social critics also observed that the inventions of the industrial revolution had done little to arrest the sordid condition of the poor. By 1886 Tennyson in "Locksley Hall Sixty Years After" indicted the very society he had praised in the first "Locksley Hall" for proud cities that had become little more than "warrens of the poor." "There among the glooming alleys progress halts on palsied feet."[18] Henry George, the famous proponent of the single tax, believed that the theory of continuous progress was contradicted by the rise and fall of nations.[19] He found a receptive audience for his book *Progress and Poverty* in England,

Where the condition to which material progress everywhere tends are most fully realized—that is to say, where population is densest, wealth greatest, and the machinery of production and exchange most highly developed—we find the deepest poverty, the sharpest struggle for existence, and the most enforced idleness . . . The "tramp" comes with the locomotive, and almshouses and prisons are as surely the marks of "material progress" as are costly dwellings, rich warehouses, and magnificent churches . . . The enormous increase in

productive power which has marked the present century and is still going on
with accelerating ratio . . . simply evidences the gulf between the Dives and
Lazarus . . . This association of poverty with progress is the great enigma of
our times.[20]

Technology had not realized old dreams of a perfected world. Despair
replaced the optimism symbolized by the Crystal Palace. Urban squalor,
suburban monotony, polluted water, said critics, were outward manifesta-
tions of an inner deficiency, an aesthetic decay that foreshadows moral
judgment. Industrial progress seemed tied to social decadence. The material plenty of Victorian society, suggests Pater in *Marius*, is, like the opulence of the Rome of Marcus Aurelius, but a prelude to a general social
decay, a poor substitute for humane values.[21]

By the late nineteenth century progress increasingly came to connote
struggle rather than melioration. Individuals, classes, nations, races
seemed locked in combat. Marx suggested that economic class conflict
would eventually replace competitive society with proletarian commu-
nism. Conflict between individuals, said Spencer, would produce the survival of the fittest. Karl Pearson, Professor of Applied Mathematics at the
University of London and director of its Francis Galton Laboratory of
National Eugenics, argued that progress would be achieved chiefly
through the military and commercial rivalry of nations.[22] Progress within
these schemes seemed threatening if not immoral.

Victorians certainly did not intend progress to be simply material. Arnold surely spoke for many when he distinguished between man's true
"progress in sweetness and light" and "the number of railways he has
constructed or the bigness of the tabernacle he has built." "In spite of all
that is said about the absorbing and brutalising influence of our passionate
material progress,"[23] he hoped for "a perfection infinitely greater than we
can ever conceive,"[24] a perfection in which evil and immorality would
disappear. The material progress of the industrial revolution was not sufficient without a deeply felt spiritual and moral advance.

THE VICTORIAN ADVERTISEMENT deals with the two sides of progress, the material and the moral, in a way that is amenable to analysis
through the separate spheres. Some advertisements explore material progress through images from the masculine sphere of industry and rationality. Others explore moral progress through images of the domestic
sphere of privacy and emotion. While motifs of material progress are
usually celebratory, images of the feminine sphere reveal a pervasive unease.

Productive Engines: Material Progress

Advertisements offer spectacular visions of material progress in which the
factory and the shop promise to satisfy every human want. It is a bravado,

a confidence in the mission of industry, which is one of the most striking features of the Victorian advertisement. The factory smokestack is magnificent; the railway emerges as a symbol of productive force and industrial momentum. Through the "mystery of manufacture" and every sort of "beneficial discovery" advertisements promise human perfectibility.

Repeated and grandiose illustrations of industrial production convey unbounded optimism. They promise Victorians an unprecedented capability to supply industrial goods. A full-page advertisement provides vignettes that illustrate various stages of furniture manufacture.[25] In another advertisement factory workers box, label, and roast cocoa beans; they operate a packing machine.[26] An advertisement for Huntley & Palmer's Biscuits describes "the prodigious, skillfully-ordered activities of this factory, in which some 2,000 men, women, boys and girls are biscuit making all year round." This

> affords to the thoughtful observer an excellent example of the results obtainable from the concentration of the mind on one operation. The economies exhibited within the factory gates are evidence of a continuous process of thought, acting upon a single object—cheap and perfect production.

"The mystery of . . . manufacture,"[27] according to advertisers, was that, like Charles Babbage's analytical machine, it was capable of undertaking any sort of calculation; it was "continuous," "concentrat[ed]," "perfect," so seemingly removed from human flaws.

The power of industrial production is alternately expressed in a litany of material abundance. Beginning about 1870, but with increasing fervor in the late Victorian period, advertisements focused very directly on material quantity. A mercer and draper advertise the

> finest organdie muslins . . . real china grass cloth dresses . . . fancy, striped, checked and plain silks . . . plain, corded and figured black-ground silks . . . rich, bright, wide and durable black silks . . . japanese silks . . . French prints, brilliants, piques . . . fancy dresses, alpaca, sole, 79 different shades . . . silk, wool and washing grenadines . . . white piques, sateens, cords.[28]

Maple & Co. Furniture invites "an inspection of their magnificent collection of ornamental and useful articles . . . 5,000 in stock . . . Hundreds of Thousands of Pounds worth of Manufactured goods ready for immediate delivery."[29] Progress in the Victorian advertisement involved more than a positive estimation of machines and technology. It required the capacity to fulfil any want of the age through abundance.

The very process of acquisition acquired its own appeal. As early as 1867 an advertisement for Newton, Wilson & Co. Sewing Machines shows customers shopping in a grand setting.[30] But the emphasis on the pleasure of shopping is even more accentuated by the late Victorian period. An advertisement for the Parisian Diamond Co. illustrates the elaborate interi-

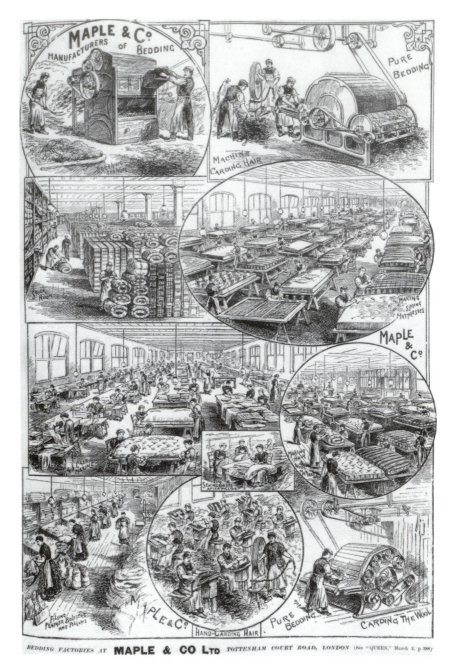

Figure 3-1. Maple & Co. Furniture, *Queen*, 1895. (British Library.)

or of "the new premises of the Parisian Diamond Co." It is "not a shop," rather "it is the shop of the future, when Industry will have wedded Art." It thereby fulfils the goals celebrated in the Great Exhibition, that very symbol of Victorian progress. The shop is a veritable "musée" replete with sculpture, a Louis-Seize suite, and a ceiling that alone would "repay a visit."[31] Even a simple visit to the "temple" or "musée" offered the consumer the potential for improvement; materialism, as a product and as a process, was commercially identified as elevating.

A conspicuous number of advertisements illustrate the facades of shops or office buildings. They borrow from an earlier tradition that pictured a tradesman's shop on his card. In the Victorian advertisement such illustrations provide an impression of the prestige, reputation, and permanence of particular businesses, but they also symbolize Victorian progress. They present a dramatic contrast between past and present; they celebrate momentum and uphold the Victorian improving impulse. According to advertisers, the material satisfaction of today merely foreshadowed the new "Golden Age . . . for humanity" in which "suffering would be spared, and how much happier life would become! In the struggle for success, none would be hampered . . . and each could put the best of his powers into both work and play." Victorians had at every turn "taken gigantic strides in the right direction."[32]

Technology and science were used to market even the most mundane products and to give them an almost magical aura. A writing table is advertised as "the latest invention."[33] The electric curler is described as an "ingenious time-saving and altogether admirable piece of mechanism."[34] Even magnets are marketed as a "beneficial discovery."[35] Advertisements consistently represent products of varying sophistication and mechanical intricacy as pinnacles of technological accomplishment. The commercial estimation of science is similarly positive. Allusions to science allow a quack device to be advertised as an impressive "electropathic belt."[36] Gillette Razors seem better because of a "microscopically smooth edge."[37] Even hair pins capture the appeal of the "scientific." Science, like technology, lent everyday products the appearance of calculated, irrefutable benefit. Nonetheless, the appeal of both was often less than rational. Both retained a mystique; their complexities were not readily understood by the consuming public. Product limitations could not be readily perceived.

Novelty was a recurrent theme. Constant emphasis on invention stressed the deficiencies of the past and the potential for perfectibility of the present. Electric Light in advertisements, for example, was only one more indication of the "old . . . gradually giving place to a [new] mode."[38] It marked the dawn of "a new era." "Patent Equilibrium Chairs," "Patent Hesperus Lights," "Patent Room Papers" offered exciting newness. A product did not have to be technically complex to tap the marketing strategy of newness. It had only to incorporate some change that made it different from the products of the past. An advertisement for a hair pin might read, "More comfortable than any other. Patent March 7, 1889, No.

4044."[39] Patents lent the product the cachet of invention, promised an exciting, but undefined potential.

Technology offered to improve every aspect of daily life. It promised a Turkish Bath in the bedroom, a reclining chair in the library, a night light in the nursery. At bath time towels might be heated in a linen warming chamber. Disinfectants such as Izal and Jeyes promised a new standard of cleanliness in the home. A wide variety of lawn mowers could adapt technology to the care of the walled garden. Vacuum cleaners could replace beating carpets. A Thermos Flask promised to "keep drinks without fire or artificial aid boiling hot, ice-cold or at any temperature required for more than twenty-four hours."[40] Electric Light would provide "light that is nearest daylight" for the "most remote resident."[41] A Hygiene Hall Stove or a similar product would enable a householder "to maintain an equal temperature in the house, a temperature of 60F" even in "the Entrance Hall."[42] For the first time the Victorians might enjoy an alternative to "sleeping in icy-cold bedrooms."[43] The advertised world of the Victorians as a direct result of technology was warmer, brighter, cleaner, more comfortable, and more ornamented than ever before. Technology in the Victorian advertisement is "beneficial," "ingenious," "time-saving," "perfect."

Material progress was so aggrandized in the Victorian advertisement that it became virtually a defining characteristic of civilization. A 1890 Vinolia Soap advertisement quotes Mark Twain from *A Connecticut Yankee in King Arthur's Court* published that very year:

> My missionaries were taught to follow the [soap] signs in their labour and explain to the lords and ladies what soap was, and if the lords and ladies were afraid of it to try it on a dog. The missionary's next move was to get the family together, and try it on himself; if any final doubt prevailed, he must catch a hermit. If a hermit could survive a wash, and that failed to convince a duke, give him up, let him alone. Whenever my missionaries overcame a knight errant on the road, they washed him and when he got well they swore him to get a bulletin board and disseminate soap and civilization for the rest of his days.[44]

Those ignorant of the merits of soap are laughable, caricatured "lords and ladies," "knights errant" from a comedic and unenlightened past. The path to salvation, on the other hand, is inextricably linked with material things.

The railway becomes a symbol for the momentum of the industrial age. A biscuit production line is transformed into a veritable "train of biscuits." A full page advertisement for Bovril illustrates a G.N.R. station crowded with winter travelers.[45] The railway functions commercially as a symbol of great industrial accomplishment, a convenience facilitated by modern technology. It symbolizes the possibilities of the industrial age: it offers the lure of unknown or unseen destinations, the thrill of rapid transit. It represents constant movement, change, the ability to transport the individual from one situation to another. The railway in the Victorian advertisement symbolizes the momentum of industrial progress. It celebrates the prowess of man.

The factory, as a productive source, acquires megalithic proportions. Epps's Cocoa devotes much of a full-page advertisement to press reports describing its new factory.[46] The new

> extensive premises have a total frontage to Holland Street Blackfriars of about 320 ft. The height from the semi-basement floor to the parapets varies from 60 ft. to 72 ft., while the clock tower stands about 110 ft., above road level, the whole forming an imposing building, whether viewed from the River Thames or the bustling thoroughfare. The total area of the various floors etc. amounts to nearly two acres, while the area of glass in the windows is about 11,000 ft.

Other segments of the same advertisement describe the building's "stupendous" or "vast scale," its "two acres of floors." They assure the reader that the new "manufactory is the largest of its kind in the country," "one of the finest and most striking pile of buildings in the metropolis." The massive scale of the factory is not menacing, beyond human control, "cyclopean" as Marx would suggest. Rather, it seems somehow redemptive. Phoenix-like, "among the imposing warehouses lining the river between Blackfriars and Southwark, Messrs Epps's new building rises radiant in the glories of red brick and an ambitious clock tower." The smokestacks are symbols of fertile productivity, impressive dominance, and the promise of satisfaction.

At every turn advertisement subjects defy limitations. Smokestacks rise into the sky, surpassing conventional heights. Production statistics promise to surpass previous records. The train presses onwards. An actress poised upon a stage before an enthusiastic audience raises a jar of Sanatogen.[47] A kitchen maid in apron and cap raises her arm high to support a jar of Lemco.[48] In advertisement after advertisement products are elevated into the sky. Products advertise that they are "obtainable everywhere." Illustrated catalogues would be sent "to any part of the world," and "all goods" would be "carefully packed and dispatched carriage paid to any part of the U.K."[49] A sense of breaking physical barriers is omnipresent in the Victorian advertisement.

At their most extreme, advertisements offer a sort of consumerist natural selection, the ultimate form of material progress. In 1868 Neave's (Baby) Food suggests "healthy childhood, promotes robust manhood,"[50] a common-sense message that seems innocuous. By 1880 Dr. Ridge's (Baby) Food suggests that "The fate of nations depends upon how they are fed."[51] In contrast to "the primitive simplicity of the garden of Eden," proper nutrition advances "the fate of the nation," its movement from primitivism to civilization, and those ill equipped are destined to lose not only "money" but "life itself." A Cocoatina advertisement asks, "Do you

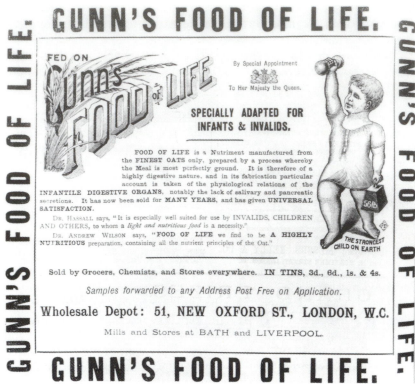

Figure 3-2.   Gunn's Food of Life, *Pick-Me-Up*, 1890. (Robarts Library.)

give your children Cocoatina? If not you place them at a disadvantage in the struggle for life with 1,000,000 children who use it daily. Eleven pence is a trifling premium to pay on a permanent insurance of health, wealth and beauty."[52] Children themselves are engaged in a fierce "struggle" against competitors. Food is continually forwarded as a sort of insurance to equip the child in the battle for life. Mellin's offers a weight chart to enable the consumer "to keep a handy, accurate record of baby's progress day by day, then week by week, then month by month, for the first two years of baby's life."[53] Another Mellin's advertisement reminds mothers that "Nature's law is that the FITTEST not the FATTEST shall survive." It assures "Mellin's Babies are always fit."[54] By 1890 Gunn's Food of Life depicts the epitome of the well-nourished child, "the strongest child on earth," as a sort of Atlas, muscles flexed, arms raised in triumph, upon whom the fate of his world depends.[55] In yet another advertisement he is a "Conquering Hero."[56] Advertisements offer a Darwinistic improvement; near physical perfection, the ultimate material form of progress, achieved through the vehicle of consumption.

THE VICTORIAN ADVERTISEMENT offered an impressive vision of material progress. Productive engines promised to gratify any want, to surpass expectations with miraculous technology, even to perfect the race. But Victorians did not embrace progress unreservedly. As much as advertisements hold the prospect of material satisfaction, they become preoccupied with the concept of moral fall.

Consuming Conflagrations: Moral Progress

Just as the advertiser places material progress in the masculine and public sphere of industry, he evaluates moral progress in the feminine and private sphere of the home. In the private sphere the advertiser offers two types of images. He presents images of pastoral simplicity, Old England, and chaste girlhood—a vision of moral restraint. But he also with surprising frequency offers images of provocative women. The first set of images constitutes an important context for the second set. The advertiser, I will argue, like his twentieth-century counterpart, realized that images of sexy women would sell products. He also recognized the erotic potential of the angel in the house. But while, like his public, he was attracted to a sexual image of hedonistic self-indulgence, even on an unconscious level, he is unable to surrender his moral vision. Accordingly, he qualifies his images of feminine sexuality, freezes them, links them to the Fall. The advertiser interprets a characteristically Victorian ambivalence through twin themes of material grandeur and moral angst.

Purity becomes the almost obsessive focus of the Victorian advertisement, fueled by adulteration scares. Advertisements for food, medicine, and soap address the Victorian middle-class passion for cleanliness. Bar graphs, medical testimony, and scientific research attest to product purity. But the identification of women with purity emerges as a veritable commercial cliché. In a Cadbury's advertisement a single female figure is enveloped by a halo configuration edged in pearl-like decoration. The caption reads "Cadbury's is the Pure Cocoa."[57] An advertisement for Fry's Cocoa pictures a young girl in her nightdress. The headline from *The Tempest*, "perfect" and "peerless,"[58] likens the girl to Miranda, the virtuous beloved of Ferdinand. Purity is personified by the female figure. She represents moral progress, but she seems scarcely hedonistic; indeed she seems to contradict the advertiser's otherwise hedonistic message.

As much by style as by substance, advertisers illustrate a nostalgic oversimplification of the consumer's moral dilemma. In an advertisement for Cadbury's, stylistic devices of the Arts and Crafts Movement—a heavy, uncarved chair, leaded windows, and the simplicity of the woman's costume—suggest the medieval period. She is fashionable to be sure, but this particular fashion connotes certain ideas as well. Arts and Crafts enthusiasts championed a communal spirit, joy in labor relieved of the demands of mechanization, the integrity of values. In this advertisement a

Figure 3-3. Cadbury's Cocoa, *Illustrated London News*, 1900. (Robarts Library.)

mother reads a "lesson" to the child seated at her feet.[59] The consumer becomes the child, admonished to pursue the "purest and best," to return to the simple pre-industrial values evoked by medieval imagery, to follow the wholesome path learned at the knee of her mother.

True progress is defined increasingly in feminine terms, according to the

"THE LESSON."

Cocoa is universally admitted to be a valuable article of diet, but to ensure the fullest benefits it must be pure and untampered with—so beware of cocoas containing questionable admixtures.

CADBURY's Cocoa is absolutely pure, and a perfect food, and can be beneficially taken by everyone all the year round. It is an ideal beverage for Children.

Figure **3-4.** Cadbury's Cocoa, *Lady's Pictorial*, 1900. (British Library.)

"riches of the heart." Eno's, in one of many advertisements with philo-
sophic messages, suggests that even amid the glorious plenty of industrial
society "man . . . lives in a fool's paradise."[60] It asks:

> What constitutes National Prosperity? Not wealth or commerce simply, or
> military achievements, but the greatest possible number of HEALTHY, HAPPY
> and GRACEFUL HOMES, where the purest flames burn brightest on the altar of
> family love, and woman her piety, forbearance, and kindliness of love is
> permitted to officiate as high priestess.

The boldface caption announces "Riches, Titles, Honour and Worldly
Prospects are Naught to a deeply rooted love."[61] Progress, celebrated in
material and masculine images of production, is ultimately evaluated in the
private sphere of the walled garden. Here in the arena of the "high
priestess," progress is defined not by access to material goods, but by a
spiritual and moral approximation of the "purest flame."

Despite material abundance and promises that "little fairies" will bring
"all that the heart can desire,"[62] the Victorian advertiser is eager to tame
passion, to reduce it to a machine at the disposal of man. Eno's quotes
Huxley's description of perfection:

> his body is the ready servant of his will, and does with ease and pleasure all
> the work that, as a mechanism, it is capable of, whose intellect is a clear, cold,
> logic engine, with all its parts of equal strength and in smooth working order,
> ready like a steam engine, to be turned to try any kind of work, and spin the
> gossamers as well as forge the anchors of the mind.[63]

The ideal is "passions . . . trained to come to heel by a vigorous will."[64]
Man is likened to an "engine," "trained to heel," dominated by "cold" and
"logic." Counter to the consumerist ethic, Eno's advises, "Teach discipline,
self-denial; make its practice pleasurable and you create for the World a
destiny more sublime than ever issued from the brain of the wildest dream-
er."[65] The advertiser seems to praise aspirations of restraint:

> Cheerful submission to superiors. Self respect and independence of character:
> Kindness and protection to the Weak; Readiness to forgive offence; a desire
> to conciliate the differences of others; and above all, fearless devotion to duty
> and unblinding truthfulness . . . Such principles if evoked and carried into
> action would produce an almost perfect moral character in every condition of
> life.[66]

But in fact in many other advertisements a conflicting image is presented;
even the most innocuous image is imbued with provocation and suggestions of sensual indulgence. Borax, not altogether incongruously, portrays
"Purity" as a phantom-like figure with bared breasts,[67] a figure clearly
sexual despite the aspirations of the ideal.

Intimations of private pleasures underpin the most apparently tame

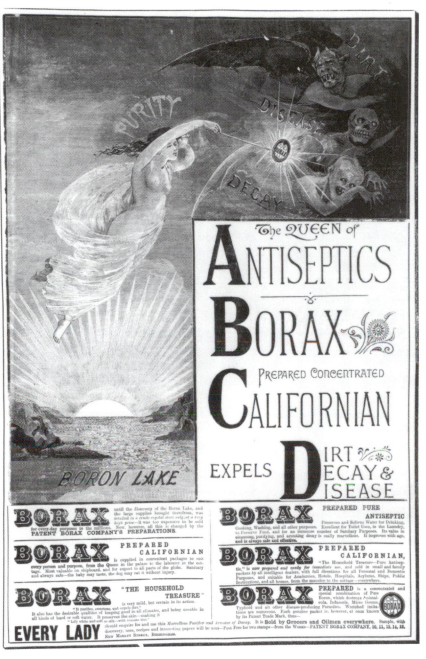

Figure 3-5.   Borax, *Lady's Pictorial*, 1885. (British Library.)

commercial portrayals. A woman slumbers on the beach. She relaxes in front of her fireplace. In evening attire she lounges in an upholstered chair. The woman in recline links the product with leisure, an essential element of the Victorian domestic ideology. But in each advertisement the focus is also the woman's sensual pleasure. She enjoys the restful rhythms of the sea; the heat and comfort of the fire; the luxurious ease of the socialite. In recline, she may appear more vulnerable, less guarded, perhaps passive, but her obvious pleasure suggests a powerfully sensual nature.

Soap advertisements expose unclean thoughts. Peter Gay has used personal correspondence and diaries to debunk the myth of the sexually anaesthetic Victorian woman.[68] Lynda Nead similarly has argued that the visual culture of Victorian Britain does not support an asexual angel as a cultural ideal.[69] In advertisements the commercial woman seems perpetually on the verge of losing control. For Lux Soap a woman, shoulders bared, casts a seductive look as she pours soap flakes into a wide dish. The box of soap is raised high above the plate, too high to facilitate practical pouring. Instead, the flakes cascade from the box in a clear attempt to imply abandon.[70] For Swan Soap a woman, her nakedness barely concealed by a diaphanous robe is attended by a servant.[71] The purpose of the ropes she adjusts is unclear, but suggestive. The soap, says the text, is "always at hand . . . [it] is dainty to sight and touch. It is fragrant and delightful to the senses. Above all it is perfectly pure. . . . Everybody likes it because it does all that it promises." Both in text and in illustration commercial depictions of the aggressively sexy woman are arresting. The dreamy sleeper, the deceptively passive recliner, and the deliberate seductress offer merely a journey further along a continuum of temptation. All may lure the viewer down a shadowy path.

Scantily clad seductresses market goods like soap to women. Created by male advertising agents, these images may have been masculine fantasies of sexy women, but the commercial success of products that used these advertising campaigns suggests that the feminine audience readily accepted the masculine fantasy as a feminine ideal. The seductress offered women an image of one aspect of their ideal selves, as sexually attractive, powerfully irresistible. In a culture that valued feminine decorum, her daring expressions of feminine sexuality appealed to the sexual side of women's nature usually repressed in public forums. The advertiser acknowledged the potent force of feminine sexuality and the desire of women for sensual pleasure.

With a superficial gloss of education and high culture, advertisers used sex to sell commercial goods. For Swan Soap two women bathers linger at the edge of a pool. One is carefully wrapped, crowned with laurel, her hands clasped demurely. She watches her companion, who, having cast aside her shawl, kneels to capture a floating bar of Swan Soap.[72] Artistic plagiarism became commonplace: the image imitates Leighton's "Venus Disrobing for the Bath" and Alma-Tadema's "A Coign of Vantage." Its subtle sensuality lies in its foreshadowing of the removal of clothes and the

Figure 3-6. Lux, *Illustrated London News*, 1900. (Robarts Library.)

metaphorical connotations of bathing. The Grecian bather engages in a sort of vaguely scholarly striptease, which the viewer may watch with impunity reassured that he or she is actually admiring high culture.

Although frequently ancient, the sexual woman might also emerge in other centuries, especially in the Elizabethan period. For example, in one advertisement a Raleigh figure assists a woman across a stream on strategi-

Figure 3-7. Swan Soap, 1902. (Bodleian Library: The John Johnson
Collection, Soap 6. Reprinted by permission.)

cally placed bars of Swan Soap.[73] Historical and foreign images were
extremely popular in the Victorian advertisement. Partly, they are used for
charm. They created pretty advertisements. In the Grecian and Elizabethan example they reminded Victorians of other eras of greatness. They
also permitted advertisers to illustrate daring expressions of intimacy that
might seem too bold for Victorian protagonists. Passionate embraces between Victorian contemporaries were unthinkable. Embraces between
Elizabethans were distant and, therefore, safe.

Foreign women, similarly, gave the advertiser latitude. A Middle Eastern image, for example, added an element of exoticism; it was an image borrowed from popular painting,[74] but a foreign setting also permitted greater pictorial license. A Parisian Diamond Co. advertisement for "Orient" Pearls pictures a Middle Eastern seductress. Her foreign appearance evokes the product name, but the contrast between image and text is also revealing. Her veil is up, her breasts are exposed, her hair down, her arms

Figure *3-8.* Swan Soap, *Illustrated London News,* 1901. (Robarts Library.)

bared. The boldface caption reads "absolutely perfect" and the pearls are described as "new and chaste ornaments."[75] The advertisement preys on a juxtaposition of the pearls, as symbols of purity, against the apparent worldliness of the wearer.

The sexualization of the Middle Eastern woman, like the appearance in

Figure 3-9. Swan Soap, *Illustrated London News*, 1900. (Robarts Library.)

Figure 3-10. Parisian Diamond Co., *Black and White*, 1910. (Robarts Library.)

other advertisements of semi-clad black female slaves as boudoir assistants (see Figure 2.10), is racist, but it is not a simple and uncomplicated image. The slave designated the white woman indisputably as mistress. But when the black woman herself assumed a sexual aspect she conveyed control of a different, perhaps even more incendiary variety. In advertisements she is about to weave the magic of her veils, a participant in the awakening of desire from a bed of rose petals. These images may indeed draw on stereotypes of the exaggerated sexual abandon of certain racial groups, but the advertiser does not focus on the black woman as victim; this would be antithetical to his commercial intent—to sell his products to women. A message of black sexual subservience is an unlikely vehicle to sell soap or diamonds to women, even ostensibly superior white women. But the white female consumer might wish to acquire the powers of sexual attraction, which the black woman in these advertisements epitomizes. The allure of the black woman must be seen within a wider context of the advertiser's general use of foreigners and the past. Both devices allowed advertisers to communicate sexual feelings without offense. Depictions of scantily clad Grecian goddesses, passionate Elizabethans, and Middle Eastern seductresses suggest hedonistic self-indulgence, but they are ultimately safely contained by the enchantment of distance. The Grecian woman and the Middle Eastern woman, unlike her Victorian sisters, might take off her clothes. Lust either centuries old or geographically distant seemed safe, removed from Victorian reality.[76]

The advertiser who uses sexuality, even unconsciously, attempts to defuse the threat of sexuality through the enchantment of distance and also sometimes by reducing the woman in particular to a sort of object, devoid of human passion. In a striking advertisement for Fry's Cocoa,[77] the head of a woman is superimposed onto a cup of steaming cocoa. On the base of the cup a caption reads "My Ideal of Perfection. Dr. Andrew Wilson F.R.S.E." Like a scientific specimen, the doctor has singled out the woman for observation. Her surreal depiction reduces her to the status of object. Like the cup, like the product, she is a base commodity, however ideal, however perfect. The verse below the cup reads "When the heart of a man/Is o'er clouded with fears/The mist is dispelled/When a woman appears/With a cup of Fry's Cocoa to cheer him." Enshrined on the cup, she is free of human fault, neither tempted nor tempting, the epitome of good, but cold and inanimate. In an advertisement for St. Jacob's Oil a Grecian female figure is frozen in stone.[78] A star radiates from her forehead. A bough of roses trails over her lap. A large owl sits in the lower right-hand corner. The slogan reads "Be Wise in Time." She seems to be Athena, who is usually represented in art and literature by her armour and an owl, and often linked with Minerva, the Italian goddess of household arts. Athena symbolizes intelligence and strategy.[79] But even the bravest woman of the past is struck down, loses her arms, suffers pain. The depiction emphasizes not her might, but her debility. Here as a low-relief sculpture, her physicality is sharply diminished. One arm is missing, the other half-obliterated by erosion. The figure's physical self is insignificant; not only frozen, it is stunted. In contrast, values—wisdom, patience, fortitude—assume prominence in the selling message. The juxtaposition of laudable values and atrophied physique is disconcerting, strangely chilling. Although the female figure may represent important ideals, it must be frozen, robbed of vitality, frozen with pain.

To surrender to desire leads in the Victorian advertisement to undefined

"No Better Food." Dr. Andrew Wilson, F.R.S.E., &c.

"My IDEAL of PERFECTION Dr Andrew Wilson F.R.S.E&

"When the heart of a man" "The mist is dispelled"
"Is o'er clouded with fears," "When a woman appears"
With a cup of FRY'S COCOA to cheer him.

Fry's PURE CONCENTRATED

300 Gold Medals, &c. **Cocoa**

N.B.—*Sold only in tins with gilt tops.*

Figure 3-11. Fry's Cocoa, *Illustrated London News*, 1900. (Robarts Library.)

disaster. For F. S. Cleaver's Trebene Soap a young girl lounges on the beach in a bathing costume.[80] Her pose suggests her attractions, while her youth connotes the innocence necessary for respectability. The attending poem, although designed to entertain, nonetheless describes her as "one little maiden," "the only person saved from the wreck." An advertisement for Field's Chamber Candles pictures a scantily clad Psyche with Cupid. Better candles, it argues, might have saved a "scandal."[81] The story of Psyche is, of course, a cautionary tale. Psyche enjoyed the attentions of a lover who only appeared to her after dark. Although content, she was overcome with a desire to see her lover. One night as he lay sleeping, she lit a candle, but a drip of hot candle wax wakened her lover, who fled never to

Figure 3-12. St. Jacob's Oil, *Illustrated Sporting and Dramatic News*, 1890.
(British Library.)

return. In the broadest sense curiosity in the story of Psyche is the agency
of tragedy, but the Victorian advertiser and the Victorian reader were also
very aware of the sexual nature of Psyche's dilemma. Cloaked in humor,
suggestions of "wrecks," of "scandals" convey an amorphous sense of the
dangers of feminine sensuality, of its consuming potential.

The woman who makes mistakes becomes a dominant commercial image, yet the negativity of this image makes it an unlikely vehicle to sell
goods to women, even when the image had a humorous presentation.
Advertisers, I suggest, gravitated to these images unconsciously. As they
pursued a hedonistic ethos, they could not entirely cast away a moral sense
that self-indulgence would be punished. Accordingly, advertisements elaborate the myth of feminine evil, which by the late Victorian period was
well established as an essential literary and artistic theme.[82] Infamous
women appear as commercial exemplars of the deleterious effects of un-
conquered passions. Eno's pictures Marie Antoinette before her execution,
as part of a series of advertisements that offer philosophical messages. The
caption reads "Lost to Human Aid."[83] In contrast, the "gentleness and
force" described in the headline refer to the qualities of love that may
redeem even the woman damned. In another series of advertisements Lady
MacBeth has a similar although more humorous role. For Pears' Soap,
Lady MacBeth asks, "What, will these hands ne'er be clean?"[84] The humor
of the advertisement is clear. Nevertheless, her infamous dilemma equates

physical cleanliness with inner purity. She is unable to attain a cleanliness that is more than skin deep. Marie Antoinette and Lady MacBeth function as commercial villainesses unrivaled by male counterparts. There are virtually no male villains in the Victorian advertisement. The appearance of Marie Antoinette and Lady MacBeth is more than simple coincidence. The demise of each followed suggested unrestrained material acquisitiveness, greed, and sexual indulgence. Both, tempted by pleasurable excess, met stern judgment.

LIKE REPRESENTATIONS OF industrial grandeur, images of women, pure or fallen, revealed Victorian attitudes about progress that were often paradoxical and contradictory. Victorian progress had a material and moral component. These components were treated very differently in the Victorian advertisement. The advertisement celebrated technological progress and embraced its hedonistic potential to gratify any human want. The Victorian advertisement also returned the consumer to an essential moral dilemma. Self-indulgence promised judgment, posed a threat to the purity represented in the feminine ideal and tainted by the Fall. Resolution could be achieved only by frozen passion and inner restraint. The self as cold engine could applaud public and masculine productive power, but remained ever vigilant, wary of a consuming conflagration, lit by the purest flame.

4

Heroes for Sale

In a changing world Victorians sought individuals to admire and examples to venerate. The very principles that animated their society elevated the Great Man, variously defined. Democracy allowed individuals to distinguish themselves through talent, intellect, or virtue. Self-help shaped inspiring portraits of excellence. The gospel of work fashioned individuals of exceptional accomplishment. Progress held the promise of human perfectibility. At the same time, Darwinism, technology, urbanization, irreligion all challenged ideas and realities that a hundred years before had seemed certain or sacred. Even the "solid-looking material world," the very focus of the advertiser's efforts, could prove to be "at bottom . . . Nothing," little more than a "shadow."[1] The advertiser might easily appear to be vendor of "the temporary and the trivial." He attempted, therefore, to associate himself with aspirations that were lofty and substantial. Accordingly, many advertisers identified their own heroes, able men (or women), figures worthy of admiration and esteem.

The Heroic Tradition and the Victorians

The advertisers' efforts to offer commercial heroes were part of a broad western heroic tradition initially prescribed by Aristotle. Aristotle's hero possessed extraordinary powers, dignity, and soul. He was larger than life, above the common level. He was an idealization, better and more virtuous than ordinary men. Nonetheless, he betrayed some mortal qualities and especially was marred by a tragic flaw. During the Romantic period a heightened emphasis on individualism translated into a preoccupation with the heroic and an adaptation of the Aristotelian model. The Romantic hero shares the basic features of the heroic tradition, but also distinctive characteristics, especially sensibility—an infinite capacity for feeling tenderness or love—and an almost satanic predisposition revealed usually in rebellion or self-absorption.[2] The Victorian advertisers' Great Man is a product of the broad heroic tradition and the Romantic legacy in particular, but it is also influenced by conceptions of individual accomplishment and personal esteem defined by the Victorians themselves.

Nineteenth-century socio-economic and technological change cultivated the expansive Victorian interest in personal fame and celebrity. Faster and cheaper printing methods and the removal of stamp duties in 1855 brought about the proliferation of newspapers and periodicals willing to focus on the sensational aspects of popular acclaim as well as notoriety. Rapid sophistication of photography lent a fresh personal quality and immediacy to stories of individual accomplishment. The spectacular popular success of the Great Exhibition of 1851 led to the founding of numerous museums, especially in the South Kensington district, which celebrated fine and applied art, and also its creators. The growth of the railway network meant that pictures and stories were easily transported all over the country. The Victorians approached their quest for heroes with new vitality.

By the mid-nineteenth century the hero formed the absorbing focus of Carlyle's famous *On Heroes and Hero-Worship* (1841). In this book, widely quoted and highly regarded by his contemporaries, Carlyle offers a view of the Hero as "the light which enlightens . . . as a natural luminary shining by the gift of Heaven," "the living light-fountain which it is good and pleasant to be near."[3] The Hero, according to Carlyle, is distinguished by insight or vision, by an understanding of inner truth, which surpasses that of other men. Insight translates into veracity of word and conduct, into absolute sincerity, which again the ordinary man may only approximate because of his own faulty vision or misapprehension. Carlyle's hero has many names—the Great Man, the Thinker, the Inventor, the Teacher. While he is, regardless of title, always a leader and a teacher, the guise in which he performs his functions is determined by his environment and the needs of his society.

> The Hero can be Poet, Prophet, King, Priest . . . according to the kind of world he finds himself born into . . . There is in him the Politician, the Thinker, Legislator, Philosopher;—in one or the other degree, he could have been, he is all of these . . . the grand fundamental character is that of the Great Man; that the man be great.[4]

Samuel Smiles, in contrast, in *Self-Help* (1859) portrays the hero as a man distinguished by behavior. According to Tim Travers, Smiles identifies three types of hero.[5] The first is the man who labors energetically to improve his social and moral condition. Through his own efforts he attains

moral, financial, and political independence. The social and economic
conditions he encounters in his efforts to achieve this goal are basically
unalterable or favorable. He overcomes external conditions through moral
habits. His aims are realized through the conquest of the self. The second
and third models are variations on the same theme. The second class of
hero reveals his disregard for the self through performing socially beneficial work under extreme difficulties. The third type of hero functions as a
contagious moral example. His life is influential and inspiring; he spurs
others to reform and becomes himself an impetus for the improvement of
others. Travers claims that in each incarnation, the Smilesian Hero is
distinguished by his internal battle with evil, his disregard for self, and the
infectious quality of his exemplary behavior and character.[6]

This concern with a moral and upright life is also evidenced in other
Victorian models of heroism such as the traditional farmer or the medieval
craftsman. Genre paintings of the 1850s and 1860s (e.g., Birket Foster's *The
Milkmaid* (1860), Ford Madox Brown's *The Hayfield* (1855), Charles Allston
Collins' *The Good Harvest of 1854* (1855), William Maw Egley's *Hallo Largess*
(1862), Richard Redgrave's *The Valleys Also Stand Thick with Corn* (1865))
praise the traditional farmer. In these paintings the farmer becomes a
symbol. He connotes honest labor, the virtuous life removed from urban
temptation. He offers the basic elements of existence as opposed to manufactured and frivolous extravagances. His labor is relatively independent,
his employment secure, his task deceptively simple. Similarly, the medieval
craftsman was praised by Ruskinian social critics and Arts and Crafts
enthusiasts. Like the farmer, the medieval craftsman is independent, hard-
working, dedicated. As cultural models, both offered honest toil and seductive simplicity.

Despite cultural resonance, images of the farmer and of the medieval
craftsman were essentially reactionary; they looked back to Romantic old-
en days for cultural models. In contrast, for many Victorians, faced with
the demands of the industrial economy, the ideal citizen became the capitalist.[7] Harold Perkin especially argues that the entrepreneurial ideal had
profound cultural significance. It was the entrepreneur, after all, who bore
the risks that fueled the industrial revolution. The great inventors and
industrialists of the Victorian age—Bessemer the steel engineer, Cubitt
the builder, even Hudson the railway king—became mythical symbols of
the potential for achievement in a society that was democratic, capitalist,
and socially mobile.

Commercial Models

Advertisements offer their own models of heroism. They do not exploit
the potentially potent iconography of the humble worker or the resplen-
dent capitalist.[8] Instead, in illustrations and in testimonials they elevate
kings and queens, doctors, soldiers, actresses, politicians, authors, beauties, and scholars to heroic status.

The testimonial was a common element of the Victorian advertisement. It supplied the opinions, sometimes legitimate, but more frequently shamelessly fabricated, of Victorian celebrities and model consumers. The veracity of product endorsements is impossible to assess with accuracy. It is clear that Lily Langtry was paid for her testimonials for Pears' Soap and that H. M. Stanley provided testimonials for Edgington Tents and Vaissier Congo Soap for free. The reproduction of royal images was also clearly authorized in some instances when accompanied by a royal warrant, as we shall see. But most testimonials leave the twentieth-century observer, presumably like the Victorian consumer, to speculate about the veracity not only of claims made, but of the testimonial itself.

Even if its truthfulness was often suspect, the testimonial was clearly a very successful advertising form. Advertising trade journals praised its merits as a manipulative device. At mid-century it was usually supplementary to the principal text, an addendum attached for reinforcement and emphasis. The testimonial almost always advertised patent medicine or foods. Keating's Cough Syrup might offer the testimony of a singer[9]; Brown and Polson Corn Flour might offer a quotation from the *Lancet*.[10] By 1870 some advertisers with increasing enthusiasm employed as many as twelve to fifteen testimonials in one advertisement. Testimonials themselves became the focus, the very source of the selling message. Testimonials in these advertisements were sometimes formulaic, but more frequently they were linked only by a single characteristic shared by each author such as membership in a common profession. With the rise of the illustrated display advertisement circa 1880, the testimonial resumed its supplementary role in the advertisement, but was employed with greater frequency than ever before. By 1890 at least one-third of all advertisements for patent medicines, foods, and corsets contained one or more testimonial.

The testimonial and advertisement illustrations identified many heroes. This chapter will focus on four especially suggestive, but very different models: the expert, the adventurer, the Queen, and the actress. All were apparently very different, but each in advertisements embodied a democratic view of individual distinction.

The Expert

The expert in the Victorian advertisement possessed none of the affecting melodrama that characterizes other commercial heroes. Typically, he was a doctor, a scientist, a member of the press. Of the four models, the expert is the only commercial hero who usually attained no particular individual fame or renown. His prestige nevertheless was considerable. Advertisement after advertisement evoked his authority. More than any other model of human achievement, the advertisement relied on the expert. His was an elevating presence, a voice of calm rationality in a forum replete with exaggeration and distortion.

The stature of the expert hinged on precisely defined abilities. The expert was able to quantify the enigmas of the industrial age. Cadbury's Cocoa in one advertisement offers statistics comparing the quantities of Theobromine and Gluten, "the stimulating and flesh-forming constituents of genuine cocoa," in Cadbury's as against two inferior brands.[11] Pears' Soap quotes a doctor from the Academy of Medicine that some soaps contain "30% of insoluble matter such as lime or plaster and even contain animal nitrogenous matter which causes a chronic inflammation of the skin."[12] The scientist through numbers could address and placate fears exacerbated by the industrial system. Medical testimonies, for example, were popular particularly because they responded to pervasive concern about food adulteration (which clearly predated industrialization) and the potentially dangerous impurities of industrial products in general. The scientist as expert could decipher industrial dilemmas that seemed impenetrable to those armed with common sense alone.

The Victorian consumer admired the precise knowledge of the scientist, his ability to assess value with statistical accuracy, his potential not to be duped by the products of the industrial age. In an advertisement for Salt Regal a town crier reads a scientific report entitled "Hard Facts." Quantification, statistical proofs, hard facts are essential clues to the Victorian perception of the expert. The Victorian enthusiasm for statistics, so evident in the founding of statistical societies and journals[13] and immortalized in *Hard Times*, is embodied in the advertisement's portrait of the expert. His testimony seemed pleasantly free from emotional manipulation and offered no unsubstantiated value judgments. His opinions might seem calculating, but at least they were verifiable. The expert seemed to be the voice of cold logic amid the increasingly sensationalized puffery that came to characterize the late Victorian advertisement (although in reality his voice was as manipulative as any other commercial voice).

The expert in the Victorian advertisement is no youthful or even middle-aged genius conjuring wildly from a test-tube laboratory. He is an old man, bearded, peering somberly through a microscope. His expertise is the product of old age; the accumulation of years of experience, rather than a fleeting ray of inspiration. He exudes the unmistakable bearing of a long and dignified career. To the Victorians, facts, raw quantification, were not sufficient. Confronted with so much that was new, untested, uncertain, the Victorian revered the sure-footed solidity of experience.

The expert's ability to understand the apparently incomprehensible is often revealed in deliberately obfuscating testimony. Following a dramatic headline "Poison in Toilet Soap," an advertisement for Pears' Soap quotes Dr. Reveil of the Academy of Medicine describing inferior soaps:

> I need but state that arsenic, the acid nitrate of mercury, tartar emetic and potassa caustica form part of their ingredients, whilst they are coloured green by the sesquixodide of chromium or of a rose colour by the bisulphuret of mercury (vermilion).[14]

"Cadbury's Cocoa being absolutely pure is therefore the best Cocoa."

Figure 4-1. Cadbury's Cocoa, *Family Circle of the Christian World*, 1890. (British Library.)

The expert possesses understanding. The consumer, on the other hand, did not hope to understand the above testimony completely or to test its veracity: he was simply impressed. While the knowledge of the expert purported to be useful, the advertisement does not require the consumer to understand. The status of expert is prescribed by a knowledge of the complex, an access through learning to knowledge of the seemingly inaccessible.

The proliferation of periodicals in the late nineteenth century, especially the founding of an astounding forty-eight ladies' magazines between 1880 and 1900, did not dilute their prestige. The periodical press emerged as a celebrated expert of the Victorian advertisement. The expertise that fuels "Extract[s] from the Press" or "Opinions of the Press" in the Victorian advertisement derives from a distinctive understanding of "mysterious invention."[15] In an age in which many magazines provided weekly invention columns (i.e., *Cassell's* "The Gatherer"), the press seemed singularly able to inform Victorians about the latest novelties and innovations. For example, one product, the Patent Darning Weaver, is described in its advertisements by *The Times* as an "invention ingenious and simple"; by the *Queen* as "a clever little contrivance," and by *The Lady* as "a perfect boon and a blessing to women."[16] If the press could furnish information about the very latest inventions, it could also supply knowledge of science and technical process. *The Tablet*, mimicking the authority of the medical testimonial, could recommend Epps's cocoa because it "not only stimulates, but nourishes, far more than any drink of its kind. It contributes to the wasted tissues in its "flesh-forming' and to "animal combustion" in its heat-giving properties."[17] Alternately, the press could assert an investigative appreciation of the process of manufacture. In an advertisement for Epps's Cocoa, *Cassell's Household Guide* offered to "give an account of the process adapted by Messrs James Epps & Co., manufacturers of dietetic articles at their works in Holland Street."[18] Just as the scientific or medical expert could dissect the composition of the industrial product, the press as expert offered to demythologize the mysteries of invention, mechanization, and manufacture.

With an access to knowledge of the latest inventions, scientific theories and mechanical processes and a unique prescriptive understanding of the fashionable life, the press could assess the relative quality of consumer goods. Old Bleach Linen was evaluated as "an exceptionally strong linen, that will last for many years" by the *Queen*, as "much sounder and stronger than ordinary linens" by *Young Ladies' Journal*.[19] Press testimony was brought into the service of the most unexpected products. The *Lancet* endorsed Compagnie Coloniale Chocolates[20] and advised, in the interests of Ogden Cigarettes, that when "used with due moderation Tobacco is of value second only to food itself."[21]

The advice of the press expert was authoritative, but comforting. In an advertisement for Edward's Oriental Sauce, the *Lady's Pictorial* recommends

> If you are at your wit's end for a nice and wholesome relish to soups and fish, get some Edward's Oriental Sauce. It is pre-eminent for its delicious flavour, the pureness of the ingredients, and its genuine Oriental properties, and forms a most welcome adjunct to steaks, cutlets, game etc. It possesses one attribute which will bring it into particular favour, namely that it will keep admirably even in the hottest climates.[22]

The expert assumes a maternal voice. *Lady's Pictorial* provides a clear course of action for the woman "at [her] wit's end"; its answer is "nice and "wholesome" and pure; it recommends tasty foods, but is mindful of practical concerns about nutrition and storage. The consumer, inundated with brand-differentiated goods, bewildered by choice, depended on the expert to assume a mock-maternal role, to act as benevolent guide, to discern quality, and to assess the relative merits of a barrage of products that confronted her in the Victorian advertisement.

The commercially anointed expert—the doctor, the scientist, the press—was elevated beyond common experience by extraordinary knowledge of the new products of the industrial age. Through information, quantification, and hard facts, the expert accessed the inaccessible, understood the seemingly incomprehensible, demythologized the mysteries of invention. His expertise was the result of careful study, long hours, and experience. The consumer, through her own repeated consumption and diligent research, hoped to become her own expert. Expertise was acquired, not innate. With the desire to achieve, expertise was attainable, self-controlled and self-created. The commercial expert enshrined the promise of heroic status by merit rather than by the circumstances of birth.

The Adventurer

The commercial hero forged his own destiny and charted his own course, literally as well as metaphorically. He was an adventurer in the twentieth-century sense of a person who undertakes extraordinary enterprises (rather than in the Victorian sense of a person who lives by underhanded means). He is repeatedly elevated in testimonials that reflect a fascination with voyages to exotic places and feats of daring. But his bravery might be cultivated by many men.

According to Leo Braudy in *The Frenzy of Renown: Fame and Its History*, the attraction of adventure represented a transformation of older forms of heroism. Up to the eighteenth century the greatest, although not exclusive, expression of bravery was the duel. By the nineteenth century the duel in most European countries was either illegal or passé. Braudy asserts that the nineteenth-century British equivalent was to dare something never before attempted or even to do something foolhardy. The Charge of the Light Brigade in the Crimean War (1854) or Gordon in Egypt or Rhodes in Africa were all potentially heroic in this nineteenth-century context. Clearly, there had been heroes of this type long before the nineteenth

century, but Braudy suggests that their brand of heroism became especially
important in the nineteenth century. The world was more charted and
known; adventurers sought unfamiliar and dangerous spots. Overwhelm-
ing odds and strange settings and situations could only augment the ex-
plorer's appeal. Moreover, in an increasingly civilized world the man who
fearlessly infiltrated the ostensible hearts of savagery and barbarism was
especially prized.[23]

H. M. Stanley came in the advertisement to embody the adventuresome
hero. Stanley, a veteran of the American Civil War and former correspondent of the *New York Herald*, became famous in Britain after he rescued
Livingston in 1871. Nearly twenty years later in 1886 he was sent to Africa
by a coalition of businessmen to assist Emin Pasha in consolidating British
power in the interior of East Africa and to return with seventy-five tons of
ivory. The Emin Pasha Relief Expedition became one of the most publicized African expeditions of the nineteenth century. His two volume
account of his adventures, *In Darkest Africa or the Quest, Rescue and Retreat
of Emin Governor of Equatoria*, was widely read.[24] In England Stanley was
welcomed with balls, receptions, lectures, and parades. Advertisers hun-
grily exploited his image. Stanley legitimately endorsed Victor Vaissier's
Congo Soap and Edgington Tents, but his appearance in myriad advertisements for a wide range of other products is striking.

Stanley is pictured, for example, at a "Reception at Guildhall" in an
advertisement for Cellular Clothing.[25] In other advertisements he applauds the merits of Bovril. He praises U.K. Tea.[26] In one particularly
interesting advertisement, widely published in the summer of 1890 in a
variety of Victorian periodicals, Stanley meets Emin Pasha at Kavelli. Although engravings in the periodical press had portrayed the meeting as a
formal occasion, in the advertisement for U.K. Tea Stanley and Emin
sip tea in a tent surrounded by packing crates. The parted curtains
reveal tropical palms before a mountainous backdrop and, in the foreground, the earnest toil of native workers. The two men were complete
strangers, one German, one English, but in the advertisement they chat as
old friends.[27]

Partly, the Stanley advertisement succeeds through the appeal of Empire. Thomas Richards asserts in *The Commodity Culture of Victorian England* that the U.K. Tea advertisement and others like it reflect a jingoistic
view of Empire, in which Africa functions as the new market for surplus
goods.[28] For Richards the power of this particular advertisement lies not
in the appeal of Stanley as hero, but in the metaphorical significance of the
commodity as civilizing agent and a symbol of Englishness.[29] Richards'
argument is not without merit. Stanley's progress in Africa did transform
him into a conqueror of sorts, and clearly advertisers liked the conqueror
image. (An advertisement for Dr. Ebermann's Tooth-wash pictures
Napoleon standing in a position of strength, one foot on a rock under the
caption, "the best dentifrice in the world.")[30] In the advertisement, the
illustration of Stanley drinking tea while natives toil in the hot sun, al-

though not a bravura Napoleonic image, does suggest Stanley's relative strength. Stanley may symbolize the English conquest of Africa. Tea may function as a civilizing agent. The advertisement undoubtedly plays on both themes.

But the composition of the advertisement offers another meaning as well. The preference for an informal scene rather than a more accurate depiction permits an intimate glimpse of the famous in repose. Just as the parted curtains of the tent allow its occupants to peer out while retaining an impression of sheltered privacy, the viewer watches unobserved from the other side of the tent. Stanley's stature is not only retained, but complemented by a comfortable teatime conversation that approximates the behavior of ordinary men and emphasizes Stanley's mortality. The advertisement's fundamental appeal is the charismatic draw of one man, Stanley the adventurer, here made invitingly more accessible by a familiar tea-time ritual.

In another advertisement, this time for Liebig Extract, Stanley replicates his adventures in Darkest Africa.

On the 22nd, soon after the advance had reached camp, a cold and heavy shower of rain fell, which demoralised many in the column: their failing energies and their impoverished systems were not proof against the cold. Madis and Zansibaris dropped their loads in the road and rushed helter-skelter for the camp.

"IN DARKEST AFRICA."—**Effect of the Liebig Company's Extract of Meat on a Madi Carrier.**—"On the 22nd, soon after the advance had reached camp, a cold and heavy shower or rain fell, which demoralised many in the column: their failing energies and their impoverished systems were not proof against cold. Madis and Zanzibaris dropped their loads in the road, and rushed helter-skelter for the camp. One Madi managed to crawl near my tent, wherein a candle was lit, for in a rainstorm the forest, even in daylight, is as dark as on an ordinary night in the grassland. Hearing him groan, I issued out with the candle, and found the naked body rigid in the mud, unable to move. As he saw the candle-flame his eyes dilated widely, and he attempted to grasp it with his hands. He was at once borne to a fire, and laid within a few inches of it, and with the addition of a pint of hot broth made from the **Liebig Company's Extract of Meat,** we restored him to his senses. On the road in front of the rear guard two Madis died, and also one Zanzibari of the rear column, stricken instantaneously to death by the intensely cold rain."—*Stanley's "In Darkest Africa."*

Figure   4-3.   Liebig Extract, *Lady's Pictorial*, 1891. (British Library.)

The setting fully described, Stanley recounts a miraculous event that ensued:

> One Madi managed to crawl near my tent, wherein a candle was lit, for in a rainstorm the forest, even in daylight, is as dark as on an ordinary night in the grassland. Hearing him groan, I issued out with the candle and found the

naked body rigid in the mud, unable to move. As he saw the candle flame his eyes dilated widely, and he attempted to grasp it with his hands. He was at once borne to a fire and within a few inches of it.

Finally, near the end of his stirring testimony, the product is introduced:

> . . . with the addition of a pint of hot broth made from the Liebig Company's Extract of Meat, we restored him to his senses. On the road in front of the rear guard two Madis died and also one Zanzibari of the rear column, stricken instantaneously to death by the intensely cold rain.[31]

The celebrity battles the elements and survives while others die in the jungle. He rescues others, nurses them back to health, and yet emerges from the experience to assess the casualties. The adventurer in the Victorian advertisement reigns victorious even outside the bounds of civility. For him, no struggle is debilitating or daunting.

The nineteenth-century soldier who triumphed in Africa or the Middle East, similarly, undertook his own extraordinary enterprise. In advertisements a recurrent militaristic motif appears mostly, but not exclusively, around the time of the Boer War. The advertiser used a topical image, but he nonetheless elevated the soldier to heroic status. Liebig pictures a soldier on horseback; Bovril illustrates a soldier and a sailor raising a toast; Ogden's Cigarettes presents a group of soldiers smoking outside their tent. The military man in the Victorian advertisement is perpetually commanding. From horseback he offers a conventional image of control. With his fellows he toasts victory and alludes to the camaraderie of the armed forces, a unity bred by the shared experiences of life-threatening situations. From the tent he masters the Spartan conditions of the Middle East.

During the Boer War the military motif reaches its peak. An advertisement announces that "Soldiers of the Queen and smokers in general prefer Old Gold Cigarettes."[32] Ogden's Cigarettes under the caption "Home from the Front" pictures a collection of officers drinking port and smoking cigarettes.[33] Lemco celebrates the "41 Years in India"[34] of Field Marshall Lord Roberts. The soldier in the military advertisement embodies not only individual courage, but personifies the patriotic impulse. Themes of patriotism, like the themes of Empire that color advertisements with Stanley, inform interpretations of the Victorian military advertisement, but they do not fully explain the advertisement's depiction of the individual soldier, which, as we shall see, emphasizes his human nature.

Although military advertisements sometimes do feature officers or war leaders, they more typically praise "the soldier on the battlefield." Under the caption, "What the soldiers say about Bovril," Bovril offers a letter from Lance-Corporal Kenworthy of the 14th Hussars with General Buller's force in Natal to his mother. He writes,

> Yesterday we had reveille at half-past three and turn out half-past four, in drill order, for a day of reconnaissance, and it was the hardest I have had in the

saddle. We started trotting and galloping about six in the morning, and we were at it at six o'clock at night, had no dinner, as I had a tin of Bovril Lozenges with me, which kept me up all night.[35]

Kenworthy's letter marks him as a survivor despite physical hardship. But there is also a humble quality to his correspondence. The brave soldier is but a boy, writing to his mother, assuring her that although he had no dinner, he was well-fortified with Bovril. The domestic theme recurs.

In an advertisement for Ogden's Cigarettes, soldiers, pictured trekking "On the road to Pretoria,"[36] use a placard advertising Ogden's Guinea-Gold Cigarettes on the Veldt as a "roof to a shanty to keep the sun off a bit" and "at night . . . to keep the dampness away, two of us sleeping on it."[37] Again, hardship is implied, but the description of improvised sleeping arrangements (improbably courtesy of Ogden's advertisements themselves) injects a humble quality to the endurance of the soldier. He is not the sort of brave hero whose exploits are to be so elevated, so distant from the common condition, that reference to the basic necessities of his daily existence diminishes his stature. The hardship of the soldier is an equalizer, which places two men, previously strangers, side by side sleeping on an advertising board. The rank-and-file variant of the military motif is democratic. It buries individual differences in love of country.

The late Victorian advertisement applauds the soldier for his accomplishments, but does not ennoble him. In military fine art of the same period, Joan Hichberger argues, the soldier is idealized, presented with a passionless face set apart by physical beauty and a natural heroism.[38] In contrast to the fine art visual image described by Hichberger, the commercial soldier is not god-like. He is disheveled, strong, but rough, more popularized than idealized, without the Grecian facial features common in other advertisements.[39] His distinction is derived not from birth, but from action. His qualities of behavior are accessible to all and embody the democratic promise of Victorian heroism.

Just as the expert rises to heroic status in the advertisement as a sure and steady guide through the newly labyrinthine world of commodities, the adventurer explores his own unfamiliar territory. The appeal of the adventurer, however, is rooted not in somber counsel, but in vivid melodrama. The adventurer embraces danger, even barbarism with unfailing strength. This strength is often bravely individualistic, but it is parallelled and supported in the advertisement by potent strains of patriotism and Empire that aggrandize the individual's pursuits and raise them above the sordid level of selfish interest. Represented by figures such as Stanley or by the military icon, the adventurer seems impressive. But his appearance is average, even roughened. Many of his concerns—tea breaks, writing to his mother, sleeping arrangements—are conspicuously mundane. Advertisers, while they applaud the objectives of the adventurer with grandiose cloaks of national goals and celebrate his brave exploits in minute detail, fail to idealize the man himself. In the advertisement the adventurer is human-

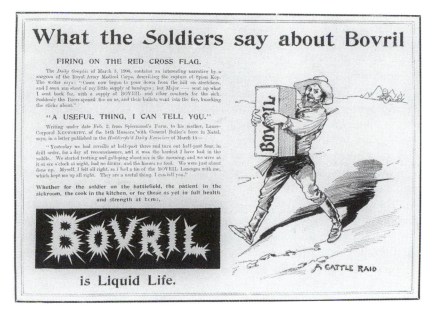

Figure 4-4. Bovril, *Illustrated London News*, 1900. (Robarts Library.)

ized, his common qualities emphasized. He is ennobled, not by circumstance, or by blood, but by action. The adventurer as hero is a proud example of distinction by achievement, who serves as a commercial vivification and exemplar of the democratic principle.

The Queen

In contrast, the Queen's heroic role in the Victorian advertisement seems to contradict broad currents of democratization. She alone was Queen. But in advertisements her unique political role is rarely highlighted; instead, advertisers promote the leveling theme of her feminine nature.

David Cannadine argues convincingly that the charismatic potential of the Queen, especially her ceremonial aspect, was promoted in the late nineteenth century. Whereas the first half of her reign was clouded by political squabbles such as the Bedchamber Crisis (1839) and later by her reclusive widowhood, in old age she became the grand old matriarch of Europe. A more national, sensational, and pictorial media that could disseminate the royal image emerged and the growth of Empire tied Victoria's image to a powerful, patriotic concept. By the Golden Jubilee of 1887 the commercial appeal of the Queen had been transformed. Manufacturers capitalized on the Queen's newfound popularity with commemorative pottery, medals, and innumerable souvenirs. Advertisers, too, seized upon the image of the Queen. Advertising journals featured articles describing Jubilee advertising techniques.

Evocations of the royal image for commercial purposes evolved in part from the use of the royal warrant. In exchange for supplying the royal household, one of the privileges accorded to warrant holders was the right to advertise the royal warrant. In theory, the royal warrant was to be displayed with taste and discretion. In practice, tradition dictated that in print advertisements the royal coat of arms should be displayed in a size never larger than the caption or product name. During the reign of Victoria, the number of warrant holders rapidly expanded (to 807), but the conventions restricting advertisements were flagrantly ignored.[40] The royal warrant became the very subject of many advertisements. An advertisement for Jay's in 1890 depicts large crests of the Queen, Princess of Wales, and Duchess of Cambridge along the left margin of an unillustrated advertisement under a gigantic boldface title. The crests themselves became the illustration, a garish focus in a print-dense advertisement.[41] Advertisements increasingly flaunted royal approval; the most tenuous connection to royalty implied a product of quality and encouraged consumers to buy a fine product favored by royalty.

If the advertiser intended merely to suggest that the Queen's use of a product connoted quality, the royal warrant was a sufficient and conventional means to communicate such a simple and uncomplicated message. But the royal image offered advertisers and the public more than one level of meaning. This is precisely the quality that made it so attractive. A product used by royalty held the promise of transformation; all consumers could feel like royalty through simple acts of consumption. An advertisement for Glenfield Laundry Starch features a stunning illustration of the Princess of Wales in an elaborate gown.[42] The beauty of the illustration is captivating. The engraving is fine; the very detail of her gown absorbing. The text announces that the product is "exclusively used in the Royal Laundry," "H.M. Laundress says it is the finest she ever used." Bold letters spell out the product name at the bottom of the advertisement. The intent of the advertisement is clear. The starch is so good it can be used successfully on such an expensive and elaborate gown and produce stunning results. But the promise of Glenfield Starch is democratic. Merely by using Glenfield Starch the humble consumer hopes to achieve some smaller, humbler, but in their own way, impressive results. Her home, if only in the laundry, will become like the palace. The consumer will, like the princess, become more beautiful than before; her behavior even in the smallest detail, royal, even if the supposed metamorphosis is superficial, confined to the exterior qualities improved by laundry starch.

The image of members of the extended royal family was often crassly sensationalized. A pictured Princess Marie of Greece, for example, might improbably request an "urgent telegraphic order" of "six bottles of Harlene" Hair Restorer.[43] But the Queen herself was almost always dignified with a more complex social role. Although the charismatic, ceremonial aspect of her role was heightened during the latter years of her reign, the Queen's popular image was conditioned as much by gender as by gran-

MESSRS JAY

Have the honour to announce that they have imported for the present season very elegant Novelties in

MANTLES, COSTUMES, AND MILLINERY,

WHICH MAY BE WORN IN OR OUT OF MOURNING.

MANTLES.

MESSRS JAY are constantly receiving from Paris MODEL MANTLES of the most *recherché* character. These models, after they have been copied, are offered at far lower prices than they could be bought at in Paris, and are suitable for ladies who are not in mourning.

MILLINERY.

MESSRS JAY are constantly receiving new MILLINERY from the first houses in Paris, and the most approved forms are at once copied to suit every degree of Mourning.

COSTUMES.

NOVELTIES in COSTUMES, designed by the leaders of fashion in Paris, are forwarded to Messrs JAY continually during the London season.

SPECIAL NOTICE.

MESSRS JAY'S choicest NOVELTIES are neither Illustrated nor shown in the Windows of their Establishment.

FASHION.

"I cannot do better than give you an account of my visit to the widely-known "establishment of Mr Jay, in Regent-street.
"Mr Jay has recently made considerable alterations in his already very com-"modious and extensive premises, and the taste and style for which he has "always been celebrated in all matters of dress has not failed him in the art of "decorating. There is a special room devoted to grey, the numerous shades of "which, and the extent to which this colour is in vogue, make it necessary to "give it this importance. The most exquisite taste has been displayed in the "choice of the models from Paris.
"I saw a charming dress of puce foulard and laine, the check of the foulard "being sufficiently large, for, though in flowered materials the designs will be small "in checks, the size will be limited to the taste of the wearer.
"The small tippets of jet and lace that are evidently to be very much worn are "too numerous to describe individually. Large jet epaulettes, collars, and bell-"shaped net sleeves were the principal features. Many were made in the zouave "form, the zouave being heavily embroidered and trimmed with jet, to my mind "the prettiest being in the form of a close-fitting body of velvet, with lace sleeves "falling to the elbow, and arranged in epaulette fashion on the shoulder.
"The cloaks shown by Mr Jay this season surpass his usual standard. I "could not have done better, therefore, than describe the novelties at Mr Jay's "establishment, for all that emanates from it carries an especial stamp for "uniqueness, as he neither allows his choicest novelties to be sketched or "exhibited in the window."—*Life, April 19, 1890.*

NOVELTIES AT JAY'S.

"As usual at this season of the year, Jay's Mourning Warehouse, Regent Street, "is to the fore with a splendid assortment of new materials for summer wear. To "the fact that grey is the prevailing colour this season is attributable the number-"less shades of that favourite tint on view at this house. Black grenadine will also "be much worn, and in this material there is an endless variety of designs amongst "those at Jay's. In silks, brocades will this year take the lead, the patterns being "mostly small and detached, the floral designs being specially attractive and hand-"some in the extreme.
"Then there is a new silk by Bonnet, of Lyons, made specially and solely for "Jay's, well adapted for deep mourning. In the mourning department the firm have "some beautiful nun's veilings of exquisite texture."—*Court Circular.*

NEW PARIS MILLINERY.

"Dainty and delicate confections in the way of hats and bonnets fresh from the "most famous Parisian *ateliers* may be seen just now at Jay's."—*Lady's Pictorial.*

NEW MANTLES.

"The week before last we had occasion to mention the novelties in materials "just received by Messrs Jay from Paris, and now we have been favoured with a "private view of the new Parisian mantles, capes, and jackets that have arrived "within the last few days. These we may say at once are all extremely dis-"tingue, and though there may be some that will require trifling modifications "to suit the quieter English taste, there are others that will be seized upon "immediately as positive gems in the matter of artistic taste and elegance."—Court Circular.

MOURNING.

"In reply to many inquiries, we recommend the Maison Jay.
"This house, long established, makes mourning a speciality, and is excelled "by no other house in London or Paris for the beauty of the work, the quality of "the material, or the style of manufacture."

MOURNING ORDERS IN THE COUNTRY.

Messrs JAY'S experienced Assistants and Dress-fitters travel to any part of the kingdom, free of expense to purchasers. They take with them Dresses, Mantles, and Millinery, besides Patterns of Materials, all marked in Plain Figures, and at the same price as if purchased at the warehouse. Reasonable estimates are also given for Household Mourning.

JAY'S, REGENT STREET, LONDON.

HER MAJESTY THE QUEEN.

H.R.H. THE PRINCESS OF WALES.

H.R.H. THE LATE DUCHESS OF CAMBRIDGE.

To LADIES Jay's FOR BLACK BLACK & WHITE and all Shades of GREY GOODS THE LARGEST THE CHOICEST The BEST Selection IN THE WORLD REGENT STREET LONDON W.

Printed and Published by the Registered Proprietor, HORACE COX, at 346, Strand, in the Parish of St. Mary-le-Strand, London, W.C., in the County of Middlesex, Saturday, May 3, 1890.

Figure 4-5. Jay's, *Queen*, 1890. (British Library.)

Figure 4-6. Glenfield Starch, 1869. (Bodleian Library: The John Johnson Collection, Soap 7. Reprinted by permission.)

deur, as Dorothy Thompson has so convincingly demonstrated. She acquired the image of a mother-figure who stood above the coarse realities of politics.[44] She presided over her family and her Empire with a maternal devotion shaped as much by her femininity as by years of political experience. The commercial interpretation of the image of the Queen reveals this tension between the womanliness of the Queen and her political role as head of state.

Commercial interpretations of the Queen's symbolic political role are suggestive. During the Jubilee year, an advertisement for Matchless Metal Polish features cameos—of the Queen, the Prince of Wales, and Princess Alexandra—under the slogan "A Matchless Reign and a Matchless Polish."[45] In addition to a patriotic appeal—"Be Loyal! Don't Purchase For-

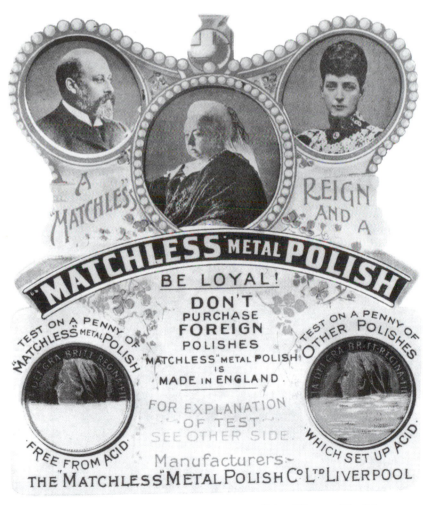

Figure 4-7. Matchless Metal Polish, n.d. (Bodleian Library: The John Johnson Collection, Oil and Candles II. Reprinted by permission.)

eign Polishes"—Matchless appears simply to draw upon its long-standing product name to praise the Queen and to provide itself with a novel and timely mnemonic. But the advertiser also reveals attitudes about the Queen, of which he was probably not even conscious. Although ostensibly matchless, the advertisers do not portray the Queen in unrivaled splendor, but instead depict her with her successors, an image that suggests the continuity of the crown as institution, rather than the singularity of the Queen's personal accomplishment. The advertiser may have intended simply to present as many royal figures as possible in one advertisement. But this device alone conveys a particular attitude about the Queen, even if it is unconscious. The Queen appears as an impressive thing that temporarily outshines the rest, but is ultimately replaceable. She is a commodity at the peak of her popularity, surrounded, not threatened by successors, but destined ultimately to be supplanted by a newer, more vibrant product.

In contrast, advertisers reveal considerable enthusiasm for the matriarchal aspects of the Queen's popular identity. In an advertisement for Sunlight Soap an organ supports sheet music for "God Save the Queen!" The caption reads "Harmony in every Home where Sunlight Soap is used."[46] A pun is the selling device. Sunlight becomes an agent of harmony at home; the Queen an agent of harmony in the nation. A woman will buy Sunlight to avoid domestic difficulties or dissention; the Queen prevents discord on another sort of domestic level. The organ, as a symbol of Christian virtue and wholesome family entertainment as well as grand cathedral celebrations, underscores the parallel maternal and national functions. The Queen in this context seems benevolent, her motivations the innate product of feminine nature rather than potentially sinister political intention. The Queen's role, like that of the angel in the house to which all women aspire, argues the advertisement, is redemptive, conciliatory, attractive, but ultimately innocuous, restricted by virtuous aims and the interests of harmony. The Queen embodies qualities that may be shared by every woman.

The role of a queen seems benign when it is overshadowed by quintessentially feminine objectives. A series of advertisements for Liebig Extract describe European queens and their palaces. The biography of the Empress of Germany is most telling.[47] Although she is depicted as being "untiring in the discharge of the numerous functions which her exalted position imposes on her,"

> The most prominent characteristic of H.M. is her domesticity: her greatest concern is for her family, and she takes the deepest interest in her children's eduction and recreation. As a model wife and mother, the Empress is universally popular with all classes of her people . . . The Emperor once said of her "I wish every German girl would follow the example of the Empress and devote their lives, as she does to the cultivation of the 3Ks—Kirche, Kinder and Küche—Church, Children and Cookery.

Figure 4-8. Sunlight Soap, 1895. (Bodleian Library: The John Johnson Collection, Soap 6. Reprinted by permission.)

The maternal role distances the queen from the political arena. It also furnishes a kinship with other women. Queens, as much as ordinary women, are elevated by their maternal function. It is through excelling in this role that a queen may distinguish herself most impressively, become a "model," an "example." The domestication of the royal image encourages the humble consumer to strive to attain the royal ideal: to excel through achievement and merit in her maternal role, to celebrate an essential equality among mothers, rather than to gaze awestruck at the class-specific dignity of a queen's ceremonial role.

Indeed, the grandeur of monarchy is dwarfed by the commanding needs of maternity. An advertisement for Atkinson & Barker's Royal Infants Preservative pictures the Queen and a mother with her baby. Given the considerable attention paid to the Prince of Wales's feathers in the frame, the mother is presumed to be Alexandra. She sits in a throne-like chair holding her infant; the Queen appears to sit beside her.[48] The mother and child thereby form the focus of the advertisement; the Queen is consigned to an unlikely supporting role. She is a grandmother. The secondary importance of the Queen is reinforced by the captions at the top of the advertisement. The first reads "Important to Mothers." The second announces "Patronized by Her Most Gracious Majesty Queen Victoria and all the Royal Family." The appeal to mothers takes precedence over the royal warrant. The Atkinson & Barker advertisement attempts to evoke the prestigious patronage of royalty, but is careful to flatter its consumers by raising maternity above royal status. The Queen in all her magnificence is overshadowed by the supremely elevating role accorded to motherhood. The Queen is not denigrated by these priorities, but humanized. Just as Stanley acquires a friendly aspect in a makeshift tea-time scene, here the Queen, although stiff and formal, is also a grandmotherly figure absorbed in family rather than political functions. The intimacy of both scenes allows the reader to observe the famous in a private moment and to ponder the equalizing consequences of the hero's human nature.

The Queen is everywoman, not only mother, but even a knowing shopper. In a widely published advertisement the Queen admires My Queen Vel Vel (Velveteen). Shopping, as a feminine function, possessed none of the elevating characteristics of maternity, yet here it is the focus of the Queen's interest. The Queen is surely happy to know, the advertisement suggests, that My Queen Vel Vel is "simply perfect, with the lustre and finish of silk velvet, but lighter to wear and less liable to spot or plush [at] . . . one-sixth of the cost."[49] Even though she is the Queen, she can appreciate value and durability as well as beauty. The Queen in these advertisements emerges as a domesticated monarch who embodies not the accoutrements of class, but interests shared by all women.

An earlier version of the same My Queen Vel Vel advertisement in 1887 included a complex backdrop detailing the Queen's domestic environment. The advertisement shows an elaborate clock, a palm, a basket of flowers, lace curtains, a screen, all suggestive of the Queen's material wealth.[50] The

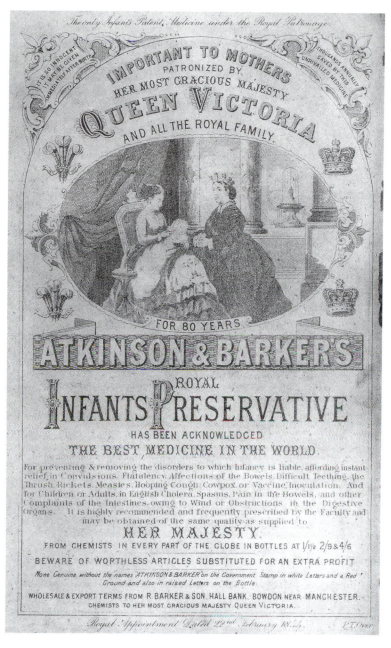

Figure 4-9. Royal Infant's Preservative, 1872. (Bodleian Library: The John Johnson Collection, Food 8. Reprinted by permission.)

Figure *4-10.* My Queen Vel Vel, *Lady's Pictorial*, 1893. (British Library.)

luxurious setting emphasizes the luxurious quality of the velveteen. Velveteen appears to be only one of the many trappings of royalty. The removal of the setting in the second version of the advertisement changes the focus. The advertisement's emphasis switches from luxury to the Queen's feminine knowledge as shopper. The Queen is humanized as shopper, but authoritative nonetheless. In both advertisements the Queen is attended by two assistants, either ladies-in-waiting or shop clerks. These assistants both connote the privilege of royalty, and project an impression of service specifically around the purchase of the product. The Queen is distant and formidable in these advertisements; staring into space. As Queen, only accustomed to the finest, she recognizes quality immediately; she idly gestures approval. The process of consumption acquires an elevated quality, a royal aura; it merits the most discerning judgment. The consumer newly appreciates the humble shopping expedition as a queenly endeavor.

The Queen as shopper defies the banality often suggested by monotonous repetition of Jubilee portraits and kitsch motifs of Empire. It reveals that despite widespread gratuitous exploitation, advertisers evolved a developed and substantive interpretation of the Queen's social role. Royal figures in general were imbued with a glamor that distanced them from average consumers. The aggrandizing effects of the Queen's political role, however, were defused with humor and with abstractions celebrating the continuity of monarchy as an institution, rather than the Queen's individu-

al power. The advertisement did not always explore the charismatic ceremonial aspect of the Queen. It often preferred her domestic character. In
many advertisements the Queen was mother and shopper, elevated by
maternity and discerning judgment; she was a purveyor of harmony instead of opulent splendor. The Queen as commercial heroine embodied
womanly qualities accessible to all; she was the product of femininity
fulfiled, rather than a personification of a comparatively cold system of
class distinction and constitutional sovereignty.

The Actress

The actress was an altogether different commercial heroine whose celebrity
crossed barriers of class and morality. Her stature was clearly not a product
of womanly virtue. Risqué portraits in the late Victorian and Edwardian
press highlighted her distance from the maternal ideal. Instead, she was a
feminine version of the adventurer—an extreme expression of some qualities of her sex, which were democratized and idealized in the commercial
forum.

The commercial elevation of the actress seems to defy an antitheatrical
prejudice that scholars often attribute to the nineteenth century.[51] By 1830
the actor was still regarded as a social and artistic outcast. He might
possess few skills and was bound by no standards or ethics. He was often
idle, bohemian, even illiterate. His reputation was completely at odds with
prevailing ideals of earnestness, self-restraint, thrift, and hard work. For
the actress social stigma was even more severe. Her work, unlike painting
or music, removed her from the genteel circle of the home. It necessitated
public exposure and immodest dress. It situated her in neighborhoods in
which shared accommodation was common and crime was rampant. It
required her to play villains and sirens. All these conditions conveyed the
impression that she was a woman of easy virtue.

By the late nineteenth century, as the number of actresses proliferated,[52]
a prejudice lingered, but in a qualified and diminished form. The widening
sphere of employment for women and a fashion for a quieter, more polite
style of acting defused some of the stigma. But the actress was also helped
by shifting attitudes at the highest level of Victorian society. Queen Victoria herself had favored Covent Garden for opera and ballet in the early
years of her reign. Yet in the late nineteenth century she emerged as an
aficionado of the theatre. Stanley Weintraub, in his biography of Queen
Victoria, suggests that, despite mourning, the Queen enjoyed plays, including musicals, often brought to her at great expense.[53] The Queen sat
in the first row for a performance at Windsor Castle of *The Gondoliers*, for
example, in 1891; she brought Clara Butt to perform at Balmoral. The
Queen's patronage of popular entertainers reveals an increasing social acceptance of the theatre and of actors, which was perhaps symptomatic of a
broader trend toward diversity in London society experienced in the late
nineteenth century.

Nonetheless, the Victorians continued to distinguish between an enjoyable public performance and shameful private notoriety. The excesses of the theatrical world, especially its flagrant disregard for convention were titillating but disturbing. The Prince of Wales' own exploits within the theatrical milieu elicited widespread public disapproval. Lady Frederick Cavendish writing on June 30, 1879, described the infiltration of Sarah Bernhardt, "a woman of notorious, shameless character," into the circle of the Prince of Wales as an "outrageous scandal."[54] Hostesses were similarly alarmed by the rise of the "cult of the professional beauties"—Mrs. Cornwallis West, Mrs. Edward Langtry, Mrs. Luke Wheeler—whose beauty was captured by the camera. Their likenesses were displayed in shop windows and became bestsellers. The inclusion of such women at parties held for the Prince of Wales became practically de rigueur. At the same time a large section of Society regarded the beauties not only as vulgar, but as contributors to the decay of the social fabric.[55]

Victorians were especially critical of the self-display that was a necessary part of the actor's craft. According to Jonas Barish, Victorians did not fear the mimetic side of the theatre, but shrank from its uncontrollable egoism.[56] The moral peril of the stage in advertisements is comfortably linked with the familiar commercial theme of feminine vanity, enmeshed with the commercial interpretation of the feminine ideal.

The actress in the advertisement becomes a siren, praised in the advertisement not only for her beauty, but also for the promise of sexuality she represents, a promise frequently ennobled with Grecian motifs. In an advertisement for Pears' Soap five women in Grecian costume—Miss Fortescue, Mad. Adelina Patti, Mrs. Langtry, Mad. Marie Roze, and Miss Mary Anderson—emerge from "The Temple of Beauty."[57] Miss Fortescue and Mrs. Langtry played Galatea in *Pygmalian and Galatea*, and this is probably the reason for the vaguely ridiculous and imitative behavior of the women as they emerge from the temple. Sexual suggestion, already connoted by the general reputation of actresses (even as it diminished in the late nineteenth century), is accentuated by the presence of Miss Fortescue, who in the 1880s was the focus of unpleasant publicity in a breach-of-promise suit. On the other hand, as seen in another context in Chapter 3, Grecian appearance defuses the threat of the actresses' sexuality (or at least disguises it in elevating garb). It also obscures her class associations. Like the soldier or adventurer, the actress in Grecian dress becomes an ideal, representative of no particular class. Her admired qualities are broadly accessible. Advertisements promise that, with the right equipment, the consumer, too, could affect the beauty for which the actress received considerable acclaim.

Advertisers, however, assert that the genius of the actress is more than her ability to affect beauty. An advertisement for Phosferine elevates the actress with particular qualities of character. The advertiser asserts "All over the world vast audiences have been thrilled and stirred by the rare

Figure 4-11. Pears' Soap, 1887. (Bodleian Library: The John Johnson Collection, Soap 4. Reprinted by permission.)

combination of great beauty and great genius possessed so markedly by Mrs. Brown Potter."

> To the matchless charm of womanhood, this famous actress adds a temperament which clothes itself at will with all the moods and passions of human nature. Thus the actual perfection and thoroughness of her work produce such exhaustion that Phosferine alone enables her to withstand great emotional strain.

The woman here, although "perfect," is far from rational (a male ideal exemplified by the expert). She is overwhelmed by enacting "passion" and "mood." She herself writes,

> After the fatigue of a long tedious journey or of playing a particularly strenuous part like Mme X when the muscles are limp and the nerves of the whole body are quivering and jangled, there is no finer restorative. If anything can add to my own appreciation, it is the fact that my mother enjoys splendid health and entire freedom from influenza and neuralgia ever since she began to take Phosferine.[58]

The actress is exhausted. This emphasis is natural enough in an advertisement for a restorative tonic. But the juxtaposition of qualities is interesting. She is oppressed by work, careworn by "fatigue," "limp," "quivering and jangled," but a dutiful daughter who considers her mother's health along with her own. However dutiful, though, she is admired for her passion for her art, her ability not to exercise restraint, but to simulate emotional extremes.

The actress offered sensuous beauty. Her seductive aspect was softened by Grecian costumes and redemptive assertions of familial concern and punishing duty. Nonetheless, her distinction, like that of the Queen, lay in the innate "charm of womanhood" and in the expression of the "moods and passions" of a common "human nature" rather than the peculiarities of personality, class or occupation.

THE VICTORIAN ADVERTISEMENT offered the consumer a beguiling vision of heroism. Its models were apparently dissimilar. The expert, the adventurer, the Queen, and the actress seemed to embody very different qualities and experiences. The expert is coolly rational; the adventurer is brave and daring; the Queen is motherly and discerning; the actress is overcome by mood and physical delicacy. Commercial models unerringly conform to the doctrine of the separate spheres, yet the broad context is progressive. Democratic principles transcend sex role stereotypes. The expert enshrined distinction by merit, the potential of learning shaped by hard work, and the trials of time. The adventurer carved his own world, created an identity through raw courage rather than genteel pretension. The Queen as beneficent matriarch espoused a leveling interest in harmony and maternal devotion. The actress's cultivated beauty and sensual indulgence allowed her to rise above the antitheatrical prejudice and the barriers of class. The hero in the Victorian advertisement reflected varieties of democratic aspiration that promised material gratification for even the humblest consumer.

5

Anxiety in the Victorian Advertisement: Evangelical Forms and Material Deliverers

Throughout the nineteenth century change enveloped Victorian society. By the 1880s many consumers feared that progress might be short-lived. The Great Depression, the rise of socialism, trade-union activity, the proliferation of evolutionary theories, and increasing questions about belief, religion, and morality seemed to augur the precipitous decline of a great empire. Beatrice Webb wrote of "a growing uneasiness."[1] *Punch* lampooned the popular fin-de-siècle mood.[2] As consumer insecurities flourished and multiplied, late nineteenth-century advertisers recognized a commercial opportunity. With almost pernicious zeal, they offered a hedonistic solution—material deliverance from every care and heavenly rewards predicated on the transformative experience of consumption.

Anxiety in the Late Victorian Period

Although the Victorian middle class had welcomed considerable prosperity throughout the second half of the nineteenth century, by the last decades of the nineteenth many people were anxious about conditions at home and in the world at large. Whether fears were realistic or simply perceived, anxiety was considerable. As we shall see, anxiety provided ample fodder for advertisers to peddle very material, ultimately hedonistic solutions.

Rising expectations fueled a pervasive sense of domestic inadequacy.[3] Housewives felt compelled to experiment with new concepts and new products. The distance between social aspirations and reality created con-

stant tensions. Outside the walled garden, the consumer feared the lurid
spectacle of moral turpitude. By the late nineteenth century prostitution
scandals, the repeal of the Contagious Diseases Acts, and rescue missions
had seemed to reveal a disturbing deviancy. Moral complacency was shat-
tered. Indeed, public response to W. T. Stead's 1885 exposé of child prostitution in London, "The Maiden Tribute of Modern Babylon" in *The Pall
Mall Gazette* seems to Judith Walkowitz to be symptomatic of a general
cultural paranoia overtaking Britain in the late nineteenth century.[4]

Within this context the apparent conflict between science and religion
took on new significance. It seemed to many Victorians that T. H. Huxley
was right when he wrote of a "New Nature" created by science, which, in
transforming the quality of life, also required an almost complete reorien-
tation in thought and expectations of people and society. Between 1850 and
1900 Huxley, professor of biology and chief apologist for Darwin, John
Tyndall, physicist, Herbert Spencer, philosopher of evolution, W. K. Clif-
ford, mathematician, and Sir Francis Galton, eugenicist and statistician,
emerged as the most able champions and publicists of science. Collectively,
they encouraged ordinary Englishmen to use rational, scientific ideas to
solve their problems. In doing so they advocated a shift away from the
Christian tradition that was potentially threatening not only to believers,
but to those who feared the erosion of the very basis of morality and law.[5]

Contemporaneously, there was a reversal of the economic prosperity
that had characterized the mid-Victorian period. A succession of disas-
trous harvests were exacerbated by the increasing availability of imported
produce, especially wheat, made newly attractive with improved transpor-
tation and technology of refrigeration. Prices fell; bankruptcies among
farmers became common. As the population drift from the country to the
town accelerated, agricultural production declined.[6] The deplorable state
of agricultural affairs was worrisome for a nation that considered its rural
community to be its backbone. Industrial expansion, which had typified
the British economy during the mid-Victorian years, began to wane.[7] As
production fell, the rate of capital investment also declined. The Great
Depression of the 1880s, real or perceived, animated an increasingly mili-
tant working class. The success of new unionism, exemplified by the London Dock Strike of 1889, was compounded by the advent of English
socialist parties in the 1880s. While H. M. Hyndman's Marxist Social
Democratic Federation (founded in 1882) may have had little prospect of
electoral success, the Fabian policy of permeating existing political parties
seemed more ominous. In 1893 the Independent Labour Party was founded. Although most working men had been granted suffrage in 1867 and
1884, admitting the working class to power still seemed incredible. Popular
interpretations of social darwinian theories about the struggle for existence and the survival of the fittest made the unrest of the workers seem
especially menacing.[8]

As the ostensible foundations of national greatness seemed to slip away,
Britain faced the prospect of international decline. The expansion of Ger-

man and American influence was achieved at Britain's expense.[9] By 1883
J. R. Seeley argued in his *Expansion of England* that Britain must create
an Empire if she were not to be eclipsed by new giant states. In a changing international world Britain felt increasingly insecure. The inadequacy
of her defences had been predicted since the military and administrative fiascos of the Crimean War. Invasion novels, beginning with George
Chesney's *Battle of Dorking* (1871) were fantasy, but in combination with
alarmist press speculations about national security, they fueled popular
support for naval expansion, an issue that in part drove Gladstone into
retirement.[10] By the time of the Boer War, historians agree that despite
British victory, there was a clear sense that the victory had not been easy.

J. R. Reed, historian of the *Decadent Style*, argues that *The Decline and
Fall of the British Empire* (1905) in fact expressed a popular view—Britain
faced not only military and financial competition, but the actual physical
degeneration of its citizens.[11] Eugenicists heightened concern. Francis
Galton published *Inquiries into Human Faculty* in 1883. William Booth's *In
Darkest England and the Way Out* (1890) and T. H. Huxley's *Social Diseases
and Worse Remedies* (1891) spotlighted serious social ills. Evolution might
after all be degenerative as well as progressive.[12] Physical degeneration,
an inadequate defense, economic decline, religious scepticism, moral
turpitude—all were causes for alarm. At every turn, Victorian consumers
confronted not merely individual concerns about meeting rising material
expectations, but sobering national questions of moral, financial, and military security.

Commercial Interpretations

In this chapter I will argue that advertisements exploited late Victorian
anxiety by using evangelical language and visual motifs. Evangelicalism
had been such a major element of nineteenth-century British culture that
by the late Victorian period some of its patterns and styles of thinking
remained after its theological content had begun to evaporate. The advertiser did not favor evangelical religious precepts, but he used familiar
evangelical forms and language to communicate a hedonistic message.
Advertisers mirrored pre-conversion angst. Advertisers admonished, instructed, cautioned, and scolded. They urged the consumer to improve, to
reform, to cast aside old habits in favor of new, more enlightened ways.
Their offer was clear. Life could be perfected, free from care. All that was
required was one simple act—consumption. This was more than a
Weberian equation of Christian virtue and worldly success. It was the
secular, vulgarized expression of popular religion. Miraculous deliverance
was predicated on unceasing self-examination. But once the choice was
made, the transformation was dramatic. The Victorian advertisement assumed an evangelical appearance, but subverted its content in a hedonistic
direction. Consumers were guided by a materialistic voice to salvation not
through conversion, but through consumption.

The commercialization of evangelical experience coalesced around twin threats, from without and from within. Threats from without, those threats posed by the outside world that were largely beyond individual control, were easily adapted to the commercial forum. Identifiable, impersonal, they might be sensationalized beyond all realism, yet not offend. Threats from within, individual faults that imperiled material success, were trickier, required a gentler touch. Overstatement might appear to be insulting and alienate the consumer. The skillful interpretation of each was imbued with the appearance of religious qualities. The dramatization of both sorts of danger enabled the advertiser to suggest the emotional extremes of evangelical religion and to mimic its saving function. But the transformative action, consumption and its heavenly vision, material plenty, were clearly hedonistic.

External Threats

Advertisers, drawing on a cultural understanding of a terror that precedes deliverance, depicted horrifying agents of worldly destruction. Real life was full of chilling possibilities. Each might be grotesquely exaggerated, provide a frightening impetus for transformative action. Disease, fraud, child injury, larceny, fire, age, and marital discord were turned into effective instruments that forced a decision, that allowed products to seem miraculous. Through a very particular means, the secular expression of evangelical experience, these external threats furthered the advertiser's purpose and emerged as an expected, even clichéd element of the Victorian advertisement.

Disease

Recovery from disease in the advertisement becomes the physical analogue to the evangelical experience of conversion. Swooning women collapse into the arms of concerned friends. Boldface captions offer "A Way of Escape!," a means to "Save Yourself."[13] A complaint as innocuous as a toothache becomes a "monster vanquished."[14] Fairy-like creatures triumphantly slay the dragon of disease. Illness is horrific and terrifying, fantastic and real. Recovery is dramatic and miraculous, fraught with emotion.

Scientific development and epidemiological coincidence laid the foundations for the advertisers' efforts. The first half of the nineteenth century raised public awareness about the scientific investigation of health. There were considerable advances in medical education (e.g., Apothecary Act 1815, Anatomy Act 1832), strides in pharmacology (e.g., the discovery of morphine, quinine, codeine) and improvements in the classification of common diseases (e.g., scarlet fever, diphtheria, typhoid, typhus, syphilis, gonorrhea). Yet in the treatment of diseases the methods employed by physicians and surgeons remained relatively antiquarian and largely ineffective. Three frightening waves of contagious disease, 1831–83 (influenza

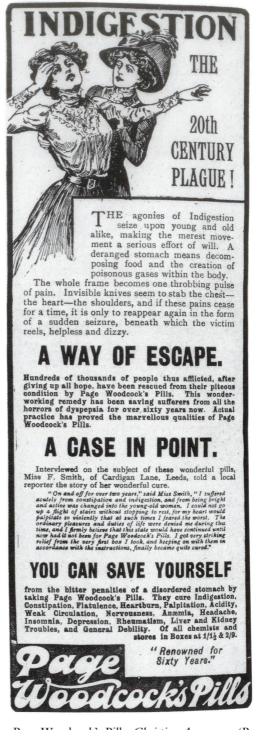

Figure *5-1.* Page Woodcock's Pills, *Christian Age*, 1910. (British Library.)

and cholera), 1836–42 (influenza, typhus, smallpox, scarlet fever), and 1846–49 (typhus, typhoid, cholera) exacerbated an unease about the apparent impotence of the medical establishment when confronted with infectious disease. Epidemics were mysterious and terrifying. They defied all known and conventional precautions. They observed no economic or geographical boundaries. Widespread public belief that disease was generated from filth and transmitted by a noxious invisible gas contributed to a sense of siege. Diseases appeared, disappeared, and reappeared; anxiety intensified.[15] This was one area about which people even at mid-century could not feel calm and assured. As adequate treatments eluded the scientists, panaceas flourished.

By 1880 patent medicine advertisements could easily make up 25% of all advertisements. There were pills for gout and wafers for biliousness. There were galvanic belts, magnetic appliances, and electric towels for fatigue; steel pills for feminine ailments; anti-fat pills for weight loss; cod liver oils, "soothing syrups," gripe waters and powders for children. There were dozens of all-purpose medicines suitable for any complaint "from whatever cause arising."[16] Even non-medicinal products, Bovril and Lemco Beef Extracts, promise to act as restoratives. Durables offer to address the fear of infectious disease in more substantial terms. The Berkenfeld Filter, "in use in all the leading hospitals," offers to "remove all germs from water."[17] The Aymard Patent Milk Sterilizer could sterilize "Raw Milk . . . one of the Most Dangerous Foods!" Sterilizers, filters, pills, and syrups all promise to rid the consumer of nebulous "impurities"[18] and guarantee miraculous health.

Preposterous claims went largely unchecked. According to the Royal Commission Report of 1914, "In the case of most newspapers these advertisements [constituted] one of the most considerable sources of income while a number of small provincial newspapers could hardly [have existed] at all without secret remedy advertisements."[19] Control over fraudulent or dangerous claims did not come from the government, which excluded patent medicines from the Food and Drug Act of 1875, and "most newspaper proprietors [did] not regard it as incumbent upon them to test the good faith of secret remedy advertisers any more than of advertisers of other goods."[20]

Despite fraudulent practice, patent medicine advertisements flourished, especially in the religious press. Whereas clothing or food advertisements dominate general interest, sporting, society, and ladies' magazines, in religious periodicals the sheer frequency of patent medicine advertisements is conspicuous. For example, patent medicine advertisements in 1890 make up 29% and 39% of all advertisements in the *Family Circle of the Christian World* and *Christian Age*, respectively, compared to only 11% in the *Illustrated London News*, 3% in *Queen*, and 5% in *The Lady*. Although the latter publications may have had a somewhat more affluent readership, the disparity does not seem to reflect class bias. The Royal Commission Report of 1914 confirmed widespread interest in patent medicines and speculated

that the middle class was more interested in these products than the
working class:

> the middle class certainly are enormous takers [of patent medicines] propor-
> tionately . . . certainly the middle class provid[es] a very large proportion of
> purchasers, because, as against their rather greater degree of enlightenment, is
> to be set the fact that they can more easily spend 2s 9d and 5s 6d than a strictly
> working man.[21]

The particular popularity of patent medicine advertisements seems to reflect readership interest, as much as class. The commissioners offered an
explanation from the *British Medical Journal*:

> It is a fact that quack medicines have more vogue among nonconformists than
> among sects of a different theological shade. This is reflected in the religious
> newspapers. The Free Churchman likes to show his independence and disci-
> pline by flouting the medical profession.[22]

More than simply a habit of theological independence, religious readers
were perhaps attracted to the familiar message of deliverance integral to
the advertisers' efforts.

The panacea, by definition, offers a universal remedy, a physical form of
deliverance, characterized typically by dramatic differences in the before
and after condition. An editorial advertisement for Siegel's Curative Syrup
is entitled "The Ups and Downs of Life." In the first picture advertisers
show

> a man in the full enjoyment of health and happiness. He has come home from
> his daily labour, and his little children are fondling about him, eager for his
> caresses.

The second picture presents the same man, now diseased:

> His head is resting upon his hand for it feels dull and heavy. His eyes are
> closed, because rolling them in their sockets gives pain. There is a collection
> of water in his mouth, and he is often sick at the stomach. There is a fullness
> about the heart after eating with a distress of breath. His sleep is often
> disturbed by unpleasant dreams.

Determined not to give in to his disease, in the next picture,

> he pushes his little children away from him. . . . The children are not allowed
> to play "because it will disturb papa." The man is indeed ill; for he has pains
> about his chest and sides; sometimes in the back. . . . He has a bad taste,
> especially in the morning, a sort of sticky slime collecting about the teeth,
> which gives his breath an offensive odour. The appetite is poor, and there is
> heavy load in his stomach. . . . The bowels have been costive and he has
> frequent hot flushes. His stomach is often sour and spits up his food.

Eventually, he is "Obliged to give up his business, for he is so feeble he cannot walk or even stand erect." For a full page the advertisement describes the graphic details of his illness.[23] Ultimately, the product is restorative, the agency of his miraculous recovery.

The theme is given comic relief in an advertisement for the Electropathic Belt. A girl clings to a rocky cliff. A dragon rises out of the sea.[24] The advertisement provides a commercial variant of a stock image. The text explains

> The above beautiful allegory aptly illustrates the position of a large portion of afflicted humanity at the present age. The Andromeda of to-day, or it may be her husband, or a sister, a cousin, or an aunt of that interesting damsel is assailed by the pestiferous breath of the remorseless demon Disease: she faints and droops under its baneful influence, but being chained to the rocks of prejudice, ignorance, and incredulity, she is unable to resist or impede the advance of the monster, who threatens each moment to enfold her in his deadly grasp. From the summit of the rocks the modern Aesculapius has exhausted the puny armoury of his profession. . . . When lo! there approaches from the distance, a figure of commanding presence, who bears aloft a weapon of the highest finish, and most unerring precision fresh from the prolific armoury of science. The Perseus of the Allegory, at whose approach the demon has hurriedly retreated, hands Andromeda the charm (bearing the mystic inscription "Electropathic Belt"), bids her wear it, and promises that it will effectively protect her against the advance of all such insidious enemies . . . henceforth she will rely for protection on the priceless treasure she has become the possessor of.[25]

Advertisers hope that "the intelligent reader will grasp the moral at a glance." Material acquisition will improve the consumer, rescue her from demons, and facilitate her deliverance.

Amid the creeping threat of disease, the consumer must remain ever vigilant. She must "fortify" herself.[26] Like the unconverted who might succumb to sin at any time, the ill-equipped consumer is vulnerable, unprotected. In an advertisement for Zam-Buk Disinfectant, germs are "magnified," a process by which they look more horrible and which emphasizes the apparent stealth of disease.[27] Advertisers draw on relatively recent scientific discoveries—Lister's advocacy of carbolic acid to clean wounds circa 1865 and Pasteur's elaboration of germ theory circa 1880. In advertisements these discoveries are dramatized. Without magnification, lethal germs are invisible interlopers. One must be "farseeing" to detect them.[28] The most mundane activity becomes fraught with danger.

> If the skin is in an unhealthy condition, a small cut, crack or scratch may be sufficient to set up blood poisoning or chronic skin disease. Housework with its dust and dirt, abounds with disease germs eager for the chance to enter any tiny sore and provoke dire mischief.[29]

Figure 5-2. Electropathic Belt, *Graphic*, 1885. (Robarts Library.)

Figure 5-3. Zam-Buk Disinfectant, *Home Chat*, 1910. (British Library.)

Infection assumes a predatory aspect. Disease is the killer, the consumer the hunted. Nubolic asks parents to use Nubolic Soap "For the Children's Sake" to prevent "a score of those irritating little disorders which we all know are incidental to children and school-life," but ends with a frightening promise to guard against serious illness "when infection stalks abroad."[30] The sense of attack is heightened in another Nubolic advertisement by an arrow that pierces a bar of soap.[31] Sanitas echoes the attack imagery with a reference from the *Lancet* to the "invasion of the human body."[32] All threats are potentially obliterated by one simple and sustained act of consumption. Nubolic "Keeps the Wolf of Infection from the Door."[33] The consumer is the lamb, sweet and innocent, the prey, easily lead, in need of shepherding. The allusion highlights the guileless innocence of the unconverted who may nonetheless make a fatal mistake, who must be urged by fear of irreparable error to reform and to change.

As influenza epidemics raged, advertisements use battle imagery as an immediate parallel for the real-life experience of war. The bold headline of a Bovril advertisement announces "Influenza, the Enemy at Home." Other large captions identify Bovril as "the resisting power. Bovril repels the Enemy." The text draws on "reports" "from all sides" and promises "protection from an attack."[34] Lemco "is the parting shot at Influenza."[35] The retreat of influenza, the consumer is warned, is "more dangerous than its attack." Two soldiers fire a cannon in the accompanying illustration. Battle imagery and text convey an unmistakable sense of conflict and unease, to be relieved and soothed by the act of consumption. Perhaps not incidentally in evangelical Christian culture the battle image functions as a metaphor for the experience of the sinner before conversion.

Without the transformative action of consumption, death will be terrible. In the evangelical experience death augured divine judgment. At that point the failure of the sinner to decide was particularly threatening. But fatal illness also presented opportunities. The ultimate state of the immolation of the self was illness and dying, when the self could be completely dissolved and purity assured. The very extremity of death intensified the pressure to choose. The threat of death recurs throughout the Victorian advertisement, but in each instance the horrors of death may be avoided by one simple decision—to buy the product. A Lifebuoy advertisement is typical. It appears to rely on a scientific testimonial from Dr. Karl Enoch, Chemisch, Hygienisches Inst., Hamburg. Each sentence, however, ends with a bald statement of death underscored twice for dramatic emphasis. Bacteria rather than people die, but the prospect of reversal is clear.

> Obstinate Typhoid Microbes . . . were dead within two hours. . . . Microbes . . . were taken from persons who had died. . . . Microbes . . . were dead within five minutes. . . . Diphtheria Microbes were killed. . . . Microbe life was entirely extinct. . . . Lifebuoy . . . is a powerful . . . exterminator.[36]

The iteration of "death," "killed," "extinct," "exterminator" effectively fosters panic while in the trademark picture, a craggy sailor holds a life preserver with the comforting caption "for saving life." The trademark and name of the product raise the soap to the status of deliverer; a decision to use it frees the individual from potentially terrifying consequences.

The product is linked to the nurturing protective atmosphere of recovery. For Bovril a child is seated comfortably in a chair.[37] A large, plumped pillow supports her back, an ample blanket is draped securely around her shoulders, she is properly bundled, peacefully reading a book. While the child may seem diminutively helpless, swamped by her coverings, the consumer is also attracted to the cozy warmth of her protective cocoon. Similarly, Nubolic's caption promises "Sweeter Homes."[38] The accompanying illustration is idyllic. A large house in the style of an English cottage is surrounded by trees. The sun shines on the horizon. A lake in the foreground and the rickety fence create a pastoral mood. Two stick figures suggest a mother and child. The home is a refuge, an oasis. "On summer's sultriest day," the text assures, "you'll find delightful freshness in the home where Nubolic Disinfectant Soap is used." The threats cultivated in influenza advertisements are defused by images of protection that prompt the consumer almost to yearn for the comforting warmth of the sick-bed and the security wrought by maternal hands. In varying degrees, these images of protection offer a heavenly alternative to the incipient danger symbolized by images of the embattled and the hunted and suggestions of a horrible death.

The popularity of disease and remedy advertisements in the religious press in particular is surely suggestive. In text and in image, commercial depictions of disease simulate popular religious experience. Before consumption the individual, alone and ill equipped, encounters terrifying threats. He is, in the popular metaphors of Christianity, a soldier in battle, a lamb threatened by wolves. His experience is intensely personal, raw with emotion. As he confronts his own mortality, he must decide. By one single action, consumption, his life is transformed. Pain, suffering, and worry disappear. The individual is comforted, soothed, transported to the commercial idyll of "sweeter homes." The physical effects of the panacea mirror the spiritual consequences of conversion.

Disease was a potent danger, but hardly singular. Despite the popularity of the recovery theme, many advertisements focus on other external threats. These, too, reveal the commercial relevance of evangelical experience.

Adulteration

Adulteration, the invisible, potentially fatal contamination of common foods and medicines, was a popular although often secondary focus in advertisements for food, medicine, and toiletries. In these advertisements constant vigilance about product purity and veracity evokes the evangelical wariness of the taint of sin. Since mid-century adulteration had been widely publicized and commercially exploited. A royal commission report in 1854 drew public attention to the issue by reporting the incidence of

Sweeter Homes

On Summer's sultriest day you'll find delightful freshness in the home where NUBOLIC Disinfectant Soap is used.

NUBOLIC cleanses and it disinfects ; it safeguards health besides.

NUBOLIC
DISINFECTANT SOAP

Three sizes of Nubolic are sold by all Grocers, Oilmen, and Stores.
Full lb. (16 ozs.), 3½d. ; ¾ lb. (12 ozs.), 3d. ; ½ lb. (8 ozs.), 2d.

PRIZES. There are 1,000,000 Prizes, value £100,500, for those who save the wrappers from Nubolic Soap. Closing date for next distribution September 30th. Every prize is guaranteed full value. List and particulars free from your dealer, or direct from

JOSEPH WATSON & SONS, Ltd., Whitehall Soap Works, Leeds.

Figure 5-4. Nubolic, *Home Chat*, 1910. (British Library.)

foreign matter in foods such as insects in sugar or alum in flour. The deliberate adulteration of food was common and before 1860 was virtually unrestricted. The Pure Food Act of 1860 involved no mandatory system of enforcement. It was not until 1872 that an act strengthened penalties and inspection procedures.[39] Public awareness was fostered by cautionary articles in family magazines.[40] Publicity focused not only on concerns about health, but also on the dark and pervasive duplicity that adulteration implies. The *Quarterly Review* wrote, for example,

> The grossest fraud reigns through the British public commissariat. Like a set of monkeys, every man's hand is seen in his neighbour's dish. The baker takes in the grocer, the grocer defrauds the publican, the publican "does" the pickle manufacturer and the pickleman fleeces and poisons all the rest.[41]

Underpinning the cynical humor was a mounting alarm. Even patent medicines, perhaps most especially patent medicines, the consumer suspected were not what they seemed. Ultimately, in 1914 a Royal Commission Report on Patent Medicines found that many products were ineffective, addictive, or even lethal. Steedman's Soothing Powder, for example, was found to contain 27.1% calomel. Advertised doses were sufficient to be toxic.[42] Government prosecution of one well-known remedy, Collis Brown's Chlorodyne, revealed that it was an opium preparation.[43] Even the apparently benign could prove sinister.

Seizing upon public fears, advertisers promise products that are "harmless,"[44] "pure," free from "injurious chemicals."[45] At great length advertisers reassure. Medicines will not kill the patient; they are non-poisonous. Koptica Cure typically advertised that "Koptica is guaranteed free from Strychnine, Arsenic, Colchicum, Belladonna, Henbane, Aconite and all other injurious drugs and can, therefore, be taken by the most delicate with the greatest confidence that it is thoroughly harmless."[46] Constant reassurances in patent medicine advertisements appear to comfort. But they also raise the temperature of alarm. If one product is safe, the implication is any of the competing products might prove fatal. Only a particular product may redeem.

Advertisers urged consumers, weaned on the virtues of self-examination, to check and recheck all sorts of products for the veracity and legitimacy of trusted brand names. "Be sure they are Carter's" warns Carter's Liver Pills. Another brand might be not only ineffective, but injurious. Carter's was safe.[47] Distinctive labeling promised the consumer the assurance of the product's quality. Liebig Extract directs consumers to "see [the] signature (as above) in blue ink across the label of each jar of genuine extract."[48] Constant commercial awareness of fraud fostered a sense that as much as consumers were threatened by invisible germs, they were equally threatened by unscrupulous people. Moral turpitude is everywhere, leading men to advertise false claims, to misrepresent themselves and their products, and to tamper with the purity of the product. The threat of adulteration was more than a physical problem of chemical formulation; it was a physical manifestation of sin, that essential agency of evangelical decision.

Child Injury

Failure to decide for consumption might jeopardize innocent children. Advertisements sensationalize parental fears. Captions like "Babies on Fire"[49] or "Do Not Let Your Child Die"[50] attract attention, but the substantive text is more alarming. Mothers may not "realize how [their] little ones suffer,"[51] that their children "are weeping in the play-time of others."[52] Advertisers ask

> Your Children. Are they healthy and strong, full of life and merriment, always active, bright and happy, bonny pictures of health and the joy of parents who love and take a proper delight in the well-being of their little ones? Or are they peevish, pale and thin, languid and weak, looking extremely delicate, without much appetite, and without the inclination to run about and play as healthy children should? Is there a gradual loss of plumpness, a pale drawn face with dark circles under the eyes and a dull, heavy expression . . . is there something wrong with these children?[53]

Yet advertisers "believe that parents would willingly make great sacrifices to see the infant grow to maturity."[54] They offer infant management books, *Bringing Up Baby* or *Advice to Mothers*. More important, they encourage parents to "protect" their children through consumption. Any number of remedies—the right soap, the right food, the right medicine—can be restorative; through their use parents may be assured that their children will always be "bright, intelligent and . . . good-tempered.[55]

Beyond the cradle, "a daughter's happiness" depends on using the right product. A mother must ask herself at

> one of the most touching moments . . . when she is alone with her daughter for the last time before her wedding . . . if it were possible to have done more to secure her daughter's happiness. . . . Does [she] know what Sunlight Soap can do?[56]

In an advertisement, similarly, for Dr. Williams' Pink Pills for Pale People, the text describes "the girl of to-day who will be the woman of tomorrow":

> How much depends upon this "to-day" for her! She does not know it; perhaps her mother has only an inkling. But between the to-day when she is a girl and the tomorrow when she will be a woman, her life's happiness and health are in the balance.[57]

The advertisement appears to allude to menstrual pain or anemia. She might be "pale, sunken-eyed, back-achy, sallow, breathless, languid and

Figure 5-5. Sunlight Soap, *Black and White*, 1893. (Robarts Library.)

bloodless at this time," but through consumption of Dr. Williams' Pink Pills for Pale People she will "develop into full-breasted, healthy blooming womanhood." Advertisements contrast the invalid with the bride, the dying child with the thriving toddler, in order to dramatize the transformative effects of a single decision.

Burglary

Disease, adulteration, even infant death, although frightening, seemed random. Victims of burglary, on the other hand, understood that they had been chosen, and it is precisely this element of choice that is highlighted in the Victorian advertisement. Although members of the prosperous middle class were not generally imperiled by violent crime, they were certainly aware of a high rate of theft and burglary and that they were often specifically identified as targets. Larceny, embezzlement, receiving stolen goods, fraud, forgery, and currency offenses accounted for 85% of indictable committals during the Victorian period. Larceny alone constituted 80% of all committals to trial. According to David Philips, as the level of prosecution increased, middle-class people became conscious of their vulnerability.[58] They realized that they owned more worth stealing. Cases of middle-class larceny, embezzlement, forgery, and especially fraud became a staple diet for novelists and journalists.[59] Authorities, too, alerted middle-class residents to the possibility for crime within their own neighborhoods. "The

miles of suburban streets which exist are most difficult to guard with the
small numbers of men at our disposal," wrote the Superintendent of Is-
lington division, "whilst the inhabitants appear to be less careful than in
more densely populated neighborhoods."[60] Police circulated notices to
householders and from the 1870s night patrols of detective officers were
instituted in middle-class neighborhoods. Just as burglars deliberately
chose certain houses to attack, the consumer was urged to make a deliberate choice not to be a victim.

In advertisements, consumption will provide the ultimate protection. A
well-known advertisement for Clarke's Pyramid Light announces in boldface: "Caution—To Prevent Burglaries." The famous illustration shows
the pyramids lit up. The text instructs

> A Pyramid Night Light should be lighted in the front and back of every house
> as soon as it is dark. Housebreakers have the greatest dread of a light. The
> police recommend a "Pyramid" Night Light as the best safeguard. Almost all
> the burglaries perpetrated might have been prevented and much valuable
> property saved, if this simple and inexpensive plan had always been adopted.
> The "Pyramid" Night Lights are much larger and give double the light of the
> common night lights, and are therefore particularly adapted for this pur-
> pose.[61]

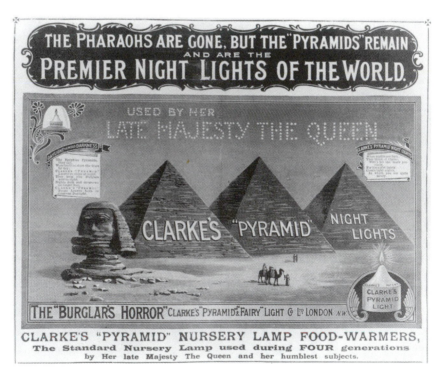

Figure   5-6.   Clarke's Pyramid Lights, *Illustrated London News*, 1901. (Robarts
Library.)

The light is so bright, so effective, that it may illuminate even the pyramids. The problem is as old as the pyramids as well. It requires a decision to opt for the surety of the light rather than to risk the perils of darkness.

Age

Through consumption, consumers might be born again. Women, anxious about aging, might be rejuvenated, seem younger, fresher, invigorated. An advertisement for Rowntree stereotypes stages of life. It advises that Rowntree Cocoa "is equally beneficial and acceptable to romping boys and delicate girls, tired women and robust men."[62] The assumption that in maturity men are "robust" and women are "tired" reveals a Victorian concern. The sheer quantity of physical work required to maintain cleanliness, that shining evidence of respectability, might render women prematurely decrepit. Sunlight Soap focused on this theme in a series of well-known advertisements with the famous caption "Why does a Woman Look Old Sooner than a Man?"[63] The text asks "Why does a woman's health so often break down at an early age?" Sunlight conjectures

> Put a man at a washing tub, let him get heated with the hot suds until every pore is opened, then let him stand over the filthy steam that comes from scalding and boiling clothes and his health would certainly break down before long and yet this terrible ordeal is exactly what a woman has to go through on washing day and besides while overheated at the hot work, she has to risk her life by going out into the open air to hang up clothes. These facts which are known to every housekeeper, readily explain why so many women look old while yet young in years.

The "terrible ordeal" of women, the "break down" of her health can all be avoided by the right soap. An advertisement in the same series describes her "careworn look, broken health and premature old age." Another envisions her "worn out and dejected," losing "rest, recreation and nerve power," succumbing to "heartbreaking worry and premature decay."[64] It speculates that

> the wonder is how any woman lives through it [wash day]—many don't. The sudden change, from the hot perspiring sour and wet steaming room inside to the cold air outside produces the natural result: cold, followed quickly by pneumonia or diphtheria, or some kindred disease, ending in the death of the poor victim. Friends call it a dispensation of Providence. What the woman really died of was *poor soap*, hard labour and exposure. Health is a Preservation of Beauty, a necessity to Happiness and the lives of your children. Don't grow old before your time.[65]

The choice is clear: disease or happiness, the purgatory and taint of those who cannot decide (or make the wrong decision) versus the bliss of those redeemed.

Like the patent medicine advertisement, Sunlight alarms with visions of disease and death. The consumer is again the "poor victim." Before-and-after pictures dramatize the depravity of her condition. Slumped over, head in her hands, surrounded by piled baskets of laundry, she seems pathetic. Consumers are directly reminded of Providence, but encouraged to help themselves. After using Sunlight Soap, in the illustration rows of happy women, "smiling faces all around," contentedly stand before their wash basins, as bars of Sunlight Soap surrounded by rays of light are elevated in the distance. Product change becomes redemptive. It liberates women from "arduous toil."[66] It creates "a cheerful old soul."[67] "Only a woman's love for cleanliness encourages her to toil unremittingly in the struggle with dirt."[68] The struggle with dirt becomes analogous with the struggle with sin; a constant trial, but one that envisions a miraculous redemption, in which the inner goodness of the cleansed is revealed and justly celebrated.

Marital Discord

Marital bliss became a secular variant of the metamorphosis that might be engineered by consumption. An Eno's advertisement crystallizes the marital ideal. A bride and a groom are pictured, separated by a poem. They lean anxiously toward each other. He, gazing rapturously, tells her "Eno's Fruit Salt will give us a long and happy life together." The boldface title emphasizes the importance of love. It implores "Riches, titles, honour, power and worldly prospects are naught to a deeply rooted love." Attentive, placing their love before all else, the Eno's bride and groom embody the Victorian conception of the romantic couple.[69] For many women, the ideal seemed to elude them beyond the wedding day.

The Divorce Act of 1857 and discussion surrounding the Married Women's Property Acts in the later nineteenth century gave very public voice to concerns about marital discord. In *The Road to Divorce* Lawrence Stone argues that nineteenth-century middle-class women strove to keep even unhappy marriages together. This contention is supported by the relatively low rate of divorce despite an enormous drop in the cost of divorce following the 1857 legislation.[70] Upper-middle-class women were mainly concerned about the protection of their property, not equal access to divorce.[71] With few careers open to them, the consequences of a divorce could be even worse than those of a bad marriage.[72] Advertisers deftly connected commercial products with the desirable goal of marital harmony and the material and emotional security it represented.

In contrast to the saccharine couple of the Eno's advertisement, there are many advertisements that graphically depict the trials of marital discord. An advertisement for a patent medicine features a dejected woman experiencing a "fit of the blues."[73] She sits in neglected silence, while her husband beside her reads the newspaper. The advertisement implies that sluggishness makes her a less than lively companion. Her exaggerated

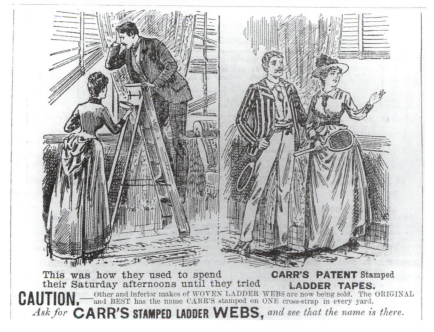

THE ILLUSTRATED LONDON NEWS

This was how they used to spend   **CARR'S PATENT** Stamped
their Saturday afternoons until they tried   **LADDER TAPES.**
CAUTION.——Other and inferior makes of WOVEN LADDER WEBS are now being sold. The ORIGINAL and BEST has the name CARR'S stamped on ONE cross-strap in every yard.
Ask for **CARR'S STAMPED LADDER WEBS,** *and see that the name is there.*

Figure 5-7.   Carr's Ladder Tapes, *Illustrated London News*, 1889. (Robarts Library.)

expression suggests her despair. She is ignored. In other advertisements wives elicit their husband's disapproval. Sunlight Soap warns "Don't let steam and suds be your husband's welcome on wash-day." A dismayed husband walks in the door to find his wife bent over a basin, enveloped in steam.[74] In both advertisements the product promises to transform the woman and reawaken her husband's interest. An advertisement for Carr's Ladder Tapes entitled "This was how they used to spend their Saturday afternoons until they tried Carr's Patent Ladder Tapes" illustrates the life-altering effects of consumption.[75] In the before picture he stands on a ladder, the blinds hopelessly askew. Holding one hand to his head, he scowls, unable even to look at his wife, who almost beseechingly offers the ladder tapes. In the second advertisement the blinds are already installed. The couple stands side by side, arms linked, looking, not away from each other, but in the same direction. They smile, they wear their tennis clothes and carry rackets. They share an ideal pursuit of affluent leisure. They embody the happy consequences of one crucial and transformative decision.

Victorian advertisers imagined all sorts of external threats to material affluence—disease, fraud, larceny, old age, infant injury, and marital discord. Commercial interpretations had striking religious overtones. In advertisements for patent medicine the individual is defenseless, vulnerable.

The prospect of death intensifies the pressure to choose. The consumer feels like a soldier in battle, a lamb among wolves. Consumption wipes away all pain. The torture of disease and the sweetness of recovery function as a physical analogue to the spiritual experience of conversion. Advertisements for other products are often less dramatic, but similarly commercialize and secularize important aspects of the evangelical experience. In advertisements for food, vigilance about adulteration mirrors the rigors of self-examination. In advertisements for night lights the consumer must decide not to be a victim, resolve to end the conflict. For myriad other products, the before-and-after motif epitomizes the commercial and the evangelical ideal of a life transformed.

Internal Fears

Instructive and prescriptive advertisements guide consumers toward metaphorical deliverance from internal conflicts, anxieties that arise from a perception of personal deficiency, rather than from the recognition of external threats. Advertisers urge consumers to recognize inadequacies, to admit that they are woefully unprepared, that their neighbors surpass them at every turn. Once consumers despair, advertisers reassure. The comforting advice of mothers, teachers, and confidantes converges. Every commercial voice urges Victorians to consume.

Outside the advertising arena the prescriptive format had achieved broad popularity by mid-century. Urbanization and rapid social mobility had removed the family from the instructive context of an extended network. Situated among neighbors who were strangers, the definition of roles and status acquired new urgency. Shifting material fortunes heightened the complexity. By 1850 the family owned dramatically more manufactured goods and had access to a wider choice of furniture, kitchen equipment, clothing, and foodstuffs than even fifty years before. In an urban and intensely materialist environment where it was impossible for each individual to be known for his character, assumptions were inevitably made on the basis of appearances.[76] The intensity of this pressure to live correctly and especially to demonstrate taste is reflected in the popularity of domestic economy manuals. Women bought them in the millions.[77] As Jay Mechling suggests,[78] these books often revealed more about what did not happen at home than about day-to-day reality. They criticized, and in doing so exposed the fears of their readers. These hidden fears fueled the Victorian prescriptive fascination. In the advertisement the prescriptive form assumed evangelical overtones. Education ceased to be a goal. Instead, instruction becomes an agency of a more essential experience, consumption, which alone might transport the individual to material heaven, untainted and without flaws.

The most obvious and direct sort of prescriptive advertisement offers to teach a household skill. In a Charles A. Voegler Co. advertisement a serving woman in white apron and cap asks pointedly, "Do you know how to cook fish?" She sells a 64-page book of recipes.[79] She asks the consumer to acknowledge her inability to prepare a basic food. Other advertisements describe how to "equip" a "town house or flat,"[80] how to raise children so that they "come up like flowers in the spring,"[81] "How to be Happy though Married,"[82] how to clean a carpet.[83] In these advertisements consumers are asked to admit inadequacies, but also to solve them.

In instructive advertisements, however, the consumer is inevitably subordinate. The frequent image of the blackboard slate, for example, relegates the consumer to the inferior position of learner. In an advertisement for Frazer's Sulphur Tablets toddlers hold up a writing tablet that spells out the name of the product.[84] For Brooke's Soap a sweet young girl holds up a slate with the words "Won't Wash Clothes."[85] In both advertisements the consumer, like a child, is exhorted to learn a lesson. Moreover, students in this popular form of advertisement are often wayward. For Bovril a girl offers an improbable example of Victorian student demeanor. She tips her stool. With legs boldly outstretched, ankles crossed, she smiles impishly at the viewer. Her slate offers a drawing of a cow and the caption "Try Bovril."[86] The purpose of the slate in advertisements is to remind the unknowing consumer of the product name, to suggest that like a student, the consumer is not always attentive to her lessons.

The instructive theme recurs with a variety of motifs. Advertisements simulate classroom settings. For Peek, Frean & Co. students study a map that ostensibly illustrates that "400,000,000 fairy cakes touching one another would stretch round from Pole to Pole."[87] Advertisements pose quiz questions: "Do you know how many compositions have been written for the Pianoforte?"[88]; "How do you spell Velveteen?"[89] They suggest an "instructive experiment which every reader can make in a moment." They offer study notes—"nine worth-remembering . . . points."[90] Whether by imagery of the classroom or by lesson-like text, advertisements appeal to consumers as students—incomplete, unformed, malleable.

The consumer is as unsure and ill equipped as a child. For Edward's Harlene Hair Tonic a girl sits by her mother's dressing table watching her brush her long hair. "Mama," she asks, "shall I have beautiful long hair like you when I grow up?" The mother replies, "Certainly, my dear, if you use "Edward's Harlene"."[91] The scene is familiar, endearing. The product is tied to the sweet simplicity of the mother-daughter relationship. The target consumer, presumably an adult woman, is asked to identify with the child, the person in the advertisement who does not use the product. Like the child, she is insecure. Like the child, she does not approximate the fully formed, pleasingly complete picture represented by the mother. Like the child, she may accept motherly advice comfortably and without offense. The Harlene advertisement is a dramatic example of an advertisement type—an advertisement in which a product not used by children is sold by children, an advertisement in which a child is the fulcrum of an instructive theme. In the advertisement the consumer becomes the young child, guided to the correct path by one older, wiser, and more confident. Adver-

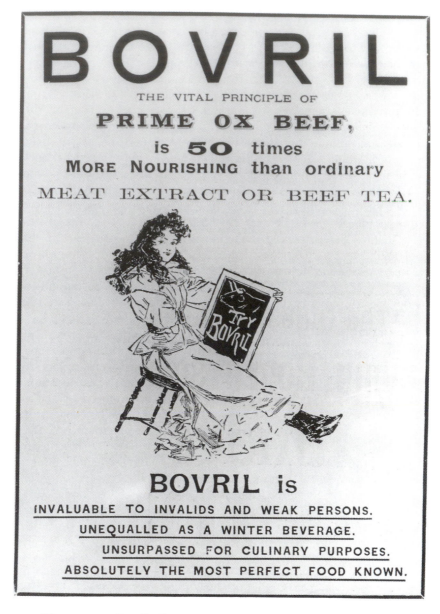

BOVRIL

THE VITAL PRINCIPLE OF

PRIME OX BEEF,

is **50** times
MORE NOURISHING than ordinary

MEAT EXTRACT OR BEEF TEA.

BOVRIL is

INVALUABLE TO INVALIDS AND WEAK PERSONS.

UNEQUALLED AS A WINTER BEVERAGE.

UNSURPASSED FOR CULINARY PURPOSES.

ABSOLUTELY THE MOST PERFECT FOOD KNOWN.

Figure 5-8. Bovril, *Illustrated London News*, 1894. (Robarts Library.)

tisements of this type conjure warm memories of childhood, but they also subtly patronize the consumer by implying a child-like absence of material sophistication.

Guided by commercial teachers and mothers, the consumer may also be led by knowing friends. Compo Soap pictures an attractive woman who leans confidentially over a fence. The caption reads "Ask your neighbour

"Mamma, shall I have beautiful long hair like you when I grow up?"
"Certainly, my dear, if you use **'Edward's Harlene'.**"

Figure 5-9. Edward's Harlene Hair Tonic, n.d. (Bodleian Library: The John Johnson Collection, Beauty Parlour I. Reprinted by permission.)

whose house is conspicuously clean, whose work worries her least, whose leisure time is greatest *how* she manages. She will say—I do all my cleaning with Compo."[92] The path is clear, obvious. It has only to be illuminated. A Rubinstein cosmetics advertisement masquerades as a short story. Entitled "The Secret of the Duchess—A Story with a Moral" by "Gadfly" the advertisement recounts a tale of "two friends," "the Duchess" and "Mary." The two women discuss the importance of virtue and beauty as feminine attributes. Suddenly Mary begins to sob.

> "Can't you see, can't you understand? Harry will be home in a fortnight . . . I am beginning to fear that I have waited too long. It is five years since Harry went to South Africa; I had some beauty then. Oh, don't you understand? It would matter nothing to me how much Harry might have changed; but will my change matter to him? From his letters I can see that he makes no allowances for the time that has slipped away. He speaks of me as his "beautiful Mary" and expects to find me just as he left me, and when"—her voice faltered a little—"when he sees how I have changed he will be disappointed in me. Oh Alice, that is what I dread—I can't tell you how much!"

Anxious to console her tearful friend, the Duchess confides her secret—Mme. Rubinstein. "In her eagerness," Mary asks, "do you really think that Mme. Rubinstein could help me?"

> Next morning saw the two ladies at Mme. Rubinstein's Maison de Beauté. . . . It was the first of a succession of visits paid by Miss Etheridge to the clever Viennese beauty specialist, for there was a long neglect to be repaired. But when, a fortnight later, she stood face to face with Harry at Southampton she had the joy of hearing from his own lips the words she most desired to hear—words that told her how well employed had been the time she had spent at Mme. Rubinstein's. "Why Mary," he cried joyfully, holding her at arm's length and surveying her with eyes that beamed with proud proprietorship, "you haven't aged a day! You are just the same beautiful Mary that I left behind me, whilst I have been growing old out there."[93]

Underlying both advertisements is a sense that other women are better informed—that the answers are clearer to some than to others. One woman confides the answer to another. The consumer is beguiled by a familiar feminine form—the best friend with a secret. She is an untutored innocent set on the right road by a trusted confidante.

Overtly didactic Eno's advertisements accentuate the pressure to choose. One Eno's caption, like an evangelical preacher, exhorts, "Yesterday is dead! Tomorrow! is not yet born! To-day! is only yours!"[94] Yet another quotes Tennyson:

> Out of eternity this new day is born,
> Into eternity at night doth return,
> Behold it aforetime, no eyes ever did,
> So soon it for ever from all eyes is hid.

> Here hath been dawning another blue day,
> Think, wilt thou let it slip useless away?[95]

A lighthouse towering above treacherous rocks in the same advertisement epitomizes the saving function of the product, the urgency of a decision.

The product in the instructive advertisement is ever a fortuitous deliverer. The unprepared hostess caught in some unenviable fix is a recurring theme. In one advertisement "the principal dish has been forgotten."[96] In another a woman has lost her Bovril and must halt her cooking until she finds it.[97] The answers for these women are clear. For the "Unexpected guest," the smiling hostess "bring[s] on one of McCalls Paysandu Ox Tongues."[98] For "The Hostess who is anxious that the dinner shall be a success . . . high-class cookery and also economy are achieved by the use of Bovril."[99] In these advertisements unhappy states—the "anxiety" of the hostess, the "unexpected[ness]" of the guest, the forgetfulness of the cook—give way to happy results—fun parties, tempting dinners, satisfied guests. The consumer is asked to assess her own preparedness, to regard the brief anxiety of self-assessment as a desirable, necessary prelude to the miracles of consumption.

Cautionary tales dangle before the consumer commercially defined pinnacles of perfection achieved by consumption. For Liebig Extract a woman performs kitchen marvels:

> Here at the kitchen table stands
> The fairest cook I know—
> She who presides the household o'er,
> From roof all down below.
> With bright sweet face and white small hands
> For there no stain e'er clings—
> No care is ever mistress there—
> She deftly bakes and sings.
>
> Why should she not? The days are gone
> When cooks must rule the roast.
> The housewife reigns the kitchen o'er,
> Just where she's needed most.
> The Magic Extract tells the tale
> Of meals that never mar
> The soulful peace of home, and is
> The modern family jar.
>
> Oh, Mr. Liebig! Thanks to thee
> And to thy company too
> The home that has the Extract has
> The bliss no ancients knew!
> Peace reigns therein from early morn
> Until the midnight call,
> Each hour has Liebig in his praise
> And crowns him King of all.[100]

Her "white small hands" are unstained by labor, yet her work is "deft."
Like a queen she "reigns" and "presides." Her secret "Magic" creates
"soulful peace" and "bliss no ancient knew." Through the miracles of
consumption she attains aspects of the feminine ideal. The Liebig woman
is a "queen" through kitchen "magic." Her accomplishments are exaggerated for effect; they demonstrate the transformative agency of consumption, the remarkable rewards offered to those who decide to buy that
particular product.

The product holds the promise of heavenly rewards. An advertisement
for Fry's Cocoa illustrates a house and the faces of two adults and two
children. The text mimics the rhythm of a child's verse:

> This is the Home that Fry built. This is the maid with the merry laugh who
> lives in the Home that Fry built. This is the boy with the ruddy cheeks who
> romps with the maid with the merry laugh who lives in the Home that Fry
> built. These are parents, healthy and strong, who use the cocoa of great
> renown, that feeds the maid with the merry laugh and also the boy with the
> ruddy cheeks who live in the Home that Fry built.[101]

The advertisement presents a story-book version of reality, an elusive fairy-
tale vision, which is so perfect that it both reminds the consumer of her
own inadequacy and urges her to reform.

The miracle of consumption depends on this essential willingness to act.
In another Liebig advertisement a little maid again practices her "Liebig
art." But this time the poem after the first stanza continues,

> Her little lecture would you hear?
> 'Tis this: "This extract is, my dear,
> The extract pure of beef prepared
> So that its flavour's not impaired
> By fat, or grease or gelatine—
> An extract wholesome, rich and clean.
> Its genuineness you may assure
> By J. Von Liebig's signature,
> On every single jar in blue—
> So let no fraud be palmed on *you*.
>
> "The Liebig *Company* alone
> Can make this extract be it known.
> And if your kitchen drudgery
> You'd greatly lighten come to me—
> And when you've found your toil made light,
> You'll be, like me, a Liebigite."[102]

She tutors her fellows with a "little lecture." The consumer, poor drudge,
must clarify her goals, as well as improve her practice. When she resolves to
change, the little maid will show her the way. The adoption of a new

product becomes like a conversion experience in which the poor sinner confesses her faults, her willingness to change, and is guided along the right path by the already converted.

The prescriptive advertisement offers the simple answers of the classroom slate, the assurance of maternal wisdom, the easy confidences of a trusted friend. All three point to consumer deficiencies. On the other hand, fairy-tale visions of commercial paradise hold the promise of heavenly perfection. The individual has only to choose. Internal fears, like external threats, may be swept away by a single decision. Advertisers thus successfully supply the essential elements of a provocative model—the angst of the unconverted, the assistance of the chosen, the bliss of the decided. In doing so, they react to the pressures of the mass market and the anxieties that typified late Victorian experience. Paradoxically, they use evangelical language and forms to support a hedonistic message.

6

Community and the Individual

Conventionally, historians have argued that the traditional experience of community, resonant with positive associations, declined in the nineteenth century under the weighty pressures of industrialism. The family left its village support networks, moved to the city, and retreated behind the sheltered hedges of suburbia. Consumerism seems at first glance to fit this pattern. Advertisements might seem in Marxian terms to glorify a commodity fetishism predicated on selfish greed, a greed antithetical to most abstract ideals of community. But in fact consumerism redefined rather than abandoned the relationship between the community and the individual. Individuals might be joined by self-illusory hedonism, by the shared experience both of being consumers and enjoying the anticipation of satiation. This was a sort of community, even though it was not tied to one specific physical place. Accordingly, products are not always peddled in the Victorian advertisement with particular reference to the satisfaction of individual needs. With surprising frequency, advertisers manipulate a broad awareness of social context. Their striking use of physical and ideological settings reveals a new interpretation of community, freshly adapted for the increasingly commercial mental and physical universe of the late Victorian individual.

Community in Victorian England

Until the nineteenth century the rural village defined the British experience of community. In the village individuals depended on each other for livelihood, entertainment, welfare, and education. Relationships were personal; customs were rooted in nature and tradition.[1] The rural concept of community became part of the English national identity, indeed a social ideal. The industrial revolution appeared to spawn the weakening of community; reciprocal obligation was replaced by competitive individualism. In the urban industrial system Carlyle argued that people were connected by the cash nexus; Ruskin despaired that industry divided men as well as labor; Marx and Engels analyzed the destruction of feudal, patriarchal, idyllic relations by naked self-interest.[2] New terminology entered social discourse. Hegel introduced the concept of alienation; Durkheim wrote of anomie.[3] An ostensible shift from organic solidarity to atomizing individualism became the central preoccupation of social criticism. By 1887 it attained its classic formulation in *Gemeinschaft and Gesellschaft* in which Ferdinand Tönnies, a prominent sociologist, hypothesized that society had discarded a rural gemeinschaft pattern (in which relationships would be personal, particular, and stable) for a gesellschaft pattern (in which relationships would be characterized by competition, impersonality, and the public bonds of politics, institutions, business, and trade).[4]

Historians in the twentieth century have seen the emergence of the Victorian family as part of this cultural shift. With urbanization, historians concur that the family became increasingly self-contained, accessible but distanced physically and psychologically from relatives, friends, or neighbors. It became its own emotional center, absorbed and motivated by its intimate connection, rather than by external pressures. Romantic love replaced economic and community criteria for selecting a mate. The mother-infant relationship acquired new cultural significance.[5] As the home became a sheltered refuge from the hostile sphere of commerce, family activities were seen as private and self-interested, premised on individual needs rather than community goals. In physical terms the enclosed world of the home was expressed in the suburban villa. The distinction between public and private, however, transcended physical parameters; it became a habit of mind conditioned by a gendered definition of the separate spheres. According to this conventional interpretation, the emergence of the self-contained family is a manifestation and a sign of a broadly evidenced decline of community.

Historians have envisioned a Victorian family isolated, separate, turned in upon itself. But the private/public, individual/community polarities upon which this analysis relies are starkly artificial. The Victorian home, however apparently private or ostensibly shielded from the outside world, was routinely penetrated, indeed absorbed, by intensely commercial, overtly public preoccupations. Victorian consumerism vividly illustrates this reality. Advertised goods might be consumed privately, even sensually by individual family members. Yet consumption of the most mundane household product might assume a conspicuously public guise. The home could become a veritable showplace of social standing and taste. It was impossible to isolate family life from commercial structures. Rather, it was the hope of creating a protected sanctuary that led Victorians to sentimental-ize the domestic circle.[6] Some advertisements illustrated this sentimental vision of the domestic circle as sanctuary (cf. Chapter 2) in their articula-tion of a domestic ideal, but in reality the public and the private, the individual and the community, were hopelessly intermingled.

By the late nineteenth century notions of community were shifting. Pre-nineteenth-century definitions of community as an aggregate of people who shared a common interest in a particular locality[7] had focused on community as a place. The nineteenth-century sense of community, on the other hand, increasingly accentuated an experiential dimension. As the railway quickly transported people from distant parts of the country and as the press quickly and efficiently informed and familiarized consumers with the world outside the walled garden and the village square, location ceased to drive the concept of community. In a nascent global village, consumers felt a kinship with those whose experience of life mirrored their own. The physical realities of day-to-day life were determined as much by the stan-dardization implicit in mass production as by geographic location. People from different parts of the country who bought the same products, shared the same taste, experienced the same material universe, were connected. They understood each other, rationally and emotionally, although sepa-rated by geographic distance. They were people who shared standards of living, taste, style, and fashion. By the late nineteenth century these factors formed a more significant commonality than mere physical proximity.

The Commercial Interpretation

Advertisements portray a Victorian consumer who is self-absorbed, but not atomized or isolated, who is indeed part of a new community of consumers. Although concerned with personal pleasure, the advertisement was also a central agency of the redefinition of community, to mean not so much a physical place as a shared and hedonistic experience of being a consumer.

The Individual

Narcissism

Many Victorian advertisements provide a seductive, but jarring impression of commercial narcissism. They seem to pander to the personal pleasure of the individual, the couple, the family. In these advertisements the hedonis-tic ethos turns attention inwards.

The requirements of particular products focused attention resolutely on the individual. Each year there were hundreds of advertisements for cor-sets, shoes, dresses, coats, colognes, toothpowders, and hair tonics. These products were designed to decorate the self. From the recesses of a bou-doir a woman modeled a corset or experimented with a face cream. These sorts of products necessitated precisely these sorts of private images, but private images created a powerful illusion; Victorians seemed consumed with the importance of anointing their bodies with creams, colognes, and decorations. Decorative intent, regardless of motivation, inherently held an important promise of self-satisfaction. Victorians seemed preoccupied with themselves. Moreover, the personal nature of these products often required that the consumer be pictured in isolation. Alone, perfumed and exquisitely costumed, the consumer, however responsive to cultural expectations and the pressures of social emulation, seemed hedonistic and self-absorbed.

The prospect of self-indulgence was even more straightforward in advertisements for luxurious superfluities. Although some Victorian luxuries were convenience items, and others had a Veblenesque function, many Victorian luxuries were luxuries in the sense that they would allow consumers to luxuriate—they offered the consumer sensuous delight. Advertisements for these products especially commercialized the Victorian consumer's narcissistic proclivities through two particular feminine images—the bather and the reflected self.

Typically, the bather fixates on her private pleasure. For Pears' Soap a woman reclines in a capacious tub. (She may be Lillie Langtry or Adelina Patti, but her identity is unclear.) Elegance is suggested by the decoration

"*I have found PEARS' SOAP matchless for the hands and complexion.*"

Figure 6-1. Pears' Soap, *Illustrated London News*, 1889. (Robarts Library.)

of the tub, the graceful lines of the bench, and the potted palm behind her head. Clusters of fruit on the tub are symbols of fertility. Roses trail haphazardly on the floor, suggesting the woman's softness. A hand mirror has been cast aside on the floor, but not so far away that it is inaccessible. The woman is preoccupied with herself. She selects one of the many bars of soap from a delicately footed dish: the availability of so many bars to one bather provides an impression of wealth and carefree leisure. As she bends over the side of the tub, she clasps a semi-transparent towel to conceal her breasts. Folds of the drapery support her bared shoulders.[8] Practically every element of the composition—the fruit, the roses, the mirror, the disheveled drapery, the semi-transparent towel—promises sensual pleasure. And yet the bather does not beckon to the viewer. She is absorbed in her private indulgence.

The bather in the advertisement enjoys physical sensation, but also a dreamy half awareness. Amid tropical foliage and palatial architecture, she wades in a lily pond.[9] In classical garb and crown of daisies she absent-mindedly plucks flower petals and sets them adrift along a river.[10] Her averted attention is part of her allure. She luxuriates in physical sensation, but also the pleasure of her own daydreams. As wealthy sybarite and idle daydreamer, the bather sells soap by promoting the enjoyment of the self, physical and cerebral.

The recurring mirror motif symbolizes a dangerous tendency toward self-absorption. At its most innocuous the mirror motif links vanity with feminine nature (cf. Chapter 2). In other advertisements mirrors suggest a distorted attention to the self. In an advertisement for Gosnell's Famora[11] a woman in a kitsch classical costume holds a small hand mirror high above her head. At an unnatural angle she grins at her own reflection. Although the advertisement clearly intends to market the product as a fashionable lotion, the extremes of her costume, her facial expression and her pose exaggerate, even parody, her self-perception. Exaggerated depictions reflect more than an assumption of feminine vanity. They create a general impression of self-absorption.

These Victorian advertisements routinely decorate, anoint, and study the individual. They market personal ornament and products that will permit the individual consumer to luxuriate. Their imagery reveals the sensual delights of the recumbent bather and the self-satisfied mirror gazer. They elaborate a theme of commercial narcissism that celebrates the most personal and private pleasures.

Romantic Love

The private pleasure of individuals is similarly highlighted through a commercial emphasis on romantic love. Large numbers of advertisements present sweet depictions of the private emotional satisfaction of the couple. Another set of advertisements favors Romeo and Juliet and elopement motifs that dramatize the couple who pursue private gratification rather than the approval of the community. All these depictions sentimentalize the private pleasures of individuals.

In the Victorian advertisement romantic love is easily reduced to an attractive abstraction. Typically, for Brandauer Pens[12] a woman sits at her writing desk, staring dreamily into space. One hand is raised to her face to indicate languor, slight embarrassment, even sensual touch. A heart-shaped locket hangs from her neck. She writes a love letter, inspired by winged cupids. The image is pretty, affecting, safely within the bounds of propriety. She is alone; the couple is as physically separate as possible. In the absence of physical contact, passion is communicated through the discrete literary symbol of the cupid. Her love letter is engaging, but essentially conventional. A ring decorates the fourth finger of her left hand. She demonstrates the utmost respectability; she writes to her betrothed.

In the presence of each other the Victorian couple are inevitably separated by physical distance and by conventional behavior. For Egerton Burnett's Serges, similarly, a man doffs his hat and kneels for a young woman.[13] Shyly, she looks away, but clutches the daisies he has presented. Although he assumes the role of adoring suitor, she the role of coy object of his attention, their postures comply with Victorian notions of propriety: the two are separated physically by the steps.

Not surprisingly, suggestions of conquests in the Victorian advertisement are metaphorical rather than physical. By 1910 Quaker Oats obliquely suggests physical satisfaction. A halo-configuration encompasses the picture of a young couple in evening dress, who hold hands. She wears a heart-shaped locket and bows her head demurely. The boldface caption announces "it's the steady caller" and promises "the perfect satisfaction" with "food that does not overheat the blood."[14]

In the commercial forum the pressing suitor is often rebuffed or ignored by the object of his desire. For Ellis Davies & Co. Tea a man in period costume, complete with jaunty feathered hat, leans to kiss a maid who spurns his affections or feigns disinterest.[15] For Montserrat Lime Juice a man stares as though captivated by the beauty of a woman in Grecian costume who serenely picks limes from a vine and sets them in a basket.[16] In both advertisements the women appear disinterested. The women are removed from the potential consumer's station—either by occupation or by periodization. Although the women are conventionally resistant, in both advertisements smitten suitors, whether by snatching a kiss or by openly staring, defy conventional standards of propriety.

Married couples are illustrated in "happy reunion." They "liv[e] happy [*sic*] ever afterwards."[17] They embrace discreetly and stare into each other's eyes. In an advertisement for Aspinall's Enamel a woman paints a chair. Her husband appears behind her and taps her on the shoulder. Surprised, she turns to greet him. She quotes *Timons of Athens* v 2, "I intend but only to surprise him." He quotes *Titus Andron* iv 1: "Wert [*sic*] though thus surprised sweet girl."[18] She has surprised her husband by painting the

Figure *6-2.* Brandauer Pens, *Illustrated London News*, 1886. (Robarts Library.)

Figure 6-3. Egerton Burnett's Serges, *Graphic*, 1886. (Robarts Library.)

chair; he has surprised her by returning unexpectedly. Each surprise is pleasant; each partner clearly endeavors to please the other. They suggest a marriage sustained by romantic love and increasingly by companionable leisure (cf. Chapter 2), a marriage that satisfies the emotional needs of the couple, rather than merely the expectations of society.

The advertiser's focus on the private needs of the couple is most dramatic in advertisements that employ a Romeo and Juliet motif. Two advertisements featuring Romeo and Juliet were especially widely printed in the 1890s. A Hudson's Forget-Me-Not Soap advertisement shows Juliet leaning over the balcony to embrace her Romeo.[19] She kisses him softly on the cheek, as he clasps her right arm with his hand. A Carr's Ladder Tape variation is considerably more flamboyant. Romeo climbs a Carr's Ladder Tape to reach Juliet on the balcony. The sense of a reckless deed driven by the power of love is accentuated by one foot that dangles from the Ladder Tapes, by Romeo's outstretched arms, and by Juliet's comparative physical security on the balcony. His cape billows behind him. He carries a lute to serenade her. The moon glows, flowers trail from the railing. Juliet's hair is down, her clothing is loose, more unstructured. Each physical detail is fully fleshed, not merely suggested, by cupid-like symbols. Although the caption is deliberately practical, "A good article at a fair price is the truest economy,"[20] the product is sold partly by an amusing use of the product, but mostly by the flagrant romance of the selling image. Women are surely happy to know that "Carr's Patent . . . Ladder Tapes are made only from the very best material," their attention is undoubtedly captured by a clever unexpected image, but the sweetness of the image is the advertisement's strongest marketing feature. Women, presumably the purchasers of ladder tapes and Hudson's Soap, buy the products not because they believe soap or window blinds may bring them illicit encounters, but because of the emotive power of the abstract notion of romantic love.

An important subtext of the Romeo and Juliet motif, however, emerges when it is viewed in conjunction with another advertisement in which a girl elopes from her bedroom window. The inventive young lady slides down her bedroom window along a Carr's Ladder Tape. Her image is saccharine. She wears a flowered bonnet, heeled shoes, and stares adoringly (to her beloved) at the ground. The caption announces Carr's as "A Modern Method of Elopement." The humor is clear.[21] Like the Romeo and Juliet motif, the image is improbable; lovers do not really climb with lutes to bedroom balconies; girls do not really use ladder tapes to elope from bedroom windows. But both images not insignificantly place the love of the couple above the wishes of their parents or the demands of the community at large. Romeo and Juliet defy community interests to rendezvous at the balcony. The girl who elopes places romantic love above parental approval. Both clichés of commercial romanticism were also motifs of rebellion in which the gratification of private desires overrides community interest.

Courtship imagery in the Victorian advertisement focuses on the private

Figure 6-4. Carr's Ladder Tapes, *Illustrated London News*, 1893. (Robarts Library.)

pleasures of individuals. Amid cupids, riverside scenes, and the watchful eye of mother, Victorian couples are driven by romantic love. But the advertiser sets limits. The lovers are encumbered by social conventions; when portrayed as Victorians, they do not cast aside community standards and join in passionate embraces. However, when distanced by historicism

Figure 6-5. Carr's Ladder Tapes, *Illustrated London News*, 1896. (Robarts Library.)

or occupation, suitors stare daringly and snatch kisses. Romeo and Juliet motifs and elopement images dramatize in advertisements breaks with community expectations. In reality, as advertisements revealed, the vestiges of traditional community still prevented uninhibited physical expression. But Victorians revelled in the pleasurable connotations of an ideal of private gratification—romantic love.

Maternal Love

The commercial exploitation of the romantic couple in the Victorian advertisement is surpassed only by an increasing number of advertisements that portray the mother-child relationship. In advertisements for baby products and for a diverse assortment of adult-oriented commodities infants with their mothers form an affecting combination. These advertisements draw attention to the personal emotional gratification derived from maternity.

In advertisements the love of the mother for her child is comparable to the attention of the pressing suitors—complete, absorbed, focused. The exclusivity of the mother-child relationship is pronounced. Captions such as "Baby and I" directly suggest it.[22] Pictorially, it also becomes clear that mother and child have eyes only for each other, even though in her maternal role the mother is increasingly (in advertisements) assisted by servant labor. (Cf. Chapter 2.) A widely printed Allenburys' Foods advertisement shows a mother leaning toward her baby, holding a baby bottle for a young sitting child. The mother appears to be lying on the floor herself so that she may, eye-to-eye, coax the child to take the bottle. There is no setting. There are no other people. The relationship between mother and child is complete; they are absorbed in each other.[23] The stark absence of environment highlights the immediate demands of the mother-child relationship. In an advertisement for Beecham's Pills a mother seated in a chair, holds a dejected female child close to her.[24] The child seems forlorn. The mother's arms encircle the child, as she presents a box of Beecham's Pills. She is not an authority-figure who commands the child to take her medicine, but a figure of comfort who expresses the nurturing qualities of her feminine nature. For Clarke's Pyramid Lamps a mother feeds her child in bed.[25] The child is young, but not newborn, yet the demands of childcare have prompted the woman to take the child into her bed. The father's place has been supplanted by the child. The love between mother and child is consuming and paramount.

The relationship between mother and child is so celebrated in the advertisement that the mother becomes a sort of madonna. In an illustration for Géraudel Pastilles a mother embraces her young daughter. They are presented in a cameo configuration. The mother's hair is undressed, her clothing classicized, her arms bared. She is, like a Raphaelite madonna, elevated by the unconditional love between mother and child. The caption reads "A touching story." The text describes how the little girl, six or seven

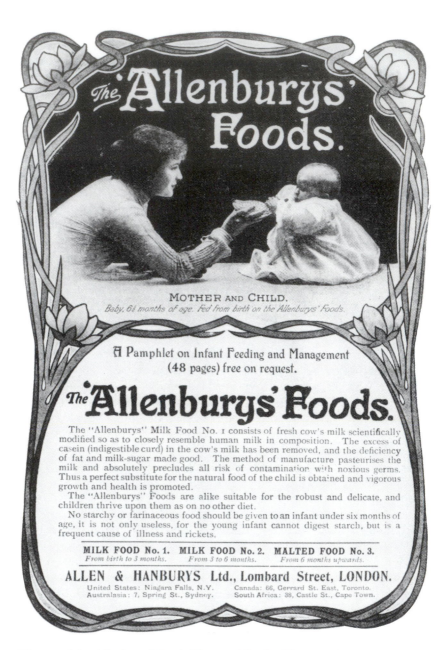

Figure 6-6. Allenburys' Food, *Illustrated London News*, 1906. (Robarts Library.)

years of age, by reading an advertisement aloud for Géraudel Pastilles, saved her mother, stricken with a serious attack of bronchitis. "Out of the mouths of babes cometh truth" announces the advertisement. The child is "like a flash of light," "in some sort inspired."[26] The love between mother and child is fierce, almost spiritual in the devotion of one to the other. Their love elevates them both and permits superhuman action. "She who rocks the cradle rules the world."[27] Eno's quotes Washington Irving,

> Who that has languished, even in advanced life, in sickness and despondency, who that has pined on a weary bed in the neglect and loneliness of a foreign land—but has thought on the mother 'that looked on his childhood' that smoothed his pillow and administered to his helplessness? Oh! There is an enduring tenderness in the love of a mother to a son that transcends all other affections of the heart. It is neither to be chilled by selfishness, nor daunted by danger, nor weakened by worthlessness, nor stifled by ingratitude. She will sacrifice every comfort to his convenience; she will surrender every pleasure to his enjoyment; she will glory in his fame and exult in his prosperity; and if misfortune overtake him, he will be the dearer to her from misfortune; and if disgrace settle upon his name, she will still love and cherish him in spite of his disgrace, and if all the world beside cast him off, she will be all the world to him.[28]

The love of mother and child is enduring, stronger than any other love.

Commercial depictions of romantic and maternal love are appealing because they create an illusion of intimacy. They expose the sexual intensity of the courting couple—through clichés like elopement, through flamboyant historical motifs, and through restrained sentimentality. They portray mother and child in their most private moments—in bed, feeding, comforting. All these situations are very private, fraught with emotion. They illustrate the satisfaction of individual needs; the couple, romantic or maternal, shut out the world at large and retreat within the sheltered arms of each other.

The Victorian advertisement with its blatant attention to personal ornament, the overt hedonism of its sensual bathers, the self-absorption of its mirror gazers, and the private emotional gratification of smitten lovers or doting mothers suggests that the commercial forum exploited highly individualistic concerns. Depictions of nude bathers, women in their boudoirs, or Romeos climbing onto a balcony seem pretty and affecting in isolation; in plentiful combination they suggest a superficial preoccupation with pleasure-seeking for its own sake. It was undoubtedly in the advertiser's interest to promote pleasure and to draw on primal responses including sexual and maternal instincts. But in isolation each of these features of the Victorian advertisement may distort the Victorian advertiser's very real sense of a world outside the walled garden. The private gratification of the hedonistic bathers must be balanced by many advertisements that transported consumers to very public vistas.

Community

In advertisements the public invades the private sphere. Even within the home, material things communicate status to the community at large. At the same time advertisements humanize the crowd, the world, the most exotic locales, and personalize political messages and nationalistic slogans. The advertisement does not focus only on private pleasure. The Victorian advertisement focuses on a community redefined by the shared experience of being consumers.

The Private Sphere Invaded

All sorts of products—tea, cocoa, biscuits, soaps—were meant to be consumed at home. Pictures of home consumption seemed practically inevitable. But as much as advertisers were eager to capture the pleasurable overtones of the private sphere, they also revealed that the home was inextricably part of the community.

The commercial depiction of the domestic hearth, the celebrated hub of the private sphere, is suffused with very public appeals to status. An advertisement for the New Patent Nursing Chair employs the familiar before-and-after motif to illustrate the beneficial effects of the nursing chair.[29] In the depiction of "home miserable" the family sits by the fire, but is disturbed by a crying baby. The mantle is materially complete. It includes a gilt mirror, a mantle clock in a protective glass globe, silver candlesticks. The scene is apparently ideal, furnished with requisite middle-class material comforts; a father home from the city, a devoted mother, everything but a thriving child. In the after picture the child smiles from his nursery chair. The decorated mantle functions in the advertisement as a visual shorthand for the comforts of a prosperous family. The product is linked with the domestic comfort a politely decorative environment suggests. The theme is perpetuated in Edwardian advertisements. The woman who reclines before a warm fire demonstrates not only the "rich decorative beauty" of her Carron firegrate, but a broad decorative context, replete with vases, mantle clocks, fresh flowers, walled sconces, and patterned carpets.[30] Advertisements that cluster the family around the hearth draw on the complex symbolism of the domestic ideology, but they are also concerned with status enhancement. The hearth illustrates the family's socio-economic status. Fine and detailed attention to mantle decoration is an essential element of the advertiser's message. Products are ideally marketed not only in conjunction with family values, but with particular reference to economic prosperity. The hearth, far from being sheltered, is itself in the advertisement a vehicle of public display.

Within "the heart of the home"[31] advertisers seize every opportunity to capture the public face of the private sphere. Decorative staircases are popular in the Victorian advertisement for precisely this reason. They are usually located in the front foyer, arguably the most public room of the house, seen by every visitor who enters through the front door. For example, for Monkey Brand Brooke's Soap a monkey slides down a polished bannister, as two little girls watch with interest in the foyer.[32] The staircase is a dramatic and beautiful architectural feature, an indication of an affluent household and a family of taste and refinement.

Commercial interpretations of the domestic environment reveal the permeability of the walls of the garden. The image of the domestic hearth concentrates on the family's preoccupation with social status conveyed through the symbolism of the mantle clock, the glass globe, the matching urns, the grand staircase. The appeal of these images is partly that they allow us to peer into the private sphere. But these central commercial symbols also reveal the pressures of the outside world that shaped and penetrated the domestic environment.

The Personalization of the Public Sphere

As much as advertisements invade the private sphere, the public arena is personalized. In advertisements impersonal conglomerations like the crowd or the world celebrate the unity created by consumption rather than the disparate isolation of their constituent elements. Neighbors talk to each other. Friends share a personal connection cemented by self-disclosure. Cold abstractions of nationhood are charmingly personified. Political process is comically humanized. In public settings, the cold impersonality of gesellschaft is rarely evidenced. At every turn the public and the private intersect and the sharp division between public and private, individual and community, is hopelessly violated.

The crowd in the advertisement, far from symbolizing urban alienation, represents a community of consumers. A 1907 Bovril campaign demonstrates this theme. One advertisement, part of a stunning series, illustrates a crowd of working-class men. The caption argues that "Three thousand five hundred such crowds as this could have been supplied with a cup of piping hot Bovril . . . Bovril repels influenza and resists colds and chills. Crowds know it!"[33] At first the advertisement seems to echo an unattractive stereotype of urban life—the faceless anonymity of the urban worker. From a distance the faces seem the same; the sense of uniformity, the absence of individuated identity, is reinforced by a sea of workman's caps. The advertisement might conjure up unhappy notions of dissatisfied workers engaged in trade union action, of the volatile urban mob, of the mediocrity of mass society. And yet, clearly, Bovril would not sell more beef tea with any of these ideas. Rather the caption is key: "Crowds Know" the benefits of Bovril. The consumer should buy the product because everyone else does. The new consumer should find out what everyone else already knows; the old consumer should be flattered that so many people share her assessment of the product. The selling message evokes the importance of shared knowledge, shared understanding. All these people, masses of people, share an understanding of the merits of

Figure 6-7. Monkey Brand Soap, *Illustrated London News*, 1891. (Robarts Library.)

THREE THOUSAND FIVE HUNDRED
SUCH CROWDS AS THIS
could have been supplied with a cup of piping hot

BOVRIL

from the Bovril sold on a single day recently.
Bovril repels Influenza and resists Colds and Chills.

Crowds know it !

Figure   6-8.   Bovril, *Illustrated London News*, 1907. (Robarts Library.)

Bovril. There is a sense of disclosure from the many to the few. All may be united by the shared action of consumption, by a shared fantasy about the beneficial effects of the product. Although apparently faceless, unknown to each other, each person in the crowd shares in a collective identity as a Bovril consumer. This message is even clearer in another advertisement in the same series in which the faces of myriad women are illustrated to sell Bovril for "Health and Beauty." The caption instructs "The Bovril sold on a single day recently was sufficient to provide a brimming hot cupful for 7,000,000 beautiful women."[34] Unlike the first advertisement in which the uniformity of the caps seems virtually dehumanizing, in this advertisement the women look remarkably different—their hairstyles, dress, hats, and facial features express their individuality and the many incarnations of feminine beauty rather than celebrate a uniform ideal. Seven million beautiful women are not standardized, robbed of individuation; they are not impersonal cogs in a gesellschaft relation; rather they are individuals connected by a shared and pleasurable experience of being Bovril consumers.

As audience, the commercial crowd expresses the bond of those unknown to each other face-to-face but united by shared experience. In an advertisement for Gramophones a crowd of women sit outside in rattan chairs and listen to music.[35] In the foreground, the dominant figures sit with their backs to us, the central figure with her head entirely concealed by her hat. Even the most distant figures in the group are not identified in clear detail. The identity of each listener is insignificant; more important is their shared experience of music. In a Christmas advertisement for the same product an ethereal "spirit of music" rises out of the gramophone as the crowds gaze with rapt attention.[36] By the nineteenth century the behavior of audiences in real life had become markedly circumscribed. Respectability required minimal display of emotion, even tears. Public displays of any sort of emotion more often than not carried negative associations of uncontrolled mobs. Audience members expected to control their own public reactions.[37] They were not joined together by personal interaction with each other, but by a shared, but often unspoken, appreciation of a performance. The experience of the audience member was in one sense like the experience of the consumer; through absorption of the self in a fantastic illusion—the fantastic performer, the fantastic product— each person could have access to a new experience or repeat old pleasurable ones. Although seemingly isolated, consumers, like audience members, might be joined by a shared pursuit of an ephemeral and elusive spirit.

Consumption promises to warm the most chilling public arena. Bovril pictures Trafalgar Square pelted with rain.[38] Before a bleak St.-Martin's-in-the-Fields darkened by stormy clouds, throngs of pedestrians obscured by umbrellas mill about a street crowded with carts and buses. The image is inhospitable not just because of the weather, but because of the harsh impersonality of one of the busiest squares of London. The text is moodily evocative. In the advertisement there is

> Cold, drenching rain, damp air that chills, chills to the marrow: underfoot a wet pavement that makes it impossible for the feet to be dry. And then, then Bovril, a cup of steaming Bovril and a warm glow straightaway spreads throughout the system. The feeling of the overpowering cold is gone and one can brave the elements again, feeling the master of them.[39]

Here the pedestrian throngs complement the chill of "drenching rain." The crowd, the busy setting, is effective because it is unwelcoming. But the simple action of consumption is an agent of courage and mastery. Just as the family prepares its members for the world outside, consumption fortifies the individual for the public sphere. The square is a seductive foil for the dramatic consequences of consumption.

The world in the advertisement becomes a physical extension of the crowd, not an alienating abstraction which swamps or intimidates the individual by its scale, but a metaphor for the expanded parameters of the shared experience of being a consumer. Advertisement after advertisement illustrates the world. Globe Metal Polish even adopts the metaphor in its brand name.[40] The text reminds consumers of the unifying effects of consumption: "If you are one of the few people who have not yet used Globe Polish . . . We invite you to try Globe Polish *to-day*." Not to use the product is to alienate oneself from a virtually universal experience. The globe becomes a symbol for "everyone"; the consumer must not feel left out. In more surreal illustrations the globe is made to seem personally controlled and manageable by monkeys that race about its circumference

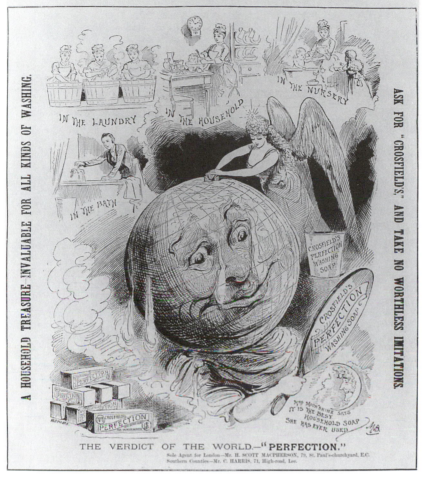

Figure 6-9. Crosfield's Soap, *Illustrated London News*, 1887. (Robarts Library.)

for Monkey Brand Soap[41] and by a cherub who is literally on top of the world for Géraudel Pastilles.[42] For Crosfield's Soap the world is even personified. As an angel scrubs away at its surface, the world examines its reflection in a hand mirror. A tiny smiling moon advises, "Mrs. Moonshine says it is the best household soap she has ever used."[43] Reduced to a caricatured person, the world is knowable, no longer faceless. The consumer identifies with the world itself, discovers a community of interests, in the pursuit of the fantasy of consumption.

The redefinition of boundaries of community, of the consumer's sense

Figure 6-10. Nabob Pickles, *Illustrated London News*, 1902. (Robarts Library.)

of commonality with other consumers, is underscored by the prominence
of exoticism in the Victorian advertisement. Many advertisements evoke
Far Eastern cultures with crudely stereotyped illustrations. On one level
these advertisements are intended to amuse. An Indian man in grossly
exaggerated costume sits cross-legged eating his "Batty's Nabob Pickles"
ostensibly reciting the rhyme "If you like the Pickles, Prithee, try the
Sauce; If one the palate tickles, The other will, of course!!!"[44] The image
borders on ridiculous; the old man is reduced to a sort of singing child.
Pioneer Tobacco employs cartoons of Eastern "foreign devils";[45] Beecham's prints an unintelligible message in fabricated oriental characters;[46]
Sapolio Cleanser pictures a Chinese gardener who advises, "The Chinese

say, 'When the wind blows your fire, it is useless to tire yourself.' About half of your toil can be avoided by the use of Sapolio."[47] Although the Indians, the Japanese, and the Chinese in these advertisements are in the loosest sense consumers, they function more as entertainers who provide a pithy aphorism, an intriguing puzzle, an amusing rhyme. They are mere curiosities, circus players in an arena of commercial goods.

Nonetheless, foreigners assume supporting roles that underline their ostensibly inferior, even indentured, status. In a typical example Moham-medans stand barefoot atop a hill marveling at stars that they believe are made bright with Brooke's Soap.[48] The racist tone is offensive today, but the Victorian intent—to seize the commercial benefit of associating the product with celebrations of cultural and racial superiority—requires that readers transport themselves outside their own culture and compare them-selves with others. This process inevitably encouraged consumers to define collective identity and to revel in collective superiority.

At the same time, consumers are repeatedly reminded that they are bonded with the people of many nations through their shared apprecia-tion and enjoyment of a particular product. An advertisement for Huntley & Palmers Biscuits informs consumers that

> The biscuit has met every civilized race under the sun. It has become as familiar to the Parisian as to the Londoner. The American, who is a born connoisseur in "crackers," adopts it as he travels over Europe; and he finds it as easily in the Swiss Mountains, in Italian cities, along the banks of the Rhine and in the silent old towns in Belgium, as at the Langham in London or the Grand Hotel in India. You cannot get beyond the reach of it "up country" in India. John Chinaman munches it; it is known to the Daimois of Japan.[49]

In another advertisement, an illustsration features an international contingent—Englishmen, Turks, Chinese, East Indians, North Ameri-cans, Scots, and Frenchmen, all in national costume—who carry an enor-mous bottle of Rose's Lime Juice.[50] International depictions present con-sumer goods as a link between nations. In an advertisement for Pears' Soap,

> Winston Churchill, the English War correspondent, says that after careful study of many nations he has concluded that the distinguishing characteristic of English-speaking people as compared with other white races is that they wash, and wash at regular intervals. "English and American," he says, "are divided by an ocean of salt water, but they are united by a bath tub of fresh water and soap."[51]

The product is the link across the ocean. However apparently dissimilar, people all over the world may share a fascination with a particular product. In some advertisements exoticism is used to unite British consumers in a joyful sense of racial superiority; in others foreigners are used to convey a

Figure 6-11. Brooke's Soap, *Illustrated London News*, 1885. (Robarts Library.)

broader unity, the unity of the world, the insignificance of geographical boundaries. Consumption and the anticipatory delight that precedes it joined people of all nations. A collective identity was created by the collective action of consuming and by collective anticipation. As much as national culture or geographic circumstance, the shared experience of being consumers became a defining mark of collective identity.

Figure 6-12. Rose's Lime Juice, *Graphic*, 1885. (Robarts Library.)

Advertisements for mass products draw upon notions of world community, but also evoke the intimate and pleasurable connections of neighborhood interaction. For Pears' Soap two maids prepare to wash the steps. A passing chimney sweep asks, "Good Morning! Have you used Pears' Soap?"[52] The maids smile in response. The exchange is familiar, perhaps a daily occurrence. They seem known to each other, part of the same community of neighborhood workers. The humble task, the easy repartee, create an impression of an old-fashioned neighborhood in which face-to-face relations are inevitably and perpetually cheerful. Their primary function is to dramatize a warm community interaction, solidified by the product.

Advertisements draw on the unifying force of self-disclosure. Neighbors confide the secret for linen "white as snow" over the garden wall.[53] Best friends whisper to each other over tea.[54] One woman confides the secret of beauty to another.[55] The secret is an essential element of the Victorian advertisement. The advertisement cultivates a central idea of community— that when people self-disclose to each other, they grow together. The psychological openness suggested by sharing a secret tightens a social bond. As neighbors share laundry secrets in the garden, the walls that separate them are lowered. The pleasing product is an agency of unity. The advertisement portrays intimate disclosure between people that contradicts the gesellschaft assumptions often imposed on late nineteenth-century consumer culture.

The cult of personality pervades the Victorian advertisement. Adelina Patti, Violet Vanbrugh, Marie Roze, Dr. Nansen, H. M. Stanley do not offer a sterile stamp of approval, but contrive a personal connection with the consumer. Testimonials of the famous simulate the easy confidences of friends and neighbors. The testimonial disclosed the most personal information about the famous—the sort of tea Stanley favored or the toilet soap used by celebrated beauties. Moreover, the testimonial itself was a sort of confidence offered by the hero to his humble followers. The cult of personality preyed upon intimate connections, the bond of being consumers, of enjoying the anticipation of consumption, a pleasure that might unite seemingly disparate individuals.

Many advertisements appeal to a public interest that transcends the satisfaction of individual needs. In one advertisement Hudson's Soap advertises "Public Health Daily Regulations" An advertisement for Eno's appeals in its largest headline to "Our Sanitary Condition. Important to All."[56] Lipton's Tea illustrates a "facsimile of the great duty cheque paid by Lipton for his week's clearance of tea!"[57] Each of these advertisements was widely printed in the Victorian press. Each is commanding, a dramatic contrast with hedonistic bathers and reflected beauties. In each advertisement products that are potentially for very private consumption—soap, pills, tea—are linked to overtly public goals—community health, sanitation, the balance of payments. This prevalent marketing strategy eschews the self-interest of buyers and sellers for a commercial brand of altruism that pushes the consumer to consider realities beyond the walled garden.

Nationalistic slogans coalesce around the war effort and the 1900–1901 trade disputes. Vinolia Soap established a war fund to which one ha'penny would be contributed for every tablet sold.[58] Lord Roberts dispatches Monkey Brand Soap "to scour the land."[59] Beecham's Pills urges that "Khaki is fashionable" but "surrender yourself unconditionally" to Beecham's Pills.[60] Images of the war tie the product to a noble and valiant cause, to the excitement and thrill of battle, and to the pull of national pride. Protectionist arguments similarly find commercial voice. Buttercup Metal Polish urges consumers with images of Britannia to "Help Home Trade." "At present" the text describes, "nearly all the polishing pastes are imported from Germany, but if you purchase Buttercup Metal Polish you will be obtaining a superior polish and giving employment to a large number of home workers."[61] Ogden's Cigarettes even more dramatically places a series of advertisements celebrating "Home Industry" that advises consumers to "nail your colours to the mast."[62] One popular advertisement pictures "Ogden's principal factory in Liverpool England" which "covers five acres of ground and employs nearly 3,000 *British* workpeople."[63] Another illustrates "a British factory employing over 2,000 British people" packing cigarettes.[64] Exhortations to buy British or to champion the war effort were straightforward appeals to the emotional force of nationalism. They identify consumption with popular national goals. But these advertisements should not be misconstrued as evidence of a gesellschaft commercial ethos in which individuals are so disconnected and isolated that they may be joined only by grandiose abstractions of nationhood and institutional authority.

Nationalistic abstractions effect intimacy through charming personifications. Powerful, but cold pictures of Britannia are balanced by affecting images of John Bull, Merrie England, lovely Erin, and bonnie Scotia. For Monkey Brand Soap John Bull relaxes in a large armchair in a panelled room before a casement window, tankard beside him. He smiles at a monkey he balances on his knee. The monkey has been "adopted by John Bull." The monkey sings, "I love John Bull and his sea-bound isle, his glorious homes and genial smile; and so long as I may, with all my might, I'll make these homes look cheerful and bright."[65] The "genial smile," the happy associations of the monkey, the attractive room and familiar pastimes of John Bull make this a cheery and beguiling reminder of national identity, attractive for personality, for our intimate connection with the scene, rather than for the cold abstraction of nationhood.

The Victorian advertisement personalizes the most public endeavor. Political issues become private, the topic of individual exchange, of anecdote, practically trivialized by their homespun presentation. A gruesome and disturbing event under commercial aegis becomes the topic of idle gossip at the local grocery. A customer asks, "Oh, Mr. Pickles, have you seen in this morning's papers that 100,000 Turks are scouring the Greek border?" The grocer replies, "Yes Madam: with Brooke's Soap. It is so good for marble, paint, crockery etc. It scours and polishes everything. Everybody uses it."[66] An international tragedy becomes the focus of commercial humor, its importance reduced to a trivial exchange between a customer and a grocer. Government process, similarly, seems a mundane affair. In an advertisement for Avoncherra Tea Gladstone presides over his cabinet. Each member is identified by the name on his cup. The group

Adopted by John Bull.

I love John Bull and his sea-bound Isle,
His glorious Homes and genial smile;
And so long as I may, with all my might,
I'll make those Homes look cheerful and bright.

FOR POLISHING
METALS, MARBLE, PAINT,
CUTLERY, CROCKERY, MACHINERY,
OIL-CLOTHS, BATHS, STAIR RODS.

Brooke's Soap – Monkey Brand.

FOR STEEL, IRON, BRASS AND
COPPER VESSELS,
FIRE IRONS, MANTELS, &c.
Removes Rust, Dirt, Stains, Tarnish, &c.

FOR CLEANING, SCOURING, AND SCRUBBING FLOORS AND KITCHEN TABLES.

Figure 6-13. Monkey Brand Soap, *Illustrated London News*, 1894. (Robarts Library.)

makes a "unanimous decision: no cabinet should be without Avoncherra Tea." The task of cabinet minister is directly personalized. The decision will enable "every one to *minister* to their own comfort and to the comfort of others." The advertisement coyly suggests that governing the country amounts to little more than each person governing himself. But the charm of the advertisement is not so much an oblique political message, but the sense that we have caught the cabinet unaware. Gladstone instructs Spencer who whitens his tea: "Steady there, Spencer, with the milk, Rosebery

BROOKE'S SOAP

MONKEY BRAND.

FOR POTS AND PANS,   FOR METALS,   FOR ZINC BATHS,
FOR WOOD WORK,   FOR MARBLE,   FOR CUTLERY,
FOR OIL CLOTHS.   FOR PAINT.   FOR SOILED HANDS.

Small Sample free to any address for one stamp.

BROOKE'S SOAP,
Windows like Crystal.

"Christian World" says:— "Possesses the necessary qualifications for removing dirt and restoring brightness."

WON'T WASH CLOTHES.

Simple Directions.

Dampen a sponge, or soft cloth rather, Rub on Brooke's Soap and make a lather, Then briskly to the place apply, Wipe with a cloth that's clean and dry.

DON'T.

Don't rub the bar 'gainst what you clean; Don't dip it in water— the Soap, I mean; Don't use it for clothes, or on silver or gold, But on everything else that's tarnished and old.

"Fun" says:— "A glorious article for cleaning Steel, Iron, Tin, Brass, Copper, and all kinds of Cutlery."

Read the Directions.

Will do everything that other Soaps will not do. Take care to buy the Monkey Brand—Ask for Brooke's.

BROOKE'S SOAP,
Tinware like Silver.

"Pictorial World" says:— "It should be tried by every housekeeper."

WON'T WASH CLOTHES.

BROOKE'S SOAP,
For Marble, For Copper, For Tin, For Oilcloth.

BROOKE'S SOAP,
Copper like Gold, Crockery like Pearl.

BROOKE'S SOAP,
4d.
per Large Bar.

"Illus. Sporting and Dramatic News" says:— "It cleans Metal, Marble and Paint effectively and rapidly."

SHOCKING !!!

CUSTOMER: "Oh, Mr. Pickles, have you seen in this morning's papers that 100,000 Turks are scouring the Greek border?"

GROCER: "Yes, Madam: with Brooke's Soap. It is so good for Marble, Paint, Crockery, &c. It Scours and Polishes everything. Everybody uses it. *EXCEPT FOR CLOTHES.*"

B. BROOKE, & CO.,
19 and 21, Queen Victoria-street, LONDON.

NO DIRT, NO DUST, NO WASTE, NO LABOUR.
SIMPLE, RAPID, CLEAN, CHEAP.

Figure 6-14. Monkey Brand Soap, *Illustrated London News*, 1886. (Robarts Library.)

Figure 6-15. Avoncherra Tea, *Illustrated London News*, 1893. (Robarts Library.)

here has not had a drop yet!!"[67] Humor is the selling vehicle; but its success depends on personalizing the abstract institutional process of cabinet decisions.

Voting becomes little more than shopping, selecting the product with the maximum appeal. Under the caption "An Appeal to the Country," Ogden's Cigarettes markets "real photographs of prominent politicians . . . in the Packets of . . . Guinea-Gold Cigarettes."[68] The choice of politician becomes, like the choice of a consumer good, merely a matter of casual perusal of a panoply of options, slickly packaged and presented. The politician and the product are equalized. Javol Hair Tonic is "Top of the Poll." Advertisement text mimics the ballot.[69] Ogden's Cigarettes are "elected with acclamation."[70] A headline referring to the "General Election 1880" asks "test questions on domestic policy" that really are concerned with washing clothes. The consumer is urged as "chancellor of the family exchequer" to "vote for Harper Twelvetrees' Villa Washer."[71] The vaunted exercise of the right of citizenship is but a trip to the grocery store, a decision to select one product or selling message over another. The process of shopping is elevated, endowed with constitutional importance, but at the same time momentous decisions of government are reduced to the most mundane sort of transaction, demystified, transformed from an action of the public citizen to an exercise of personality.

The consumerist vision does not support simple polarities; in the Victorian advertisement the gulf between individual and community, private and public, is far from clear. It is certainly true that some advertisements confirm the egoistic suppositions that underpin the domestic ideology and the gemeinschaft-gesellschaft hypothesis. Many advertisements prey upon the sensuous appeal of sybaritic luxuries; they employ provocative motifs of private bathers and self-absorbed narcissists. Saccharine images of courtship celebrate the self-indulgent satisfactions of romantic love and the thrilling prospects of elopement, even though they do ultimately respect community boundaries. The intensity of the mother-infant relationship is shamelessly exploited. Yet the depiction both of romantic and maternal love converts the public consumer into a sort of voyeur who invades the private sphere to glimpse intimate moments. The family hearth itself becomes a vehicle of the most public commercialism; the very hub of the private sphere, it nonetheless is the focus of public display. The home in the advertisement is not merely a symbol of domestic values, but a prime material indicator of socio-economic status. As the private sphere is invaded, the public arena is personalized. Daunting abstractions, the world and the nation, seem knowable through cheerful personifications. Humor reduces government decisions to trivial concerns, the process of voting to little more than a shopping expedition, circumscribed by the cult of personality. The shared and joyful experience of being a consumer joins friendly neighbors and grand celebrities, strangers in a crowd. Far from preying solely on individual aspirations, the Victorian advertisement redefines community for a mass society. Through the fantasy of consumption it offers to unite those unknown to each other even from the most distant land.

7

Social Emulation and Mass Consumption: Elitism or Material Democratization?

Since Veblen, social emulation has been a centripetal force for historical studies of the so-called consumer revolution. These studies have focused on the eighteenth century or on the efflorescence of mass production up to 1850. They have rarely concentrated on the heights of mass production and mass advertising that were achieved between 1885–1914. An examination of advertisements during these years brings into question an uncritical acceptance of the hypothesis of social emulation. Coincident developments suggest alternative explanations. The consumer revolution achieved unprecedented heights precisely during the period in which the Great Depression occurred, in which aristocratic fortunes waned and in which glaring social inequalities spawned socialist parties and collectivist sentiments. The key to consumer demand, I will argue, lay not so much in imitation of aristocratic (or even rich) behavior, as in a distinctively bourgeois pursuit of equal opportunity. This was already a virtual fait accompli politically, but remained an unfulfilled material prospect, dramatized by late nineteenth-century studies of poverty. The democratic vision and the material fantasy were surprisingly similar. Mass consumption was the material analogue of political democratization, a complementary manifestation of an increasingly hedonistic perspective.

Veblen argues in *The Theory of the Leisure Class* (1908) that wants are motivated by a desire to imitate or emulate the behavior of other consumers.[1] Consumption is not a simple matter of satisfying needs; it is a way to enhance social status. The consumer's drive to imitate the consumption of his social betters may overpower even basic instinctual needs. Some consumption is conspicuous, a symbol as well as an index of economic worth. It may also be motivated either by the bandwagon effect or by snob appeal: some people will buy a good because everyone else buys it; some people will choose not to buy a good because everyone else buys it. In both instances individual consumption is influenced by the behavior of other consumers.

But the Veblenesque perspective poses its own difficulties. It suggests that people spend large sums of money on things simply for display; many items of conspicuous consumption, though, are intrinsically attractive. The Veblenesque perspective assumes that distinction must be expressesd through imitation; in fact, individuals often draw attention to their own special qualities by innovation or by rejecting the values of the group above them. It assumes that consumption is an other-directed pattern of behavior; but private or inconspicuous consumption may also express cultural values. It assumes, further, that fashion is always introduced by the aristocracy; in fact important trends in consumption often have non-aristocratic origins. Despite these drawbacks, the Veblenesque perspective has enjoyed notable popularity among historians.

Harold Perkin has become its principal exponent. In *The Origins of Modern English Society* he argues that if consumer demand was the key to the industrial revolution, social emulation was the key to consumer demand.[2] Social emulation was particularly effective in the British context, where a comparatively open social system allowed easy interaction between individuals at different social levels and permitted greater social mobility than continental European societies. Perkin's argument is pursued by McKendrick and Plumb in their important and suggestive work, *Birth of a Consumer Society*. According to McKendrick, the source of the desire to consume may be found in the striving for vertical social mobility amid novel levels of prosperity. Emulative spending for McKendrick and Plumb seemed to be at the very root of the "Western fashion pattern."[3] J. A. Banks in his well-known *Prosperity and Parenthood* concurs that increased spending (during a later period, 1800–1850) was the result of a general expansion in conspicuous consumption.[4] Banks speculates that marriage was delayed and family size limited in order to permit a scale of expenditure that might indicate social position. Consumption of the paraphernalia of gentility—servants, a carriage, fine furniture and dress, French food and wine, seaside holidays—according to Banks was motivated by a Veblenesque concern with social emulation.

The Aristocratic Ideal

Curiously, the aristocratic ideal the middle class purportedly sought to emulate was distinctly unsympathetic to the hedonistic impulse that fueled Victorian consumerism. Originally premised on a chivalrous code of honor dating from the middle ages, the aristocratic ideal by the nineteenth century merged a cavalier tradition with eighteenth-century dandyism and paternalism. Inheritors of a cavalier tradition of the Civil War and ensuing Restoration period believed that the ideal gentleman was a Renaissance man: lover, soldier, wit, musician, he was accomplished in many fields, but ever nonchalant. The secular life of a courtier might seem hedonistic, but in fact it placed no premium on passion. Any excess of emotion was regarded as unseemly and ungentlemanly. The cavalier gentleman tried to make his behavior pleasing to others rather than to himself.

Similarly, the dandyism exemplified by Beau Brummel was only deceptively hedonistic. The ideal was perfect dress combined with refined conversation; a display of the self that often amounted to arrogance.[5] But such artificially contrived behavior and the continual struggle to ensure one's reputation meant that restraint and emotional control were essential.

Added to this premium on emotional control was a paternalistic strain. As inheritor of a feudal tradition, heir to a broadly defined sense of noblesse oblige, the aristocrat had a responsibility to protect the lower orders. Amid the wholesale abdication on the part of governors, which Carlyle decried in the early Victorian period, the responsibilities of the aristocracy seemed to decline in favor of the state. Nonetheless, the paternal ideal remained an important standard of aristocratic behavior, which praised dedication to others rather than self-gratification.

Neither paternalism, dandyism, or the cavalier tradition with their emphasis on restraint and other-regarding action could provide any meaningful impetus for mass consumption. The Veblenesque perspective assumes that broad segments of Victorian society, especially the middle class, attempted to emulate aristocratic behavior, but the ideals that underlay aristocratic action were clearly antithetical to the hedonistic impulses of modern consumerism.

Moreover, the aristocracy, supposedly the focus of imitation, began to decline in social and political power precisely during the years in which consumerism thrived. The parliament elected in 1880 was the last in which landowners had a clear majority. By 1885 they were outnumbered. The Third Reform Act of 1884, unlike its predecessors, for the first time gave working-class voters the possibility of constituting a majority of the electorate. The Corrupt Practices Act of 1883, by limiting the amount per elector that each candidate could spend, had a larger effect than the Ballot Act on the independence of voters. The County Council Act of 1888 and the London Government Act of 1889 extended democracy to the counties, to London, and to larger cities. The power of the aristocratic elite began to wane. Franchise extensions of 1867 and 1884, the secret ballot, and limitations on election expenses undermined political influence. Whereas landed families made up three quarters of the House in the 1840s, by 1886 they constituted one-half of the House and by 1906 and 1910 only one-tenth of the House.[6] A decline in land values significantly reduced agricultural rents and foreshadowed the breakup of great estates. New wealth, often American, increasingly overshadowed patrician land-based fortunes.

David Cannadine and W. D. Rubinstein have both pointed to the complexities of assessing the reasons for the decline and fall of the British aristocracy.[7] Whatever the cause, the aristocracy did decline in social, political, and economic prestige by the end of the nineteenth century. Although this declining aristocracy may have engaged in more conspicuous consumption during the Edwardian years to demonstrate its last vestiges of grandeur, it is scarcely credible that the middle class, newly influential politically and economically, would be preoccupied with imitating a fading giant. As the aristocratic power waned, material requisites were increasingly supplied by a production process obviously oriented toward the masses. Large quantities of goods were marketed not to a select aristocratic market but to middle-class and working-class consumers. Economies of scale and mechanization reduced the price of goods such as carved furniture and wallpapers that had previously been the preserve of an elite. Quantity removed the scarcity value of a broad spectrum of goods. The reduction of prohibitive prices and increases in accessibility gave many goods an unprecedented mass appeal that diluted rather than enhanced emulative status. Critics, exemplified by Henry Cole at mid-century and later by the Arts and Crafts enthusiasts, deplored the often unhappy aesthetic consequences of the marriage of mechanization and art. The deterioration of taste, the rampant philistinism of the middle class, caused Matthew Arnold to despair. Then as now, mass production implied mediocrity, rather than aristocratic imitation.

The retailing revolution further de-emphasized elite aspects of consumption. The retailing revolution was characterized by the displacement of fairs and markets by large shops with extensive inventories.[8] Although the decline of fairs and markets may have replaced a folk atmosphere with potentially luxurious shops, for the most part the retail revolution refers not to the creation of exclusive shops but to the emergence of standardized department stores. Their external use of brilliant lighting, billposting, and elaborate displays has led Asa Briggs to compare their owners to impresarios.[9] The shop that simulated a sensational P. T. Barnum experience seemed an unlikely venue for social emulation.

The department store offered vast scale, quantity, and selection. Multiples such as Lipton's, W. H. Smith, and Singer Sewing Machine Stores provided cheap pricing. The appeal of both was essentially democratic. Both could undercut the prices of traditional shops. Marked prices and the movement toward principles of self-selection and self-service removed intimidation. The elimination of credit in department stores provided equal opportunities for purchase and reduced prices. At the same time payment plans put expensive items within the reach of all. By the 1880s retailing had moved from the hands of the specialist into the hands of the universal provider. The universalism and egalitarianism that underpinned nineteenth-century mass production and the retail revolution were fueled ultimately not by social emulation, but by the middle class' high estimation of open competition.

The Entrepreneurial Ideal

This high estimation of open competition was crystallized in the entrepreneurial ideal. According to that ideal, the ideal society was competitive; the ideal citizen was a capitalist. Through hard work, an individual competing in a free and democratic society would receive rewards. This ideal was upheld by the middle class throughout the nineteenth century, but by the late nineteenth century an emphasis on the democratic aspect of the ideal represented a change in focus. In the early and mid-nineteenth century the stress had been on the entrepreneurial ideal's emphasis on a puritanical dedication to work. By the late nineteenth century, Victorians focused their attention on the democratic character of the ideal, especially equal access to the material as well as the political fruits of labor. Enjoying material rewards was implicitly hedonistic. I will provide a brief survey of the early puritanical focus in order to throw the hedonistic and democratic pattern of the late nineteenth century into sharper relief.

In the mid-nineteenth century the entrepreneurial ideal emphasized a moral conception of work. On earth, the capital that would determine social status was available to all through industriousness. An open competitive society enabled each person to rise through his own talents. With energy and ability, any man, however humble, could climb the social and economic ladder. Smiles' self-made man epitomized this ascent. The entrepreneurial ideal shaped the social philosophy of Victorianism. Work was a virtue. Similarly, thrift was desirable. Hard-earned money should be carefully saved; through the accumulation of capital the individual might prosper. Manners and good conduct were important. Through sobriety, sabbatarianism, and a decent family life the individual would avoid the temptation and vice that might distract him from his goal. The Victorian social philosophy at mid-century forwarded a Smilesian view of a society of hard-working thrifty individuals pursuing their own self-interest or competition with each other in an arena of equal opportunity.[10] This does not seem to be a hedonistic focus. Between 1850–75 the entrepreneurial ideal established its dominance in Victorian society. The triumph of the entrepreneurial ideal was, according to Perkin, evidenced in three ways; its moral victory is apparent in the imposition of puritan standards of behavior, especially honesty, temperance, courtesy, and self-help; its intellectual victory is witnessed in the entrenchment of the competitive ideal in Victorian public schools—through scholarships, the prefect system, debating, and athletics—and in its promulgation in the provincial middle-class press; its state victory is evidenced in parliamentary reforms that enabled all citizens to compete for political office and to rise in society by merit rather than privilege.[11] At mid-century the central planks of this ideal—thrift, work, puritanical behavior—seem to be remote from hedonism. But the democratic character of the ideal sowed the seeds that would permit self-indulgence in the late Victorian period.

The entrepreneurial ideal was inevitably democratic. It praised equal opportunity and accessibility. This emphasis sprang from the egalitarian ideals of the seventeenth-century Puritans and was especially attractive to men of ambition and energy within the middle class.[12] These new men demanded the abolition of patronage, protection, and monopoly. Protestants, after all, taught that all men are equal in the sight of God; therefore, all men should be equal before the law and enjoy freedom of conscience, self-expression, and political equality. The egalitarian energies of the Nonconformists were at first channeled toward political concerns.

For the first three-quarters of the nineteenth century Nonconformists concentrated on achieving political democracy. They actively pursued the Repeal of the Test and Corporation Acts, the Reform Act (1832), the Municipal Corporation Act (1835), the abolition of slavery (1833), the abolition of compulsory church rates (1868), and the abolition of religious tests at Oxford and Cambridge (1854–56). They were a driving force behind the legislation of Gladstone's Great Ministry (1868–74). The Second and Third Reform Acts of 1867 and 1884 established household suffrage. By the 1880s Perkin suggests that the Liberal Party had almost completed its democratization of Britain.[13]

When political democracy was a veritable fait accompli, middle-class attention increasingly coalesced around material concerns. Despite a clear rise in national income and in average living standards during the industrial revolution, inequality seemed at it height between 1880–1914. Although historians have focused on the immediate effects of industrialism on the standard of living during the 1800–50 period, the economic distance between the classes was still great during the late Victorian period. Dudley Baxter's 1867 survey established that 60% of national income went to upper- and middle-class families who constituted only 26% of the population. Thirty-nine percent of income went to the 74% of the population who were working class. By 1904 Sir Leo Chiozza Money made a similar estimate of the distribution of national income for the U.K. Those in "riches" over £700 a year, less than 2.9% of the population, received 34.2% of national income; those in comfort (between £160–£700), 8.7% of the population, received 14% of national income; while those in poverty, below the income tax level, 88% of the population, received only just over half (51.5%) of national income.[14] Material disparities were dramatized for a middle-class audience in sensational exposés such as Rev. Andrew Mearns' *The Bitter Cry of Outcast London* (1883) and William Booth's *In Darkest England the Way Out* (1890). Rowntree's survey of York in 1899 found that 27.84% of citizens were living in poverty, with "earnings . . . insufficient to obtain the minimum necessaries for the maintenance of mere physical efficiency."[15] The statistical proof of the extent of poverty was alarming. Journalistic accounts and photography made the relative deprivation of certain sections of the community more immediate. The working class sought redress through industrial strikes, social reform, and working-class alternatives to existing political parties.[16] Material inequity and the working-class response to it made middle-class people anxious, anxious about the potential physical degeneration of the race and about social unrest. (See Chapter 5.) But it also encouraged the middle class to seek material rewards, to attempt to realize material democracy now that political democracy was within their grasp.

Middle-class efforts for political democratization, now virtually achieved, were easily transferred to material democratization. If the Gladstonian completion of the constitutional revolution had offered a political promise of gratification, an essential aspect of the consumer revolution was the potential to realize its egalitarian premise materially. As the middle class sought material rewards for their labor, in the late nineteenth century they displayed a hedonistic cultural pattern.

In advertisements the hedonistic pattern appears at first glance to reflect the emulative drive that historians have assumed underpinned the consumption patterns of industrial society: advertisements are replete with newfound luxuries as well as necessities; they idealize the potential for leisure; they employ patrician imagery. But for the most part advertisements, far from emphasizing aristocratic character or even wealth, decidedly appeal to the theme of accessibility. This theme, I suggest, reflected a cultural emphasis in the late nineteenth century on the democratic component of the entrepreneurial ideal. Only the most expensive luxury is marketed with direct reference to aristocratic cachet. The rest are made to seem mundane and very affordable. Aristocratic imagery is almost always historicized or classicized; it seems abstract, removed from the prospect of direct imitation. On the other hand, advertisements for every type of product are suffused with mass appeal—consumer goods exist in vast quantities, with huge selections and low prices. They are accessible to all, regardless of status by birth. Mass-produced goods in the popular parlance of the advertisement were for "the million and the millionaire," "the palace and the cottage." The consumer revolution emphasizes consumption as an egalitarian vehicle, not a Veblenesque force that could only strengthen aristocratic notions which the middle class had already politically rejected.

The Elite Appeal

Luxury Advertising

Undoubtedly a large part of Victorian advertising was concerned with luxury goods. In general these goods were luxuries because they fell outside of the most basic middle-class budget. But within this broad category were three subgroups. First, there were very expensive goods—furs, diamonds, silver, phonographs. These goods were quite beyond the reach of ordinary families in the middle class, although they may well have represented a material ideal. Second, there were products that copied expensive products such as silverplate or simulated diamonds. Third, there were goods that middle-class people bought as indulgences rather than necessities. An examination of advertisements for these three types of luxuries reveals that social emulation was by no means a consistent emphasis in their marketing strategy.

The most expensive products—diamonds, furs, couturier clothes— placed lavish advertisements obviously directed toward a restricted market of the very wealthy. In these advertisements there is no attempt to capture a broad audience. Advertisements glorify an opulent interior of the Pari-

Figure 7-1. International Fur Store, *Lady's Pictorial*, 1897. (British Library.)

sian Diamond and Pearls Shop[17] or illustrate an impressive carriage outside the magnificent facade of the International Fur Store.[18] These products were clearly so expensive that there was no attempt to market them to
anything but a wealthy audience. The aristocratic aura of these advertisements was a realistic reflection of the very narrow and wealthy market for
these particular products.

Occasionally, within this category of very expensive luxuries, there is an
emphasis in some advertisements on social emulation. Advertisements for
pianos and gramophones typically picture friends clustered in a sitting
room enjoying the music of their host. Although the text may praise the
"prospect of real and endless pleasures,"[19] the social appeal is always clear:

> The Pianola Piano is always a source of real enjoyment because it means good
> music—music which you and your friends actually produce for yourselves. If
> you own a Pianola Piano you can entertain any number of people.[20]

Advertisers of pianos and gramophones hoped that the aristocracy would
buy their products, but also that they would attract some middle-class
consumers, who would like the product, but also its potential social function. Advertisers remind consumers of social emulation as a motive for
purchase. But this is a rare characteristic in advertisements for Victorian
luxuries.

Other advertisements, in which social emulation is routinely exploited,
advertise imitative products such as simulated diamonds and silver plate.
Faulkner's Jewellery, for example, advertised "Spanish crystals" "Known all
over the *world* as the *finest stones* ever produced." "Detection" was "impossible." "Defy the BEST JUDGES to tell them from DIAMONDS. The brillian-
cy and lustre are most marvellous and equal to Brilliants. . . . All stones set
by diamond-setters and beautifully finished."[21] Advertisements for electroplate were shaped by the same motivations. Sarl's Argentine silver plate
boldly advertised that it was "unrivalled amongst all substitutes for silver."[22] The motivation for purchase was aristocratic imitation, and, therefore, an emphasis on social emulation in these advertisements was a natural
focus.

Advertisements that stress aristocratic taste or habits—advertisements
for very expensive products and imitative goods—were not at all common
in the Victorian press. Far more advertisements appeared for ornament
such as jewelry, conveniences such as appliances and entertaining items
such as bicycles and cameras. These more commonly advertised luxuries
were not generally marketed with reference to a social elite, but with a
dominant focus on the democratic and hedonistic message that luxury was
affordable.

Advertisements for jewelry, including watches, emphasized economy,
but economy with a hedonistic emphasis. Unlike advertisements that
might advertise a mundane product such as cheap tea with an obvious
appeal to thrift, advertisements for jewelry, through an emphasis on low

prices and payment plans, encourage consumers to self-indulge, to spend money now rather than to save, to experience immediate gratification. Jewelery advertisers carefully marked prices in their advertisements. An advertisement for Goldsmith Alliance, for example, includes a price list with the assurance that "single-stone, three-stone, cluster and gipsy rings of every description, and at various prices, always ready for immediate selection."[23] But payment plans made the same point even more efficiently. John Bennett Ltd. advertises "engagement rings, bridesmaids' presents and Xmas gifts in great variety," watches and sapphire, diamond and ruby rings. The company boasts about its royal appointment, but the advertisement is slashed by a boldface banner announcing "gradual payment system by monthly instalments" and detailed text that emphasizes "manufacturers' prices."[24] In another advertisement, this time for watches, Benson's illustrates a "Field Watch" in "Hunting, Half-Hunting, or Crystal Glass 18-ct. Gold Cases," a product with apparent aristocratic appeal. The text has quite a different orientation. The boldface headline announces "20 monthly payments" and prints the price (£25) on each side of the illustration.[25] These advertisements are about economy. In quantitative analysis they are not distinguishable from advertisements for cheap tea. The emphasis on economy, therefore, seems static throughout the second half of the nineteenth century. But clearly there is a qualitative difference between buying a luxury on the installment plan and buying cheap tea. This distinction reveals an important deficiency of quantitative analysis. By the late nineteenth century many advertisements emphasize affordable luxury, a deceptive message that actually promoted not thrift, but hedonism.

Advertisements for watches, besides encouraging middle-class hedonism, revealed a subsidiary motivation that was also not connected with social emulation. Monthly payment plans reflected the changing status of the watch as it moved from an ornamental luxury to a practical necessity. Ingersoll pictured Father Time who "founded the Ingersoll Watch eighteen years ago—since then over 18,000,000 people have found entire satisfaction in the Ingersoll Watches."[26] The consumer who did without seemed anachronistic, but class equations were scarcely part of the selling message.

Jewelery advertisements in general, in addition to encouraging immediate gratification, emphasized selection and quantity, not aristocratic pretensions. Jewelery advertisements effect a dazzling display of infinite variety. They illustrate earrings, necklaces, brooches, bracelets, cufflinks, and haircombs all together. Pieces are rarely modeled and only the most expensive pearls or diamonds are singled out for separate attention. Like the sparkling display in a crowded jewelery case, the effect is eye-catching, the pieces more stunning in combination than in isolation. Crowded together, the pieces complement each other, simulate a setting or context, provide a general impression of prosperity. Nonetheless, these sorts of advertisements emphasize selection rather than the exclusivity of a particular

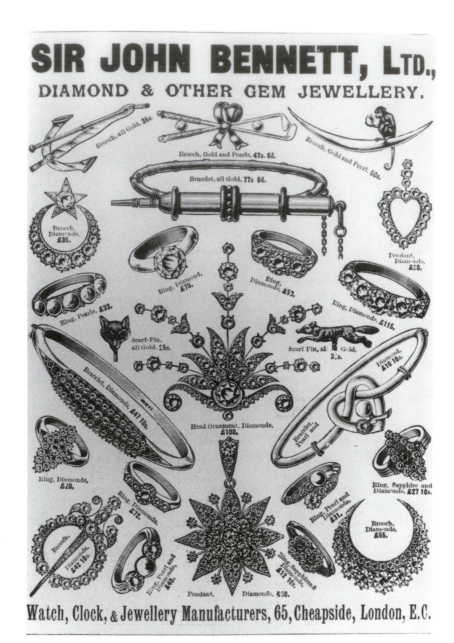

Figure 7-2. Sir John Bennett Ltd. Jewellery, *Illustrated London News*, 1900. (Robarts Library.)

piece.[27] Howell & James Ltd. in an advertisement for the "self-closing bracelet," an extremely popular item circa 1890, emphasizes novelty rather than imitation. Its patent was boldly announced and a brief text informed

> this beautiful and artistic article of jewellery is made perfectly flexible and elastic. Will fit wrist of any size. Most comfortable to wear. Never slips in whatever position placed on arm or wrist. Cannot be lost as there is no snap to come unfastened. It avoids the inconvenience of safety chains, and discomfort to wearer, of a badly-fitting bracelet of the ordinary kind.[28]

The selling vehicle is novelty, not imitation, and, secondarily, a broad rather than exclusive appeal. It will fit a wrist of any size, in any position, for any wearer. Jewelery advertisements for the most part were concerned with appealing to the consumer's quest for variety, not social position.

Bicycles, like jewelery, are sold with an emphasis on accessibility. Typically, Gamage advertises that its "Cupid" model for girls, available in "all sizes up to date" with "pneumatic tyres," is guaranteed to "bring joy and happiness to boys and girls in every Home."[29] But payment plans are omnipresent. Juno Cycles offers a monthly payment plan, "carriage paid," "discount for cash," "accessories for all kinds at lowest prices."[30] Bicycles were a means of fashionable recreation, but advertisements emphasize that they are within the reach of all.

Decorative art items, similarly, used price to suggest accessibility. By 1887 Treloar & Sons Carpets announces that "real Turkey Carpets have never been so low in price."[31] Simpitrol Lighting promises to effect light "that is nearest daylight and almost as cheap." A. Ferguson & Co., specialists in period decoration, offer "complete transformations of the most ordinary looking rooms at a very moderate cost."[32] Samuel Peach & Son, Drapery Manufacturer, explained that "The public by purchasing LACE CURTAINS for CASH, DIRECT save both the wholesale and retail profits and also the usual large margins for long credits and bad debts."[33] Advertisements for relatively expensive products by straightforwardly alleging the cheapness of their products, by announcing prices, and by suggesting the absence of middlemen hoped to convince consumers that to indulge in the purchase of a superfluous product was not really self-indulgent. The message appealed to hedonistic impulses, not social emulation.

Products manufactured and marketed for the first time during the Victorian period emphasized their broad appeal to many people rather than their favor with a social elite. Although some domestic machines were marketed with a certain amount of class consciousness—the J. J. Theobald & Co.'s Acme Knife cleaner was sold as "the Servants' Friend" and a W. J. Harris & Co. Lockstitch Sewing Machine was advertised as the "Talk of London"[34]—advertisers more generally emphasized that domestic machines could be used by all people in all classes. Evans's Matchless Kitchener emphasized its adaptability for "the smallest families as well as the largest establishments."[35] The American Challenge Stove promised assembly "by almost any inexperienced person in a few minutes."[36] The Villa Washer would "suit all classes."[37] Lawnmowers promised that they were "easy to work."[38] Packaged foodstuffs, similarly, generally emphasized their appeal for "all in the family"[39] and their efficacy for "thousands of lovely and healthy children."[40] Conveniences were marketed as luxuries for everyone, not as goods that had a social cachet.

Camera advertisements emphasize the luxurious quality of convenience rather than the cachet of personal snapshots. Kodak advertises that "Any school boy can master Kodak Photography in a few minutes." Marketed for all, including children, the product loses any aura of exclusivity. The text stresses a convenience that would make it attractive especially to the consumer who did not already pursue the hobby of photography: "The Folding Pocket Kodak goes into any pocket, yet takes photographs 3 x 2" in size. No dark room is required for changing the films."[41] But any hint of social emulation is quickly defused. One Kodak advertisement, for example, features a small vignette of a Venetian gondola. The vignette acts as the view through the camera lens. The consumer, the advertisement suggests, may take his camera on his trips abroad, a theme that has class connotations: despite the growing passion for Mediterranean travel as a polite pursuit,[42] only comfortable members of the middle class or aristocracy would be able to take snapshots in Venice. It is revealing, however, that the text of this advertisement adopts a "You press the button, we do the rest" line of argument, which switches the emphasis back to a convenience feature that can be appreciated by everyone. Advertisements for cameras, like advertisements for domestic machines, endeavored to capture the mass market by purporting that luxury was within the reach of all, rather than suggesting aristocratic imitation.

Luxurious superfluities of all types—jewelery, watches, appliances, bicycles, and cameras—were marketed almost entirely without reference to the favour of aristocrats or even the wealthy. Jewelery advertisements, by emphasizing selection and novelty rather than exclusivity, stress the mass orientation of the market. Domestic machines could be used by everyone. Aristocratic emphasis was aberrant, confined to the most obviously imitative products such as simulated diamonds and silverplate, and to very expensive purchases such as pianos and gramophones. For the most part the Victorian luxury advertisement displays a clear preference for selection and convenience, qualities appreciated by the broadest segments of the market and for immediate gratification via payment plans, a preference that ultimately overshadows a more selective pursuit of imitation.

Leisure: Its Class Dimension

The reduction of toil was the implicit and explicit promise of many commercial products. Advertisements accordingly illustrated the leisured ideal. Children at play in advertisements more often than not displayed no class

Come here you Rascal It's Pears'

Figure 7-3. Pears' Soap, *Illustrated London News*, 1894. (Robarts Library.)

orientation, but on the polo field or wrapped in fur on an ice-rink, leisured adults seemed decidedly aristocratic.

The simple dress of children and the focus on their childish delight obscures their class associations in most advertisements. For Williams' Shaving Soap two laughing boys pin another boy down and cover his face with shaving cream.[43] For Fry's Cocoa three young children make faces as they peek from behind a curtain.[44] For U. K. Tea children dressed in aprons, shawls, and bonnets enjoy a tea-party.[45] In the absence of class-specific settings or dress these children and their leisure seem classless.

Aristocratic exceptions are suggestive. For Pears' a "rascal" hides from his nanny at bath time.[46] In an advertisement for Bird's Custard Powder, a little boy sneaks "His Third Glass" of custard from underneath a table appointed with dainty cakes and gelatin molds.[47] The pleasures of aristocratic children—hiding at bath time (whether from a nanny or mother), sneaking food—are not the preserve of an elite. The child at play became a popular image in the advertisement that commercially elevated the sweet simplicity of childhood quite apart from class associations.

But adult leisure, in contrast, evokes aristocratic status or at least wealth. Gentlemen in evening dress play billiards before a warm gas fire in a comfortably appointed panelled room.[48] In evening dress a couple pursue a round of table tennis.[49] A man falls from his polo pony for Elliman's

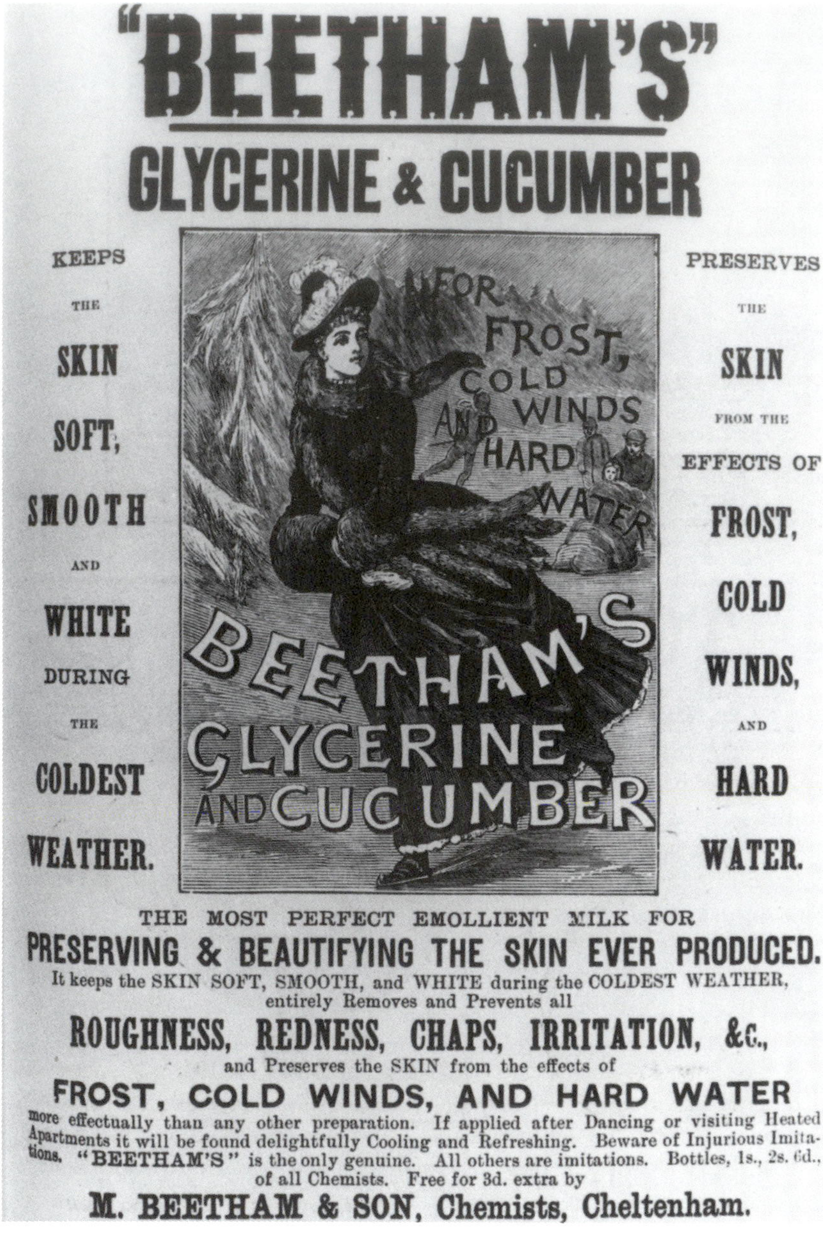

Figure 7-4. Beetham's Glycerine and Cucumber Lotion, *Illustrated London News*, 1890. (Robarts Library.)

Figure *7-5.* Fry's *Illustrated London News*, 1910. (Robarts Library.)

Embrocation.[50] A lady in fur muffler and trailing muff enjoys her skating.[51] Three friends sip Ross's Ginger Ale between tennis matches.[52] In advertisements already studied in other chapters couples departing from parties or dining by candlelight, although they may represent a middle-class ideal, are clearly more prosperous in advertisement depictions than the middle-class average. The commercial forum more often than not chooses grandiose depictions of leisure in which aristocratic pastimes are presented as an emulative ideal.

In advertisements middle-class people enjoy a more moderate form of leisure. In the evening an older man in his dressing gown sits in his wing chair and raises his cup of cocoa to his health.[53] Women happily sip Bovril from a rocking chair,[54] lean back in a settee before a warm fire,[55] recline in an easy chair.[56] For Cuticura a lady tests her golf swing before a background of sheep.[57] Although these depictions are pleasant, they are clearly not as lush or picturesque as more flamboyant depictions of the aristocracy at play.

In the commercial world leisure is the indulgence of children or the privilege of the very rich. For most middle-class people for whom it is a momentary affair—a cup of cocoa at the end of the day or a few minutes before the fire—the aristocratic model represents the hedonistic ideal. The depiction of leisure in the advertisement does seem to suggest an emphasis on social emulation.

Historical Patricians

While aristocrats appear in some advertisements as models of leisure, there are many advertisements in which aristocrats are situated in the past, in the eighteenth century or in the idealized world of ancient Greece. Here they are significantly removed from Victorian reality.

The aristocrat of the English past constitutes a pretty image, but through historical distance he seems the unlikely focus of consumer imitation. In one advertisement an eighteenth-century couple cart a lifesize bar of Swan Soap on the back of their carriage.[58] For Eno's a bowing courtier inquires after the health of a fair maiden.[59] In these advertisements aristocrats model showy costumes and exaggerated manners. In others aristocratic heritage is suggested obliquely. A woman examines her "rich store of old Bleach Linen" from the open drawers of a heavy, carved armoire. The setting and the furniture evoke a medieval chatelaine.[60] The purpose of each image is to charm and to capture attention. The consumer is not intended to aspire to the linen chest of a medieval chatelaine, the health of a courtier, or the equipage of an eighteenth-century couple. The consumer is asked rather to associate the product with the pleasures and prosperity of past days, to attribute only vague aristocratic associations, but not to engage in a precise, fashion-conscious exercise in social emulation.

Ancient Greece offered conflicting associations. Grecian imagery evoked for a Victorian audience the elitism of high art, but also the egalitarian principles of democratic political ideas. This was a compelling commercial subtext.

Classical themes had academic associations. Antiquity had provided themes for painting since the Renaissance. From the mid-nineteenth century academic appeal was enhanced by archaeological discovery. Lord Lytton's *The Last Days of Pompeii* (1834) became a widely read classic. The first systematic excavations of Pompeii and the Herculanaeum were carried out in 1861 by the Italian government immediately after the Risorgimento.[61] A company that favored classical themes was surely composed of educated men who appreciated the finest things in life, including the finest commercial products.

Academic elitism was accentuated by the fact that Grecian figures in advertisements frequently represented respected abstract ideals. In an advertisement for Pears' Soap, Truth sends a message to Mars assisted by a lamp and a mirror.[62] In an advertisement for Beecham's Pills, Health crowns Love with laurel.[63] In an advertisement for Jeyes' Disinfectant, Hygeia, as a statue in the public square, proclaims the importance of disinfectant.[64] Truth, Health, Hygiene were ideals the Victorian consumer vigorously pursued. The importance of these ideals underscored the elevating tone of the Grecian theme. Moreover, the Grecian figure performs superhuman feats. As Truth, she works a magical trick with her mirror to send an interplanetary message. As Health, holding the crown, she is ruler, a queen elevated from the common condition. As Hygeia, she towers above the tiny men and cattle below. The Grecian figure seemed to lend products an undeniable prestige.

But while the Grecian subject appeared to be the most elite sort of image, it was also peculiarly leveling. Grecian context separated visual images from Victorian class associations. An elaborate Victorian feminine costume was a sign of social status. The simply draped Grecian goddess was removed from this competition. Her dress was foreign to all—to the lower middle-class housewife and to the bejeweled aristocrat. She appealed to members of all classes. Moreover, Grecian appearance was contained within a pregnant political context; ancient Greece, for many, represented a political ideal.[65] Although links with high culture and leisured sensual indulgence seemed vaguely patrician, superior status was situated within an ideal democratic society rather than within the harsh context of the British class system. The Grecian image avoided Victorian-specific appeals to status.

Nineteenth-century social emulation was clearly softened by historicized motifs that harkened back to a golden age in which relations between social groups seemed simplified under the gauzy veil of nostalgia. During the eighteenth century fixed social place seemed clear; in ancient Greece democracy more fully realized. If nostalgic figures were patrician, they were also distanced from Victorian society. Their elite status was elevating; it complemented esteemed ideals. At the same time the eighteenth-century aristocrat and the Grecian woman did not command direct imitation, only a general appreciation of a product fit for a king or worthy of the gods.

The Mass Market

Despite Grecian imagery, festooned courtiers, medieval chatelaines, polo ponies, and billiard rooms, the display advertisement clearly sold goods for a mass market. In advertisements for regular products that were not luxuries advertisers reminded consumers of mass orientation through an emphasis on quantity, not just the quantity of goods, but the quantity of consumers, the appeal of goods to rich and poor, and the manner in which consumerism transcended class boundaries.

Advertisements for every sort of product suggested not only selection and availability, but the unfathomable vastness of mass production and used this emphasis to promote consumption. U. K. Tea provides a typical example. In one advertisement, "Tea by the Ton," dozens of tea cups that border the text provide a physical sense of the repetitive uniformity of mass production. The extensive text emphasizes scale.

A visit to the huge warehouses of U. K. Tea Co. Ltd., in Finsbury, London, is a revelation. In the first place, you have to multiply your modest pound or so of tea by thousands, and arrive at TONS before you can realise even a single days' output of this great firm . . . [tea is] mixed by huge machines, which in their turn, discharge their contents into great funnels, each holding many

Figure 7-6. U.K. Tea, *Illustrated London News,* 1892. (Robarts Library.)

Figure 7-7. Beecham's Pills, *Illustrated London News*, 1901. (Robarts Library.)

hundreds of pounds, whence the teas are conveyed to the . . . enormous containers.[66]

The advertisement captures the allure of a technically impressive process, but it also urged consumption by assuring the consumer that she was not alone: the product was consumed by thousands.

Advertisements directly suggest that rich and poor may consume the same product. A product may be enjoyed by all sorts of people, from virtually any class, any occupation. Beecham's Pills is especially direct. It pictures feet—male and female, from the most elaborately shod to the barefoot. Despite appearances, there is an important commonality. "All sorts and conditions of people in every 'walk' of life appreciate the wonderful powers of Beecham's Pills."[67] The consumer good is not simply "for the million"[68] or the millionaire. The product may defy status as well as denote it.

In the advertisement, consumption becomes an egalitarian action that works for all. Monkey Brand Soap imprints the face of a monkey on a gleaming sun that beams down upon the rooftops of a town. A stone wall charmingly defines its parameters. Spired turrets and thatched roofs convey variations of social status within the town. But the sun radiates equally to every corner. The caption reads, "Great and small it shines for all."[69] Beecham's Pills adopts the same egalitarian premise. It offers beneficial effects in "the castle or the cottage." Two vignettes, one of a towering castle,

Figure 7-8. Monkey Brand Soap, *Illustrated London News*, 1906. (Robarts Library.)

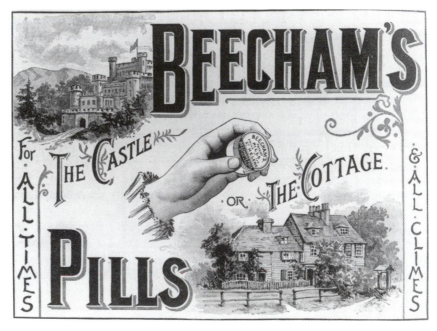

Figure 7-9. Beecham's Pills, *Illustrated London News*, 1894. (Robarts Library.)

complete with turrets, flag, and magnificent backdrop, and the other of a large house in the English style bordered by a fence, trees, and a well are bridged by a hand that extends a box of Beecham's Pills.[70] The vignettes are beguiling, attractive, clearly idealized. They are also equalized—the supposed "cottage" mimics the scale and grandeur of the castle. Consumerism purports to ignore differences in status. The product bridges differences, cuts across barriers of class and distance.

The gratification of material desires emerges as the child's commercial "birthright." Mellin's Food uses the dramatic headline "Your Child's Birthright." The substantial text explains:

> There are probably no bounds to the sacrifices a mother would make if necessary for the sake of her child. But a mother may do a great thing for her child without any self-sacrifice, by simply giving the child its birthright in the shape of proper food.[71]

Birthright conjures up a sense of the child's inheritance by virtue of birth—especially his social status and wealth. The advertisement defuses these assumptions by redefining birthright with reference to an affordable product; this child as much as any other should have equal access to Mellin's Food.

The luxurious orientation of many Victorian products did not effect an unrelentingly Veblenesque marketing strategy. To be sure, some products—artificial gems and electroplate—were overtly imitative. Others such as diamonds and furs only hoped to appeal on any serious scale to an elite. Only the most expensive Victorian products marketed to the middle class, such as pianos and gramophones, consistently exploited social emulation. In the billiard room and in the ballroom, leisure was commercially identified with the aristocracy, but more often than not commercial representations situated the patrician within the egalitarian context of ancient Greece. Advertisers encouraged consumers to spend more money on luxuries under the pretense that they were thrifty rather than self-indulgent. At the same time advertisers emphasized an expansive fellowship of spenders. They envisioned products as a bridge rather than a barrier between classes. Material satisfaction, a hedonistic ideal, was a "birthright" for the million and the millionaire, the palace and the cottage; it constituted the material analogue of the democratic revolution.

8

Conclusion

Victorian print advertisements reveal an important cultural pattern. As the hall of commerce infiltrated the very heart of the home, Victorians with increasing fervor in the late nineteenth century gravitated toward a commercial ideal of "self-illusory hedonism." But, intriguingly, advertisers set materialism within the context of pastoral romanticism, classical culture, and evangelical conversion. It is significant that each of these contexts had egalitarian connotations.

The advertisement blended the requirements of the new and improved products of the industrial age, the desires, needs, and fantasies of a feminine market and the informed opinions, social perceptions, and gender perspective of male creators. The goods sold in the Victorian advertisement were necessarily, as a result of mass production, increasingly brand differentiated, increasingly luxurious. Female consumers, in a society, which was constantly in flux and which designated for women a central role as definers and enhancers of status, sought an image of themselves as they would like to be, a projection of some aspect of their ideal selves. Advertising agents, even unconsciously, imposed their own perceptions of society and of women. Implicitly, this confluence of industrial product, female consumers, and male agents crystallized an important Victorian vision of the good life.

The advertisement defined four ideals—the ideal setting, the ideal activity, the ideal human nature, and the ideal society—that philosophers contend are the essential elements of the good life.[1] Each was hedonistic. Advertisements celebrated an artificial environment delineated by a complex assortment of manmade goods accessible to all; a life that was leisured but attained through industry and merit; heroes who were self-made not born; utopias removed from the Western fashion pattern, but suffused with communal connotations. The print advertisement elaborates the pattern of middle-class values in the late nineteenth century.

The new ideal glorified consumption for its own pleasure and to denote status (although social emulation should not be assumed). Endless fashion advertisements resembling Parisian fashion plates identified particular elements, brands, and styles of costume that might be considered "artistic" or "elegant."[2] They dictated "les dernières nouveautés,"[3] the "luxury of the age,"[4] the quintessential item that could contribute to "social success."[5] They formulated a composite of the ideal woman. She would have pale skin, lavender scent, coiffed hair, and breath "sweet as the ambrosial air."[6] At home amid literary chairs, ferns, Brussels carpets, Minton china, "mirrors . . . for reflecting the beautiful . . . candlebra . . . and . . . artistic accessories,"[7] she would enjoy the gentle comforts of family life. The foods of her own kitchen would be supplemented by the variety of packaged convenience products—cocoas, beef extracts, confectionery, biscuits. Her household would be scrupulously clean, improved by a widening array of household soaps, ammonia, laundry soaps and disinfectants, and a dazzling assortment of domestic machines. The home so exquisitely beautified, cleaned, and appointed was to be "the seat of jocund mirth,"[8] a center of harmony, shielded (often literally with stained glass) from the sordid world of industry, a veritable hothouse, an "attraction . . . after the toil and turmoil of the day" marred by "never a false note, never a jarring chord."[9] But its decoration would convey the family's social position.

Consumer goods could facilitate glorious leisure. This was a central aspect of the commercial ideal. The commercial woman sits before a warm fire, reclines at the end of the day with a hot cup of cocoa, lounges on her literary chair. As mother, she is assisted by servant labor that relieves her from the most onerous demands of domestic tasks and child care. As wife, she is the companion of her husband's leisure at parties, at candlelit dinners, at tennis. As Grecian sybarite, she lies, eyes veiled, on a bed of roses. Her leisure connotes social status, but it is also intrinsically pleasurable.

Advertisers focus unrelentingly on the sensual dimension. The ideal woman seems forever to be soaking in a capacious tub surrounded by rose petals and gauzy veils or poised on the brink of paradisiacal baths. She stares dreamily into her boudoir mirror; indeed she seems to be examining her reflection at every turn. She luxuriates in physical pleasure and her own daydreams. Daring romantic courtship imagery and suggestions of the exclusivity of the mother-infant bond implied self-fulfilment and promised the most intimate pleasures.

Industrial improvements possessed the potential to surpass the past with new and unprecedented delights. In advertisements powerful smokestacks and driving engines conveyed the prowess of mass production. Litanies of stock and images of plenty implied its limitless potential. The old was

"gradually giving place to a [new] mode."[10] The consumer could antici-
pate the dawn of "a new era." Whether temporarily disappointed or sati-
ated, she had only to await the marvels of "the latest invention," the most
recently crowned "luxury of the age." The prospect of pleasure seemed
heightened, even endless. An advertisement for a bathing pitcher, the
Philips' Toilet Aquarius, proclaimed "The main idea of [the late nineteenth
century] is making life easier. This ought to be a great recommendation in
this nineteenth century when we all want to save ourselves from toil and
use our energies in pleasure."[11] The use of "our energies in pleasure"
became the commercially defined middle-class ideal.

While it extolled superfluous variety and sensuous pleasure, the new
ideal was scarcely animated by aristocratic or even elitist pretensions. Only
the most expensive items—pianos or diamonds—or the most obvious
aristocratic imitation—electroplate or simulated gems—are advertised
with aristocratic allusions. Advertisements for most entertainments—
jewelery, bicycles, cameras—purport that they are competitively priced;
that to buy them is to enjoy pleasure today under the pretense of thrift.
Advertisers struggle to create an impression of affordability, to emphasize
broad rather than elite appeal. Instead of stressing exclusivity, advertisers
remind consumers of mass orientation—factory production, quantity, variety. Headlines proclaim "Tea by the Ton," "No Middleman," "Buy Direct." The industrial product is for the million and the millionaire, for
people in "every walk of life,"[12] "in the castle or the cottage."[13] The
gratification of material desires emerges as a commercial "birthright,"
more glittering and meaningful than the superficial gloss of entrenched
privilege.

The entrepreneurial ideal had always implicitly included the potential
for material well-being. Hard work, thrift, self-help brought material comfort. With mass production, this potential increased exponentially. By the
third quarter of the nineteenth century citizens who possessed the political
opportunity to rise in society by merit rather than privilege did not reject
the virtues that had served them well. Social mobility, such a pivotal ideal
in a relatively open class structure, might now be expressed culturally in
the celebration of the equal opportunity for all citizens to manifest their
economic, social, and political arrival in material acquisition. Just as the
Weber hypothesis concedes the right of the sixteenth-century Puritan to
achieve worldly success, the consumerist spirit of the late nineteenth century allowed the exemplar of the entrepreneurial principle to display and
even to enjoy his material profits. The advertisement was the material
expression of democratic values, the ultimate extension of the bourgeois
belief that hard work, thrift, and diligence would bring rewards.

This fundamental egalitarian premise is evidenced in the advertisement
at every turn. Advertised products transcend the boundaries of physical
and social space. Products may be "used all over the world" and enjoyed by
millions.[14] In a nascent global village thousands of consumers experience
the same physical realities of day-to-day life. By purchasing the same prod-

ucts they are united; they understand each other rationally and emotionally by sharing standards of living, taste, style, and fashion. Consumption becomes a leveller that links those of apparently distinct geographic, economic, or social circumstance. Neighbors exchange secrets over the garden gate; celebrities expose product preferences to humble consumers. Advertisements evoke the metaphor of the crowd—the sea of workman's caps, the myriad faces of beauty, the dark recesses of the audience— wherein each individual is joined with the others by the experience of consumption. The world is charmingly personified; reduced to a caricatured person, it is knowable, no longer faceless. The consumer identifies with the world itself, discovers a community of interests in the pursuit of consumption. Advertisements underscore the consumer's sense of commonality with other consumers by reshaping the boundaries of community though images of exotic foreigners. All may be united, apparently equalized, by the shared action of consumption, by a shared anticipation of the beneficial effects of the product.

Heroes embody a democratic vision. The expert—the scientist, the doctor, or member of the press—derives his prestige from merit rather than social class. His expertise is acquired, not innate—attainable, self-controlled, and self-directed. The adventurer charts his own course in an unknown world. As he braves the physical and emotional pressures of the frontier that ignore social class, he emerges victorious, triumphant through classless raw courage rather than through genteel pretension. He is ennobled by action, not status. The actress's cultivated beauty and sensual indulgence allow her to rise above the vestiges of the antitheatrical prejudices and the barriers of class. Her distinction lies in the innate charms of womanhood and in the experience of the moods and passions of a common human nature. In commercial models heroes are distinguished by qualities that are accessible to all.

Through the enchantment of distance the eighteenth-century courtier and the Grecian goddess connote enduring values. The Grecian motif frequently represents Truth, Beauty, or Justice: its English alternative, the rural idyll, conjures up Old England, the virtues of home, family, and community. A patrician veneer suggested in the classical example by its associations with education and fine art and in the English example by connotations of the fixed social place of persons during the medieval past is balanced by conflicting associations—the democratic ideals of Athens, the keyhole vulgarity of Alma-Tadema, and Ruskinian notions of a Romanticized communal ideal. Commercial utopias avoid the prospect of direct social emulation while praising universal values.

Advertisements consistently emphasize not the divisive consequences of social status, but the leveling experience of humanity. All are unified by a shared dread of the Fall that clouds material expectations. Despite eugenicist visions of perfectibility, advertisers return the consumer to a moral dilemma. As Grecian sybarite and Middle Eastern seductress, Lady MacBeth or Marie Antoinette, the commercial temptress helped the advertiser peddle his wares, but her dangerous aspect betrayed a commercial subtext of repression that identified women with Judgment and the Fall. Productive prowess seemed qualified by the universal spectre of moral transgression that ignored social class.

As consumers equally confronted the all-consuming threat of desire, they sought refuge in an equalizing promise of deliverance through one transformative action—consumption. Moral failing, innate inadequacy, a variety of external threats—disease, infant death, marital discord, burglary, adulteration—might be worse for the poor, but no one was immune. Over the garden fence or in a private confidence to a trusted friend, the consumer as humble housewife or wealthy socialite reveals her inner turmoil. Advertisements mirror pre-conversion angst. With maternal voice and prescriptive formats, advertisers admonish, instruct, caution, scold. They urge the consumer, rich and poor, to cast aside old habits in favor of new, more enlightened ways. Their heavenly promise is clear and accessible to almost everyone: life could be perfected, without a care. The consumer could keep the wolf from the door. Assurance could be hers. All that was required was one single choice. The Victorian advertisement absorbed the evangelical ethos, including its egalitarian premise. Salvation was available to all who decided. Consumers would be guided by a materialistic voice to a secular idyll, the fulfilment of the democratic dream.

Notes

Preface

1. Implicitly, this is a study of Victorian consumerism, although the term itself may be more obfuscating than helpful. The term consumerism was coined in the 1950s. It was first used by Vance Packard to refer to advertising strategies that promoted planned obsolescence and combatted a saturated market. In the 1960s it was adopted by Ralph Nader and became synonymous with the consumer protection movement. In academic context, however, it usually refers to a social movement from an ethos of production to an ethos of consumption, from a cultural emphasis on work, sacrifice, and saving to a cultural emphasis on leisure, self-gratification, and self-realization. See Paul N. Bloom and Ruth Belk Smith, *The Future of Consumerism* (Toronto: Lexington Books, 1986).

2. Walter Houghton, *The Victorian Frame of Mind* (New Haven: Yale University Press, 1957).

3. Patricia Branca, *Silent Sisterhood* (London: Croom Helm, 1975).

4. J. A. Banks, *Prosperity and Parenthood* (London: Routledge & Kegan Paul, 1954).

5. T. Schlereth, *Material Culture: A Research Guide* (Lawrence: University of Kansas, 1968).

6. Simon Jervis, *Victorian Furniture* (London: Ward Lock, 1968); Geoffrey Wills, *Victorian Glass* (London: G. Bell, 1976); Nicholas Cooper, *The Opulent Eye* (London: Architectural Press, 1977); Nicholas Pevsner, *High Victorian Design* (London: Architectural Press, 1951).

7. Harold Perkin asserts that "consumer demand was the ultimate key to the industrial revolution." See *Origins of Modern English Society* (London: Routledge, 1969), p. 91. But the only major work to focus on demand, Neil McKendrick and J. Plumb, *The Birth of a Consumer Society* (London: Europa Publications, 1982), champions a Veblenesque perspective that does not adequately address the independent vitality of the middle class.

8. Henry Sampson, *A History of Advertising from Earliest Times* (London: Chatto & Windus, 1874); Frank Presbrey, *History and Development of Advertising* (Garden

City, New York: Doubleday, 1929); E. S. Turner, *The Shocking History of Advertising* (London: Michael Joseph, 1952); John Braun, *Advertisements in Court* (London: John Murray, 1968); Diana and Geoffrey Hindley, *Advertising in Victorian England 1837–1901* (London: Wayland, 1972); T. R. Nevett, *op. cit.*

9. See especially T. R. Nevett, "London's Early Advertising Agents," *Journal of the History of Advertising*, December 1977, pp. 15–18.

10. See the evaluation of the psychologist Carol Moog in *"Are They Selling Her Lips?" Advertising and Identity* (New York: William Morrow & Co., 1990), p. 222.

Chapter 1

1. See Asa Briggs, *Victorian Things* (London: B. T. Batsford, 1988).

2. The term middle class was first cited in the Oxford English Dictionary in 1812. See Asa Briggs, "Middle Class Consciousness," *Past and Present*, v. 9–12, 1956–57. For the origins of the middle class see Peter Earle, *The Making of the English Middle Class* (London: Methuen, 1989). Contemporaries applied concrete tests to define membership—income, occupation, education, style of life. Each criterion represented an ideal, which was not always attained by every person considered by his neighbors to be middle class. Nor were middle-class attributes exclusive; workers or aristocrats might share one or several so-called middle-class characteristics. This lack of exclusivity has attracted some historians to the embourgeoisement thesis. See John Goldthorpe, *The Affluent Worker in the Class Structure* (London: Cambridge University Press, 1969). Victorians, however, did believe that a definable middle class existed. Advertisers asserted that their advertisements were directed to such a middle class.

3. The ability of typical middle-class people to employ a domestic servant or servants is controversial. E. J. Hobsbawm suggests that middle class was defined by the ability to keep domestic servants. *Industry and Empire* (Harmondsworth: Penguin, 1968), p. 157; More than one servant seems essential to this definition. The maintenance of a single daily or char was not sufficient to obviate the manual labor of the housewife or to secure leisured appearance. On the other hand, Theresa McBride in *The Domestic Revolution* (New York: Holmes & Meier Inc., 1976) argues that many members of the middle class were servantless. See pp. 20–21.

4. Within the middle class there were variations determined in part by geography. There were regional differences in the qualities attributed to the middle class, differences between urban and rural perceptions and distinctive characteristics associated with London; the outward demonstrations of status were obviously different in a northern village than in a London suburb. Other variations were clearly influenced by income. Both Branca and Banks argue that those within the lower income reaches of the middle class (say between £100–£200 per annum) lived with only modest material comforts and often without a domestic servant, whereas those at the highest income levels enjoyed considerable affluence. My use of the umbrella label middle class is not meant to ignore or to undervalue the significance of these variations, but to employ the language of advertisers themselves, who were concerned with a broadly defined national middle class, which transcended these interior distinctions. See J. A. Banks, *Prosperity and Parenthood* (London: Routledge & Kegan Paul, 1954) and Patricia Branca, *Silent Sisterhood* (London: Croom Helm, 1975).

5. Peter Earle, p. 329.

6. Colin Campbell, *The Romantic Ethic and the Spirit of Modern Consumerism* (Oxford: Clarendon Press, 1987), p. 201.

7. Each of these elements is surveyed in some detail in T. R. Nevett, *Advertising in Britain* (London: Heinemann, 1982). For the rise of the provincial press see Lucy Brown, *Victorian News and Newspapers* (Oxford: Clarendon, 1985) and A. P. Wadsworth, *Newspaper Circulations 1800–1954* (Manchester: Manchester Statistical Society, 1954–55). For the growth of the women's press see Cynthia White, *Women's Magazines 1693–1968* (London: Michael Joseph, 1969). For the technical developments that transformed the press see Colin Clair's *A History of Printing in Britain* (London: Cassell, 1956).

8. Virginia Berridge, "Popular Journalism and Working Class Attitudes 1854–1886: A Study of Reynold's Newspaper and Lloyd's Weekly Newspaper," University of London, Ph.D., 1976.

9. See Arthur Aspinall, *Politics and the Press* (London: Home & Van Thal, 1949).

10. Maples Furniture, *Court Journal*, May 7, 1870, p. 538.

11. G.N.R., *Illustrated Sporting and Dramatic News*, May 7, 1900, p. 407.

12. Such illustrations, although usually produced within the advertising agency, were sometimes actually purchased from an art gallery. Millais' "Bubbles" (1886), to the initial consternation of the artist, appeared in an advertisement for Pears' Soap; Frith's "The New Frock" (1889) appeared in an advertisement for Sunlight Soap; a Harry Furniss drawing from *Punch* appeared in a Pears' testimonial. Despite complaints from members of the Royal Academy, an advertiser who owned a picture had the right to reproduce it. Most artists reconciled themselves to popular commercial practice and objected publicly only when their work was poorly reproduced by woodcuts. Some might even hire out their services for commercial purposes. Stacey Marks drew a picture for Pears' Soap of two monks at their ablutions—"Cleanliness is Next to Godliness"; the Beggarstaff brothers and Phil May dabbled for profit in commercial illustrating. See Frank Presbrey, *History and Development of Advertising* (Garden City, New York: Doubleday, 1929), p. 98.

13. Pulvermacher's Galvanic Chain-Bands, *Illustrated London News*, December 24, 1870, p. 668.

14. Phosferine, *Family Circle of the Christian World*, July 29, 1890, p. 79.

15. Brand names and trademarks were protected against gross fraud, but it remained legal throughout the nineteenth century to use the name of a famous person without permission. A famous court case, *Carlill v. the Carbolic Smoke Ball Co.*, warned advertisers against fraudulent claims, but for the most part without effect. Government regulations and a pressure group, the Society for Checking Abuses in Public Advertising (SCAPA), founded in 1893, both focused almost exclusively on outdoor advertising. Only the Indecent Advertisements Act of 1889 that prohibited the advertising of venereal disease remedies pertained to the content of advertisements. For further details see John Braun, *Advertisements in Court* (London: David Fanning Ltd., 1965) and T. R. Nevett, *Advertising in Britain*.

16. Villa Washer, *Hand and Heart*, May 21, 1880, p. 544.

17. "Advertising Space," *Advertising*, March 1900, p. 284.

18. See Gregory Anderson, *Victorian Clerks* (Manchester: Manchester University Press, 1976).

19. J. A. Banks, *Prosperity and Parenthood* (London: Routledge & Kegan Paul, 1954).

20. S. B. Saul, *The Myth of the Great Depression* (London: MacMillan, 1969).

21. S. Mayston, "How to Reach the Woman at Home," *Advertising World*, February 1913, p. 210.

22. Several trade journals were founded in the latter part of the nineteenth century—*Advertising World* (1901–1940), *Advertising* (1891–1914), *Advertiser's Review* (1899–1904), *Advertiser's News* (1904–1905), *Advertiser's Monthly Circular* (1905), *Advertiser's Weekly* (1913–1969).

23. "The Appeal to Women," *Advertising World*, February 1913, p. 208. These observations were not the product of market research, but the intuitive response of experienced agents to the demands of the market. An 1907 an article in the *Fortnightly Review*, evaluating "The Craft of the Advertiser," cites "tracing results" by "keying" advertisements as the principle method employed by modern agencies. According to this system, advertisers simply provided a number in each advertisement to which the public could write for information, to place an order, or for a coupon, free sample, or catalogue. By providing a different number for different advertisements or different newspapers, the advertiser could assess the success of each advertisement. See "The Craft of the Advertiser, *Fortnightly Review*, February 1907, pp. 301–310.

24. Accordingly, I have focused in my analysis on advertisements that directly or indirectly target women as consumers. These advertisements, given the advertising agent's explicit designation of his market, are most representative. In the Victorian press there are advertisements that target men (e.g., advertisements for whisky), but because these advertisements represent only a small portion of all advertisements, I have not focused on them. Nor have I focused in any substantive way on the small fraction of advertisements that appeal to the children's market.

25. E. S. Turner, *The Shocking History of Advertising* (London: Michael Joseph, 1965), p. 66.

26. Mike Dempsey, *Early Advertising Art from A. and F. Pears Ltd.* (London: William Collins, 1978), p. 5.

27. House of Commons, *Report of the Select Committee on Patent Medicines*, August 1914, p. x.

28. Noble Fabric, *Queen*, 1890.

29. P. and F. Beyfuss Furniture, *Illustrated London News*, 1860.

30. Atkinson's Furniture, *Queen*, 1850.

31. Christian and Rathbone, *Illustrated London News*, 1870.

32. Smith Furniture, *Illustrated London News*, May 1, 1850.

33. Colman's Flour, *Illustrated London News*, 1870.

34. Beecham's Pills, *Illustrated London News*, 1900.

35. Hancock Jewellery, *Illustrated London News*, May 1, 1850.

36. Savory and Moore Baby Food, *Illustrated London News*, 1890; Cavé Corsets, *Queen*, 1890.

37. Glenfield Starch, *Illustrated London News*, May 1, 1860.

38. *Illustrated London News*, 1890.

39. *Court Journal*, 1890.

40. Bovril, *Queen*, 1890.

41. Willcox and Gibbs, *Illustrated London News*, 1870.

42. Aertex Underwear, *Queen*, 1900.

43. Formamint, *The Lady*, 1910.

44. Neave's Food, *Peter Parley's Annual*, 1868, p. 1.

45. Brooke's Soap, *Pick-Me-Up*, March 15, 1900, p. 401.

46. Carron Stoves, *Illustrated London News*, 1910, p. 980.

47. Autopiano, *Illustrated London News*, November 5, 1910, p. 721.

48. *Ibid.*

49. Sunlight Soap, *Black and White*, March 11, 1893, p. 305.

50. *Myra's Journal, Atalanta*, 1889, p. 14.

51. Bovril, *Illustrated London News*, January–June 1900, p. 451.

52. Cadbury's Cocoa, *Child's Companion*, 1890, back cover.

53. Hudson's Soap, *Peter Parley's Annual*, 1888, p. 11.

54. Pears' Soap, *Illustrated London News*, June–December 1890, p. 572.

55. Mellin's Food, *Illustrated London News*, January–March 1910, p. 33.

56. Aymard Patent Sterilizer, *Illustrated London News*, January–March 1910, p. 33.

57. Foot's Adjustable Chair, *Illustrated London News*, 1910, p. 843. The Library Lounge was one version of the so-called literary chair—a reclining chair that came equipped with a bookrest attached to one side.

58. Liebig Extract, *Illustrated London News*, 1890, p. 409.

59. Bird's Custard Powder, *Illustrated London News*, July 1889, p. 772.

60. Swan Soap, *Illustrated London News*, July–December 1900, p. 577.

61. Philips' Toilet Aquarius, *Illustrated London News*, July 12, 1890, p. 59.

Chapter 2

1. Sinclair's Cold Water Soap, *Family Circle of the Christian World*, 1885.

2. Anthony Wohl, *The Victorian Family* (London: Croom Helm, 1978), p. 11.

3. Leonore Davidoff and Catherine Hall, *Family Fortunes: Men and Women of the English Middle Class 1780–1850* (Chicago: University of Chicago Press, 1987).

4. Edward Shorter, *The Making of the Modern Family* (New York: Basic Books, 1975).

5. *Hand and Heart*, May 7, 1880, p. 507.

6. John Ruskin, *Sesame and Lilies* (New York: F. M. Lupton, 1896).

7. John Ruskin, *Sesame and Lilies* (New York: F.M. Lupton, 1896).

8. Ruskin, p. 79.

9. *Cassell's Household Guide* (London: Cassell, Petler and Galpia, 1869–71).

10. *Hand and Heart*, October 1, 1880, p. 6.

11. For example, Sarah Ellis, *The Women of England: Their Social Duties and Domestic Habits* (1839); John Walsh, *Manual of Domestic Economy* (1857); Mrs. Beeton, *The Book of Household Management* (1861). See Dena Attar, *A Bibliography of Household Books* (London: Prospect Books, 1987).

12. Quoted in Joseph Banks, *Prosperity and Parenthood* (London: Routledge & Kegan Paul, 1954).

13. Martha Vicinus, *Suffer and Be Still* (Bloomington: Indiana University Press, 1972).

14. Patricia Branca, *Silent Sisterhood* (London: Croom Helm, 1975).

15. Quoted from William Hyde's *College Men and Women*, 1908, is Sara Delamont and Lorna Duffin, *The Nineteenth Century Woman: Her Physical and Cultural World* (London: Croom Helm, 1978).

16. Mrs. Warren, *How I Managed My House on £200 a Year* (London: Houlston & Wright, 1864), p. iv.

17. Mrs. Mary Haweis, *The Art of Housekeeping* (London: Sampson Low, Marston, Searle and Rivington, 1889).

18. Warren, p. 5.

19. Warren, p. v.

20. Warren, p. vi.

21. Sergeant's & Co. Tea, the John Johnson Collection, Tea and Grocery Papers I, 1865.

22. Mrs. Ellis, *Daughters of England* (London: Fisher and Sons, 1845), p. 7.

23. Mrs. Ellis, *Mothers of England* (London: Peter Jackson, Late Fisher and Son Co.,1843), p. 174.

24. Lynda Nead, *Myths of Sexuality: Representations of Women in Victorian Britain* (Oxford: Blackwell, 1988), p. 44.

25. Martin Wiener, *English Culture and the Decline of the Industrial Spirit* (Cambridge: Cambridge University Press, 1981).

26. Sunlight Soap, the John Johnson Collection, June 1895.

27. Mother Siegel's Syrup, the John Johnson Collection, Patent Medicine 7, March 1880.

28. Cadbury's Cocoa, *Illustrated London News*, July–December 1900, p. 951.

29. Bile Beans for Biliousness, the John Johnson Collection, Patent Medicine 5, 1902.

30. McCaw Stevenson & Orr, *Illustrated Sporting and Dramatic News*, January 11, 1890, p. 541.

31. Melodeon, *Christian Age*, April 7, 1880, p. 4.

32. Angelus Autopiano, *Illustrated London News*, November 5, 1910, p. 721.

33. Cameron and Viall, *Court Journal*, May 4, 1850, p. 288.

34. Jay's, *Court Journal*, May 4, 1850, p. 288.

35. Baker and Crisp and Hayward Lace, *Court Journal*, May 7, 1870, p. 539.

36. Ganterie Francaise, *Court Journal*, May 7, 1870, p. 545.

37. J. Duvelleroy, *Court Journal*, May 7, 1870, p. 545.

38. Jaeger Woollens, *Court Journal*, May 3, 1890, p. 720.

39. *Court Journal*, May 3, 1890, p. 717.

40. Wills & Segar, *Court Journal*, May 3, 1890, p. 717.

41. Sandow Corsets, *Queen*, May 7, 1910, p. 53.

42. Floriline, *Illustrated London News*, Christmas Supplement, 1880, p. 14.

43. Bailey's Complexion Brush, *Illustrated London News*, May 3, 1890, p. 575. Poisonous is a suggestive word that indicates not only the potential health hazards of leaving paint on the face, but also a damaging association of makeup with women of easy virtue that prevented makeup from being a respectable subject for large-scale advertising even in the late nineteenth century.

44. Metcalfe Dressing Cases, *Court Journal*, May 7, 1870, p. 547.

45. Jay's, *Court Journal*, June 25, 1885, n.p.

46. Burgess Silks, *Court Journal*, May 7, 1870, p. 539.

47. William Buszard, *Court Journal*, May 3, 1890, p. 719.

48. *Court Journal*, May 7, 1870, p. 545.

49. Osler China and Glass, *Illustrated Sporting and Dramatic News*, November 29, 1890, p. 393.

50. *Ibid.*

51. Since Weber power has been notoriously difficult to define. Weber in *Wirtschaft and Gesellschaft* identifies two forms of power: control through social authority (patriarchal, magisterial, princely) and control through economic force. See Max Rheinstein and Edward Shil, trans., *Max Weber on Law in Economy and Society* (New York: Simon and Schuster, 1967), pp. 323–324.

52. Kate Millet, *Sexual Politics* (New York: Doubleday, 1970), pp. 101-106.

53. Kathy Davis, "Critical Sociology and Gender Relations," *The Gender of Power* (London: Sage Publications, 1991), p. 79. There is a further difficulty for historians: simply addressing the question of feminine power is to enter the politics of gender, to participate in the ongoing debate between the theoreticians and the materialists. Feminist historians have in general gravitated toward three theoretical perspectives: patriarchy, Marxism, and French post-structuralism. My choice in this book not to employ one of these theoretical perspectives is not rooted in political opposition to what Bryan Palmer has called "the implosion of theory." Partly, it is a reflection of my material training not just as an historian, but as a museologist. But it is also a response to the evidence itself. Advertisements exist in large numbers and constitute a source almost unexplored by historians: it is my intent to expose readers to a broad spectrum of these advertisements, rather than, as is often appropriate with a narrowly defined and often more familiar group of documents, to subject them to more detailed and theoretical analysis. See Joan Scott, *Gender and the Politics of History* (New York: Columbia University Press, 1991); E. P. Thompson, *The Poverty of Theory* (New York: Monthly Review Press, 1979); Bryan Palmer, *Descent into Discourse* (Philadelphia: Temple University Press, 1982).

54. Juliet Mitchell argues that consumer consciousness, although it may have tried to manipulate women, cultivates attitudes that allowed women to "rebel in their own terms." See *Woman's Estate* (New York: Random House, 1973), p. 69.

55. Beecham's Pills, *Illustrated London News*, 1890, p. 255.

56. Richard Jenkyns, *The Victorians and Ancient Greece* (Oxford: Basil Blackwell, 1980), p. 14.

57. Richard Jenkyns, *Dignity and Decadence: Victorian Art and the Classical Inheritance* (London: Harper Collins, 1991), p. 20.

58. Jenkyns, p. 25.

59. Borax, *Lady's Pictorial*, 1885.

60. Osler China and Glass, *Illustrated Sporting and Dramatic News*, November 29, 1890, p. 393. For a full treatment of sexual themes see Chapter 3, "Productive Engines and Consuming Conflagrations."

61. See Adeline Tinter, "The Sleeping Woman: A Victorian Fantasy," *Pre-Raphaelite Review*, v. 2, 1978, pp. 12–26, and Susan Casteras, *Images of Victorian Womanhood in English Art* (Cranbury, New Jersey: Associated University Press, 1987).

62. Pears' Soap, the John Johnson Collection, Soap 5, June 4, 1887.

63. Nina Auerbach, *Woman and the Demon: The Life of a Victorian Myth* (Cambridge: Harvard University Press, 1982).

64. Hodkinson Venetian Blinds, the John Johnson Collection, Houses II, 1889.

65. Holloway's Pills, the John Johnson Collection, Patent Medicine 5, 1902.

66. Aspinall's Enamel, the John Johnson Collection, Oil and Candles, n.d.

67. Matchless Metal Polish, the John Johnson Collection, Oil and Candles I.

68. Aspinall's Enamel, *Illustrated London News*, July–December 1889, p. 292.

69. Floriline, *Illustrated London News*, October 1, 1910, p. 516.

70. Anne Hollander, *Seeing Through Clothes* (New York: Viking, 1978), p. 397.

71. Erasmic Soap, *Lady's Pictorial*, July 3, 1897; Beecham's Glycerine and Cucumber Powder, *Home Chat*, December 30, 1885.

72. Bovril, *Sphere*, January 22, 1910, p. iii.

73. Maples Furniture, *Court Journal*, May 7, 1870, p. 538.

74. Hewetson Furniture, *Illustrated London News*, January 3, 1895, p. 31.

75. J. C. Drummond, *The Englishman's Food* (London: Jonathan Cape, 1939), p. 372.

76. Neave's Food, *Little Wide Awake*, 1886, back cover.

77. Meredith & Drew Biscuits, the John Johnson Collection, Food 1, n.d.

78. Singer Sewing Machines, *Family Circle of the Christian World*, January 14, 1890, p. 18.

79. Willcox & Gibbs, the John Johnson Collection, March 1871.

80. *Ibid.*

81. *Ibid.*

82. Willcox & Gibbs Sewing Machines, the John Johnson Collection, Sewing Cottons and Machines, December 1, 1869.

83. Patent Nursery Chair, the John Johnson Collection, Houses II.

84. Willcox & Gibbs Sewing Machines, the John Johnson Collection, Sewing Cottons and Machines I, November 1871.

85. Sunlight Soap, *Illustrated Sporting and Dramatic News*, 1893, p. 665.

Chapter 3

1. J. B. Bury, *The Idea of Progress* (New York: MacMillan, 1937).

2. Warren W. Wager, *The Idea of Progress Since the Renaissance* (New York: John Wiley & Sons Inc., 1969), p. 3. A widely held interpretation suggests that the idea of progress is a secularized version of the Christian belief in Providence. See Christopher Lasch, *The True and Only Heaven: Progress and Its Critics* (New York: W.W. Norton, 1991), p. 40.

3. Alan Gilbert, *The Making of Post-Christian Britain* (London: Longman, 1980), p. 47.

4. Quoted in Buckley, p. 36.

5. Quoted from *Lives of the Engineers* in Martin J. Wiener, *English Culture and the Decline of the Industrial Spirit 1850–1880* (Cambridge: Cambridge University Press, 1981), p. 81.

6. Quoted in Buckley, p. 34.

7. Quoted in Buckley, pp. 9–10.

8. Nicholas Pevsner, *High Victorian Design* (London: Architectural Press, 1951), p. 18. The Duke of Wellington speaks of his daily visit.

9. Quoted in Pevsner, p. 16.

10. Quoted in Asa Briggs, *Victorian People* (London: Penguin Books, 1954).

11. Quoted in Buckley, p. 34.

12. Quoted in Buckley, p. 45.

13. Buckley, p. 36.

14. Wiener, p. 38.

15. Quoted in Wiener, p. 39.

16. J. S. Mill, *On Liberty* (New York: W.W. Norton, 1975), p. 56.

17. Quoted in Wiener, p. 146.

18. Quoted in Jerome Buckley, *Tennyson: The Growth of a Poet* (Cambridge: Harvard University Press, 1960), p. 233.

19. Lasch, p. 64.

20. Quoted in Buckley, p. 55.

21. Buckley, p. 81.

22. Wagar, p. 106.

23. Quoted in Buckley, pp. 61–62.

24. Quoted in Buckley, p. 47.

25. Maples Furniture, *Queen*, March 16, 1895.

26. Cadbury's Cocoa Essence, *Christian Age*, July 14, 1880.

27. Epps's Cocoa, *Christian Age, op cit.*

28. Baker & Crisp, *Queen*, May 7, 1870.

29. Maples Furniture, *Court Journal*, May 3, 1890.

30. Newton, Wilson & Co. Sewing Machines, *Peter Parley's Annual*, 1867, p. 3.

31. Parisian Diamonds, *Lady's Pictorial*, August 7, 1897.

32. Formamint, *Illustrated London News*, January–March 1910, p. 359.

33. "The Minister," *Illustrated London News*, January–June 1900, p. 588.

34. Electric Curler, *Illustrated London News*, 1890, p. 349.

35. Parkes' Compound Magnets, *Family Circle*, April 14, 1885.

36. Harness' Electropathic Belt, *Illustrated London News*, May 31, 1890, p. 703.

37. Gilette Razors, *Illustrated Sporting and Dramatic News*, May 7, 1910, p. 402.

38. Simpitrol Lighting, *Queen*, May 7, 1910, n.p.

39. Kirby Beard, *Queen*, June 3, 1890.

40. Thermos Flask, *Queen*, May 7, 1910.

41. Simpitrol Lighting System, *Queen*, May 7, 1910.

42. Hygiene Hall Stove, the John Johnson Collection, Fire Grates and Cooking Ranges I, 1881.

43. *Ibid.*

44. Vinolia Soap, *Lady*, May 1, 1890.

45. Bovril, *Lady*, May 1, 1890.

46. Epps's Cocoa, *Family Circle*, April 27, 1880, p. 204.

47. Sanatogen, *Illustrated London News*, January–March 1910, p. 241.

48. Lemco, *Illustrated London News*, July–December 1900, p. 823.

49. Hitching's Ltd. Baby Cars and Carriages, *Lady's Pictorial*, October 20, 1900.

50. Neave's Infant Food, *Peter Parley's Annual*, 1868, p. 1.

51. Dr. Ridge's, *Illustrated London News*, 1880, p. 599.

52. Cocoatina, *Black and White*, April 9, 1898, p. 507.

53. Mellin's Food, *Illustrated London News*, 1910, p. 520.

54. Mellin's Food, *Illustrated London News*, March 5, 1910, p. 361.

55. Gunn's Food of Life, *Pick-Me-Up*, May 10, 1890, p. 96.

56. Ridge's Food, *Lady's Pictorial*, July 29, 1893.

57. Cadbury's Cocoa, *Illustrated London News*, July–December 1900, p. 785.

58. Fry's Cocoa, *Illustrated London News*, July–December 1900, p. 2.

59. Cadbury's Cocoa, *Lady's Pictorial*, December 8, 1900.

60. Eno's, *Routlege's Annual Advertiser, op. cit.*

61. Eno's, *Illustrated London News*, January–June 1890, p. 153.

62. Williams' Shaving Soap, *Illustrated London News*, January–June 1900, p. 660.

63. Eno's, *Illustrated Sporting and Dramatic News*, May 7, 1910, p. 393.

64. *Ibid.*

65. Eno's, *Illustrated London News*, January–June 1900, p. 94.

66. Eno's, *Illustrated London News*, April 19, 1890, p. 50.

67. Borax, *Lady's Pictorial*, 1885.

68. Peter Gay, *Education of the Senses* (New York: Oxford University Press, 1984).

69. Lynda Nead, *Myths of Sexuality: Representations Women in Victorian Britain* (Oxford: Basil Blackwell, 1988).

70. Lux Soap, *Illustrated London News*, January–June 1900, p. 237.

71. Swan Soap, *Punch*, August 27, 1902.

72. Swan Soap, *Illustrated London News*, September 7, 1901, p. 359.

73. Swan Soap, *Illustrated London News*, November 10, 1900, p. 699.

74. For example, Edwin's Long's "The Babylonian Marriage Market" (1875) was one of the most popular pictures of its day. Cf. Richard Jenkyns, *Dignity and Decadence*, pp. 119–120.

75. Parisian Diamond Co., *Black and White*, April 9, 1910, p. 513.

76. Peter Gay, *The Bourgeois Experience* (New York: Oxford University Press, 1984), p. 392.

77. Fry's Cocoa, *Illustrated London News*, January–June 1900, p. 585.

78. St. Jacob's Oil, *Illustrated Sporting and Dramatic News*, July 26, 1890, p. 681.

79. Michael Grant/John Hazel, *Who's Who in Classical Mythology* (London: Weidenfeld & Nicolson, 1973).

80. Trebene Soap, *Peter Parley's Annual*, 1886.

81. Field's Chamber Candles, the John Johnson Collection, Oil and Candles 1.

82. H. R. Hays, *The Dangerous Sex: The Myth of Feminine Evil* (New York: G. P. Putnam's, 1964), p. 228.

83. Eno's, *Illustrated London News*, 1900, p. 357.

84. Pears' Soap, *Illustrated London News*, January–June 1900, p. 63.

Chapter 4

1. Thomas Carlyle, *On Heroes and Hero-Worship* (London: Chapman & Hall Ltd., 1897), p. 63.

2. Peter Thorslev, *The Byronic Hero* (Minneapolis: University of Minnesota Press, 1962).

3. Carlyle, p. 2.

4. Carlyle, pp. 73–74.

5. Tim Travers, *Samuel Smiles and the Victorian Work Ethic* (New York: Garland Publishing, 1987), pp. 172–175.

6. Travers, pp. 172–175.

7. Harold Perkin, *The Origins of Modern English Society 1780–1880*, p. 221.

8. Although some manufacturers, Bovril and Fry's in particular, favored campaigns in which hardy laborers are warmed and fortified by hot beverages, and many other advertisers evoked pastoral imagery, workers generally were not preferred subjects in the Victorian advertisement. Nor did the capitalist assume a conspicuous presence. In American advertisements of the 1920s the entrepreneurial ideal took on pictorial form as a stereotyped businessman. Older men were depicted as business executives, younger men as salesmen aspiring to management positions. The typical citizen in these advertisements was bound for the office or humped over a desk. But these images do not appear in the Victorian advertisement. See Roland Marchand, *Advertising the American Dream*, pp. 189–190.

9. Keating's Cough Syrup, *The Lady*, 1850.

10. Brown and Polson Corn Flour, *Queen*, 1860.

11. Cadbury's Cocoa, *Christian Age*, July 14, 1880.

12. Pears' Soap, *Court Journal*, September 27, 1890, p. 1699.

13. See M. J. Cullen, *The Statistical Movement in Early Victorian Britain* (London: Harvester Press, 1975).

14. Pears' Soap, *Court Journal*, September 27, 1890, p. 1699.

15. Philip's Toilet Aquarius, *Illustrated London News*, 1890, p. 59.

16. The Patent Darning Weaver, *Illustrated London News*, July–December 1889, p. 450.

17. Epps's Cocoa, *Family Circle of the Christian World*, April 27, 1880.

18. Epps's Cocoa, *Illustrated London News*, 1890, p. 441.

19. Old Bleach Linen, *Court Journal*, April 26, 1890.

20. Compagnie Coloniale Chocolates, *Queen*, 1870.

21. Ogden Gold Cigarettes, *Illustrated London News*, July–December 1900.

22. Edward's Oriental Sauce, *Queen*, May 30, 1885.

23. Leo Braudy, *The Frenzy of Renown* (New York: Oxford University Press, 1986), p. 507.

24. Thomas Richards, *The Commodity Culture of Victorian England* (Stanford: Stanford University Press, 1990), p. 136.

25. Cellular Clothing, *Illustrated London News*, January–June 1890, p. 830.

26. U.K. Tea, *Illustrated London News*, January–June 1890, p. 249.

27. Richards, p. 139.

28. Richards, p. 131.

29. Richards, p. 139.

30. Ebermann's Tooth-wash, *Queen*, May 3, 1890.

31. Liebig Extract, *Lady's Pictorial*, March 14, 1991.

32. Ogden's Cigarettes, *Illustrated London News*, June 6, 1900, p. 31.

33. Ogden's Cigarettes, *Illustrated London News*, July–December 1900, p. 955.

34. Liebig, *Illustrated London News*, January–June 1900, p. 165.

35. Bovril, *Illustrated London News*, January–June 1900, p. 585.

36. Ogden's Cigarettes, *Illustrated London News*, January–June 1900, p. 557.

37. Ogden's Cigarettes, *Illustrated London News*, July–December 1900, p. 137.

38. Joan Hichberger, *Images of the Army: The Military in British Art 1815–1914* (Manchester: Manchester University Press, 1988).

39. Bovril, *Illustrated London News*, January–June 1900, p. 585.

40. For a complete history of the royal warrant see Tim Heald, *By Appointment* (London: Queen Anne Press, 1989).

41. Jay's, *Queen*, May 3, 1890, p. 4.

42. Glenfield Starch, the John Johnson Collection, Soap 7, November 1869.

43. Harlene, *Illustrated London News*, 1900.

44. Dorothy Thompson, *Queen Victoria: Gender and Power* (London: Virago, 1990), p. 125.

45. Matchless Metal Polish, the John Johnson Collection, Oil and Candles II.

46. Sunlight Soap, the John Johnson Collection, Soap 6, 1895.

47. Liebig Extract, the John Johnson Collection, Food 6*.

48. Royal Infant's Preservative, the John Johnson Collection, Food 7, n.d.

49. My Queen Vel Vel, *Lady's Pictorial*, September 21, 1893. See Thomas Richards' interpretation in "The Image of Victoria in the Year of the Jubilee," *Victorian Studies*, v. 31, 1987, pp. 7–32.

50. My Queen Vel Vel, the John Johnson Collection, Women's Clothes, December 17, 1887.

51. Jonas Barish, *The Antitheatrical Prejudice* (Berkeley: University of California Press, 1981), p. 348.

52. The 1841 occupational census lists 387 actresses and 987 actors in England and Wales. By 1911 there were 9,171 actresses, 9,076 actors. See Christopher Kent, "Image and Reality: The Actress and Society," in Martha Vicinus, *A Widening Sphere*, pp. 94-116.

53. Stanley Weintraub, *Victoria: An Intimate Biography* (New York: E. P. Dutton, 1987), p. 522.

54. Quoted in Philip Magnus, *King Edward the Seventh* (London: John Murray, 1964), p. 153.

55. *Ibid.*

56. Barish, p. 348.

57. Pears' Soap, the John Johnson Collection, Soap 4, 1887.

58. Phosferine, *Christian Age*, May 6, 1910, p. iii.

Chapter 5

1. Beatrice Webb, *My Apprenticeship*, Chapter 4, quoted in F. Harrison, *Dark Angel* (London: Sheldon Press, 1977), p. 61.

2. R.K.R. Thornton, *The Decadent Dilemma* (London: Edward Arnold, 1983), p. 9.

3. See *Prosperity and Parenthood* and *Silent Sisterhood*.

4. Judith Walkowitz, *Prostitution and Victorian Society: Women, Class and the State* (Cambridge: Cambridge University Press, 1980), p. 247.

5. Frank Miller Turner, *Between Science and Religion: The Reaction to Scientific Naturalism in Late Victorian England* (New Haven: Yale University Press, 1974), p. 12.

6. T. W. Fletcher, "The Great Depression in English Agriculture 1873–1896," *Economic History Review*, 2nd series, vol. 13, April 1961, pp. 417–439.

7. S. B. Saul, *The Myth of the Great Depression* (London: MacMillan, 1972).

8. Bernard Semmel, *Imperialism and Social Reform* (New York: Doubleday, 1960), p. 9.

9. Even in manpower, Britain suffered a decline. During the years 1870–1914 the British population increased more slowly than any other European state. When Germany unified, its population was 41 million, 10 million more than the U.K. By 1914 this gap had doubled. In the U.S. population by 1914 approached 100 million and was still expanding dramatically. G. R. Searle, *The Quest for National Efficiency* (London: Ashfield Press, 1971), p. 9.

10. Searle, pp. 7–9.

11. John Reed, *Decadent Style* (Athens, Ohio: Ohio University Press, 1985), p. 3.

12. Thornton, p. 14.

13. Page Woodcock's Pills, *Christian Age*, May 6, 1910.

14. Eau de Suez, *Queen*, May 1, 1880.

15. See F. B. Smith, *The People's Health* (London: Croom Helm, 1979) and Anthony Wohl, *Endangered Lives* (London: Dent, 1983).

16. Clarke's Blood Mixture, *Family Circle of the Christian World*, July 29, 1890, p. 18.

17. Berkenfeld Filter, *Illustrated London News*, January–June 1900, p. 204.

18. Parr's Pills, *Family Circle of the Christian World*, June 15, 1880, p. 287.

19. House of Commons, *Report of the Select Committee on Patent Medicines* (London: H.M. Stationery Office, August 1914), p. xi.

20. *Ibid.*

21. House of Commons, p. 181.

22. House of Commons, p. 114.

23. Siegel's Syrup, the John Johnson Collection, Patent Medicine 7, May 1880.

24. The advertisement plays on the artistic popularity of the Perseus and An-

dromeda story. In the 1850s John Bell's statue "Andromeda" had met wide acclaim and had been purchased by the Queen. By the late nineteenth century painters picked up the image. Andromeda was painted once by Leighton, by Poynter twice, and in two forms by Burne-Jones as part of a cycle representing the whole Perseus story. See Richard Jenkyns, *Dignity and Decadence*, p. 116.

25. Electropathic Belt, *Graphic*, February 14, 1885.

26. Salt Regal, *Illustrated London News*, January–June 1890, p. 31.

27. Zambuk Disinfectant, *Home Chat*, August 20, 1910, p. 489.

28. Nubolic, *Illustrated London News*, 1910, p. 325.

29. Nubolic, *Home Chat*, August 10, 1910, p. 489.

30. Nubolic, *Illustrated London News*, February 26, 1910, p. 325.

31. Nubolic, *Illustrated London News*, 1910, p. 325.

32. Sanitas, *Queen*, April 9, 1910.

33. Nubolic Soap, *Illustrated London News*, 1910, p. 325.

34. Bovril, *Illustrated London News*, January–June 1900, p. 641.

35. Lemco, *Illustrated London News*, 1900, p. 238.

36. Lifebuoy, *Illustrated London News*, July–December 1894, p. 123.

37. Bovril, *Illustrated London News*, July–December 1894, p. 123.

38. Nubolic, *Home Chat*, August 20, 1910, p. 493.

39. Bruce Haley, *The Healthy Body and Victorian Culture* (Cambridge: Harvard University Press, 1978), p. 12.

40. "The Adulteration of Food: How to Detect and Avoid It," *Cassell's Family Magazine*, 1877, pp. 462–464.

41. *Quarterly Review*, vol. 96, 1854, p. 493.

42. *Ibid*.

43. See Terry Parssinen, *Secret Passions, Secret Remedies* (London: Institute for the Study of Human Issues, 1983).

44. Izal, *op.cit*.

45. Lifebuoy Soap, *op. cit*.

46. Koptica Cure, *Family Circle*, January 14, 1890, p. 18.

47. Carter's Liver Pills, *Illustrated London News*, 1900, p. 34.

48. Liebig Extract, *Family Circle*, May 5, 1880, p. iii.

49. Cuticura, *Illustrated London News*, 1900, p. 242.

50. Fenning's Children's Powder, *Hand and Heart*, October 22, 1880, p. 64.

51. Cuticura, *Illustrated London News*, July–December 1890, p. 510.

52. Formamint, *Illustrated London News*, 1910, p. 797.

53. Dear's Children's Tonic, *Pick-Me-Up*, December 22, 1894, p. 191.

54. Ridge's Food, *Family Circle of the Christian World*, August 17, 1880, p. 109.

55. Frame Food, *Illustrated London News*, January–March 1910, p. 180.

56. Sunlight Soap, *Black and White*, March 11, 1893, p. 305.

57. Dr. Williams' Pink Pills for Pale People, *Black and White*, January 28, 1899.

58. David Philips, *Crime and Authority in Victorian England* (London: Croom Helm, 1977), p. 177.

59. David Jones, *Crime, Protest, Community and Police in 19th Century Britain* (London: Routledge & Kegan Paul, 1982), p. 8.

60. Quoted in Jones, p. 127.

61. Pyramid Night Lights, *Illustrated London News*, 1890, p. 480.

62. Rowntree, *Illustrated London News*, July–December 1900, p. 866.

63. Pears' Soap, *Illustrated London News*, July–December 1890, p. 541.

64. Pears' Soap, *Illustrated London News*, July–December 1890, p. 503.

65. Pears' Soap, *Illustrated London News*, July–December 1890, p. 638.

66. Sunlight Soap, *Illustrated London News*, July–December 1890, p. 764.

67. *Ibid.*

68. Sunlight Soap, *Illustrated London News*, July–December 1890, p. 503.

69. Eno's Fruit Salt, *Illustrated London News*, January–June 1890, p. 153.

70. Even though the cost of divorce dropped from £2,000 to £150–500, during the next fifty years only a few hundred couples divorced per year.

71. Lawrence Stone, *The Road to Divorce* (Oxford: Oxford University Press, 1990), p. 363.

72. Stone, p. 384.

73. Purgen Aperient, *Illustrated London News*, October 12, 1911, p. 549.

74. Sunlight Soap, *Queen*, February 25, 1905.

75. Carr's Ladder Tapes, *Illustrated London News*, July 20, 1889.

76. Jenni Calder, *The Victorian Home* (London: Batsford, 1977).

77. Dena Attar, p. 13.

78. Jay Mechling, "Advice to Historians on Advice to Mothers," *Journal of Social History*, v. 9, 1975, pp. 44–63.

79. Charles A. Voegler Co., *Illustrated London News*, October 18, 1890.

80. Gas Light and Coke Co., *Queen*, May 7, 1910.

81. Quaker Oats, *Christian Age*, March 6, 1910.

82. Ogden's Cigarettes, *Illustrated London News*, November 9, 1901.

83. Boreas Vacuum, *Queen*, May 7, 1910.

84. Frazer's Sulphur Tablets, *Christian Age*, July 16, 1890, p. iii.

85. Brooke's Soap, *Pick-Me-Up*, March 15, 1890, p. 401.

86. Bovril, *Illustrated London News*, July–December 1894, p. 689.

87. Peek, Frean & Co., *Illustrated London News*, July–December 1900, p. 357.

88. Orchestrelle Co., *Illustrated London News*, January–March 1910, p. 362.

89. Louis' Velveteen, *The Lady*, March 22, 1900.

90. Vilixir, *Christian Age*, May 6, 1910, p. vii.

91. Edward's Harlene, the John Johnson Collection, Beauty Parlour 1.

92. Compo Soap, *The Lady*, March 22, 1900.

93. Mme. Rubinstein, *Queen*, May 7, 1910, p. 57.

94. Eno's, *Illustrated London News*, May 23, 1891, p. 689.

95. Eno's, *Graphic*, May 28, 1881, p. 535.

96. McCalls Meats, the John Johnson Collection, Food 4, December 1890.

97. Bovril, *Illustrated London News*, November 10, 1900, p. 707.

98. McCalls Meats, the John Johnson Collection, Food 4.

99. Bovril, *The Lady*, November 25, 1897.

100. Liebig Extract, *Illustrated London News*, March 28, 1891, p. 423.

101. Fry's Cocoa, *Illustrated London News*, October 1, 1910, p. 519.

102. Liebig Extract, *Illustrated London News*, 1890, p. 409.

Chapter 6

1. Lynda Nead, p. 44.

2. Lasch, p. 137.

3. Christopher Shaw/Malcolm Chase, *The Imagined Past: History and Nostalgia* (Manchester: Manchester University Press, 1989), p. 6.

4. Bender, p. 18.

5. See, for example, Edward Shorter, *The Making of the Modern Family* (New

York: Basic Books, 1975) or Leonore Davidoff and Catherine Hall, *Family Fortunes* (Chicago: University of Chicago Press, 1987).

6. Shorter, op. cit.
7. Bender, p. 16.
8. Pears' Soap, *Illustrated London News*, March 9, 1889, p. 314.
9. Pears' Soap, *Illustrated London News*, June 1, 1889, p. 703.
10. Beecham's Pills, *Graphic*, Summer Number 1889, p. 35.
11. Gosnell's Famora, *Home Chat*, June 6, 1900, p. iii.
12. Brandauer Pens, *Illustrated London News*, September 25, 1886, p. 243.
13. Egerton Burnett's Serges, *Graphic*, August 21, 1886, p. 195.
14. Quaker Oats, *Illustrated London News*, 1910, p. 481.
15. Ellis Davies Tea, *Graphic*, April 9, 1887, p. 391.
16. Montserrat Lime Juice, *Graphic*, June 12, 1886, p. 651.
17. Carr's Ladder Tapes, *Illustrated London News*, March 28, 1896.
18. Aspinall's Enamel, *Graphic*, May 11, 1889, p. 519.
19. Hudson's Soap, *Lady's Pictorial*, April 5, 1890.
20. Carr's Ladder Tapes, *Illustrated London News*, April 22, 1893, p. 505.
21. Carr's Ladder Tapes, *Illustrated London News*, April 4, 1896.
22. Odol, *Illustrated London News*, 1910, p. 108.
23. Allenburys' Food, *Illustrated London News*, 1910, p. 31.
24. Beecham's Pills, *Lady's Pictorial*, January 3, 1891.
25. Clarke's Lamps, *Illustrated London News*, 1890, p. 480.
26. Géraudel Pastilles, *Pick-Me-Up*, December 31, 1892, p. 239.
27. Eno's, *Illustrated Sporting and Dramatic News*, December 6, 1890, p. 408.
28. *Ibid.*
29. Patent Nursing Chair, the John Johnson Collection, Houses II.
30. Carron Firegrates, *Illustrated London News*, April 2, 1910, p. 513.
31. Pears' Soap, *Queen*, March 4, 1905.
32. Monkey Brand Soap, *Illustrated London News*, April 4, 1891, p. 455.
33. Bovril, *Illustrated London News*, January 12, 1907, p. 75.
34. Bovril, *Illustrated London News*, January 26, 1907, p. 151.
35. Gramophone, *Illustrated London News*, April-June 1910, p. 942.
36. Gramophone, *Illustrated London News*, Christmas 1910, p. 35.
37. Richard Sennett, *The Fall of Public Man* (New York: Alfred Knopf, 1977), pp. 206–207.
38. Bovril, *Sphere*, January 8, 1910, p. iii.
39. *Ibid.*
40. Globe Metal Polish, *Illustrated London News*, May 8, 1907, p. 775.
41. Monkey Brand Soap, *Illustrated London News*, November 18, 1893, p. 653.
42. Géraudel Pastilles, *Illustrated London News*, March 4, 1893, p. 286.
43. Crosfield Soap, *Illustrated London News*, March 19, 1887, p. 335.
44. Nabob Pickles, *Illustrated London News*, April 26, 1902, p. 625.
45. Pioneer Tobacco, *Illustrated London News*, August 18, 1900, p. 251.
46. Beecham's Pills, *Illustrated London News*, August 18, 1900, p. 251.
47. Sapolio, *Illustrated London News*, July–December 1889, p. 577.
48. Brooke's Soap, *Illustrated London News*, Christmas Number, 1901, p. 39.
49. Huntley & Palmer Biscuits, the John Johnson Collection, Food 1, 1877.
50. Rose's Lime Juice, *Queen*, August 14, 1885.
51. Pears' Soap, *Illustrated London News*, October 19, 1901, p. 587.
52. Pears' Soap, *Illustrated London News*, January–June 1890, p. 253.

53. Sunlight Soap, *Illustrated London News*, June 24, 1893, p. 775.

54. Mazawattee Tea, painting by G. Sheridan Knowles, R. I., the John Johnson Collection, Tea and Coffee I, 1892.

55. Mme. Rubinstein's Maison de Beauté, *Queen*, May 7, 1910.

56. Eno's, *Illustrated London News*, May 23, 1891, p. 689.

57. Lipton Tea, *Illustrated London News*, July–December 1894, p. 27.

58. Vinolia Soap, *Illustrated London News*, January 6, 1900, p. 33.

59. Monkey Brand Soap, *Illustrated London News*, March 10, 1908, p. 345.

60. Beecham's Pills, *Illustrated London News*, January–June 1900, p. 623.

61. Buttercup Metal Polish, *The Lady*, July 1, 1897, p. 29.

62. Ogden's Cigarettes, *Illustrated London News*, March 10, 1900, p. 343.

63. Odgen's Cigarettes, *Illustrated London News*, December 21, 1901, p. 983.

64. Ogden's Cigarettes, *Illustrated London News*, November 23, 1901, p. 802.

65. Monkey Brand Soap, *Illustrated London News*, March 31, 1894, p. 405.

66. Monkey Brand Soap, *Illustrated London News*, June 19, 1886, p. 668.

67. Avoncherra Tea, *Illustrated London News*, February 18, 1893, p. 223.

68. Ogden's Cigarettes, *Illustrated London News*, October 6, 1900, p. 505.

69. Javol Hair Tonic, *Illustrated London News*, January 20, 1906, p. 96.

70. Ogden's Cigarettes, *Illustrated London News*, July–December 1900, p. 546.

71. Villa Washer, *Hand and Heart*, April 9, 1880, p. 445.

Chapter 7

1. Colin Campbell, *The Romantic Ethic and the Spirit of Modern Consumerism* (Oxford: Clarendon Press, 1987), p. 43.

2. Harold Perkin, pp. 96–97.

3. Neil McKendrick and J. H. Plumb, p. 11.

4. Joseph Banks, p. 52.

5. See Ellen Moers, *Dandyism* (London: Secker & Warburg, 1960) and Mark Girouard, *The Victorian Country House* (New Haven: Yale University Press, 1987), p. 13.

6. David Spring (ed.), *European Landed Elite in the Nineteenth Century* (London: Johns Hopkins University Press, 1977), p. 24.

7. David Cannadine, *The Decline and Fall of the British Aristocracy* (New Haven: Yale University Press, 1990); W. D. Rubinstein, *Men of Property: The Very Wealthy in Britain Since the Industrial Revolution* (London: Croom Helm, 1981); W. D. Rubinstein, *Elites and the Wealthy in Modern Britain* (New York: St. Martin's Press, 1987).

8. W. Hamish Fraser, *The Coming of the Mass Market 1850–1914* (London: Archo Books, 1981).

9. Asa Briggs, *Friends of the People* (London: B. T. Batsford, 1956).

10. Derek Fraser, *The Evolution of the British Welfare State* (London: MacMillan, 1973).

11. Perkin, p. 298.

12. Perkin, pp. 225–230.

13. Harold Perkin, *Rise of Professional Society* (London: Routledge, 1989), pp. 41–42.

14. Harold Perkin, *The Rise of Professional Society*, pp. 29–30.

15. Quoted in John Burnett, *Plenty and Want* (London: Methuen, 1966), p. 126.

16. Perkin, p. 36.

17. Parisian Diamonds, *Lady's Pictorial*, August 7, 1897.

18. International Fur Store, *Lady's Pictorial*, November 17, 1900.

19. Pianola Pianos, *Illustrated London News*, February 19, 1910, p. 285.

20. Pianola Pianos, *Illustrated London News*, June 11, 1910, p. 929.

21. Faulkner's Diamonds, *Illustrated London News*, July–December 1889, p. 541.

22. Sarl Plate, *Illustrated London News*, January–June 1850, p. 104.

23. Goldsmith's Alliance, *Illustrated London News*, 1880, p. 312.

24. John Bennett Ltd., *Illustrated London News*, December 15, 1900, p. 905.

25. Benson's Watches, *Illustrated London News*, January–June 1900, p. 29.

26. Ingersoll Watches, *Christian Age*, May 6, 1910, p. v.

27. Goldsmith's Alliance, *Queen*, May 3, 1890, p. xxx.

28. Howell & James Ltd., *Queen*, May 3, 1890, p. xxvi.

29. Gamage Cycles, *Chums*, v. 7, 1891, p. 272.

30. Juno Cycles, *Chums*, v. 7, 1898, p. 624.

31. Treloar & Sons, *Illustrated London News*, June 18, 1887, p. 703.

32. A. Ferguson & Co., *Queen*, May 7, 1910.

33. Samuel Peach & Sons, *Christian Age*, May 5, 1880, p. iii.

34. W. J. Harris Sewing Machine, *Queen*, May 3, 1890, p. xliv.

35. Evan's Matchless Kitchener, *Peter Parley's Annual*, 1863, pp. 10–11.

36. American Challenge Stove, *Family Circle*, April 14, 1885, p. 180.

37. Villa Washer, *Hand and Heart*, May 21, 1880, p. 554.

38. Excelsior Lawnmowers, *Queen*, May 3, 1890, p. xvi.

39. Pink's Jams, *Christian Age*, May 6, 1910, p. 11.

40. Ridge's Food, *Lady's Pictorial*, August 5, 1893, p. xvi.

41. Kodak, *Chums*, v. 7, 1898/1899, p. 624.

42. See John Pemble, *The Mediterranean Passion* (Oxford: Clarendon Press, 1987).

43. Williams' Shaving Soap, *Illustrated London News*, April 14, 1900, p. 525.

44. Fry's Cocoa, *Illustrated London News*, July–December 1894, p. 87.

45. U.K. Tea, *Illustrated London News*, January–June 1890, p. 122.

46. Pears' Soap, *Illustrated London News*, July–December 1894, p. 27.

47. Bird's Custard Powder, *Illustrated London News*, Christmas Issue 1906, p. 40.

48. Gas Heating, *Court Journal*, May 25, 1910, p. 699.

49. Gamage Table Tennis, *Chums*, 1902, p. 224.

50. Elliman's Embrocation, *Illustrated London News*, January–June 1890, p. 57.

51. Beetham's Glycerine & Cucumber Lotion, *Illustrated London News*, July–December 1890, p. 731.

52. Ross's Ginger Ale, *Illustrated London News*, April–June 1900, p. 991.

53. Fry's Cocoa, *Illustrated London News*, February 5, 1910, p. 213.

54. Bovril, the John Johnson Collection, Food 5.

55. Carron Firegrates, *Illustrated London News*, April 2, 1910, p. 513.

56. Fry's Cocoa, *Illustrated London News*, 1910, p. 365.

57. Cuticura, *Illustrated London News*, July–December 1900, p. 549.

58. Swan Soap, *Illustrated London News*, July–December 1900, p. 953.

59. Eno's, *Queen*, May 28, 1910, p. 4.

60. Old Bleach Linen, *Court Journal*, April 26, 1890, p. 695.

61. Jeremy Maas, *Victorian Painters* (London: Barrie & Jenkins, 1969), p. 178.

62. Pears' Soap, the John Johnson Collection, Soap 5, December 1892.

63. Beecham's Pills, *Illustrated London News*, 1890, p. 255.

64. Jeyes' Disinfectant, *Lady's Pictorial*, September 16, 1893.

65. Jenkyns, p. 14.

66. U.K. Tea, *The Illustrated London News*, October 22, 1892, p. 529.

67. Beecham's Pills, *Illustrated London News*, May 25, 1901, p. 769.

68. Opaline, *Queen*, May 7, 1910.

69. Monkey Brand Soap, *Illustrated London News*, January 27, 1906, p. 130.

70. Beecham's Pills, *Illustrated London News*, January 27, 1894, p. 128.

71. Mellin's Food, *Illustrated London News*, June 8, 1901, p. 839.

Chapter 8

1. Yi-Fu Tuan, *The Good Life* (Madison: University of Wisconsin Press, 1986).

2. J. Duvelleroy Fans, *Court Journal*, May 3, 1890, p. 724.

3. Jay's, *Court Journal*, June 25, 1885, n.p.

4. Jaeger Woollens, *Court Journal*, May 3, 1890, p. 720.

5. Sandow Corsets, *Queen*, May 7, 1910, p. 53.

6. Floriline, *Illustrated London News*, Christmas Supplement, 1880, p. 14.

7. Osler China, *Illustrated Sporting and Dramatic News*, November 29, 1890, p. 393.

8. Mother Siegel's Soothing Syrup, the John Johnson Collection, Patent Medicine 7, 1880.

9. Angelus Autopiano, *Illustrated London News*, November 5, 1910, p. 721.

10. Simpitrol Lighting, *Queen*, May 7, 1910, n.p.

11. Philips' Toilet Aquarius, *The Illustrated London News*, July 12, 1890, p. 59.

12. Beecham's Pills, *Illustrated London News*, May 25, 1901, p. 769.

13. Beecham's Pills, *Illustrated London News*, January 27, 1894, p. 128.

14. U.K. Tea, *Illustrated London News*, February 6, 1892, p. 185.

Bibliography

Victorian Periodicals

Advertiser's Monthly Circular and Prices, January–November 1895.
Advertiser's Review, April 1899–24 December 1904.
Advertiser's Weekly, April 1913–1969.
Advertising: A Monthly Journal for Every Advertiser, 1891–1914.
Advertising Review, 1936–1940.
Advertising World, 1901–1940.
Atalanta, 1888–1893.
Black and White, 1891–1899.
Cartwright's Lady's Companion: A Journal for Women and Girls, 10 December 1892–
    27 February 1915.
Cassell's Family Magazine.
Chatterbox, 1871–1877.
The Child's Companion, 1824–1889.
Children's Friend, 1824–1882.
The Christian: A Weekly Record of Christian Life and Testimony, Evangelical Effort and
    Missionary Enterprise, 1870–1964.
The Christian Age: Sunday Reading for the Home, 1871–1917.
The Christian Million, October 1883–December 1905.
The Christian World: Family Circle Edition, 1 January 1878–December 1897.
Chums, 1892–1914.
The Court Circular: A Journal of Fashion, Literature, Science and Art, 26 April 1856–
    July 1911.
The Court Journal, 2 May 1829–13 March 1925.
Every Boy's Annual, 1873–1887.
Every Girl's Annual, 1882–1888.
The Graphic, 1869–1932.
The Grocer, 4 January 1862–30 October 1886.
Hand and Heart, 1881–1903.

Hearth and Home: An Illustrated Weekly Journal for Gentlewomen, 21 May 1891–
    29 January 1914. (incorporated with *Vanity Fair*)
Home Chat: A Weekly Journal for the Home, 23 March 1895-11 February 1956.
Home Chimes, 1884–1894.
Home Circle, 20 April 1901–5 December 1914.
Home Friend, 1885–1856.
Home Sweet Home: A Journal of Stories and Pictures for Everybody, 18 March 1893–
    13 April 1901.
Illustrated London News, 1842+.
Illustrated Sporting and Dramatic News, 28 February 1874–22 January 1943.
Ladies' Field, 19 March 1898–25 March 1922.
The Ladies' Monthly Magazine, 1852–1891.
The Lady, 19 February 1885+.
The Lady's Newspapaer and Pictorial Times, 2 January 1847–27 June 1863 (incorpo-
    rated with *The Queen*).
Lady's Pictorial, 5 March 1881–26 February 1921.
Lady's Realm, 1896–1909.
Ladies' Review, 9 April 1892–December 1908.
Little Folks, 1875–1907.
Little Wide Awake, 1880–1888.
Madame, 21 September 1895–7 June 1913.
Myra's Journal of Dress and Fashion, February 1875–August 1912.
Peter Parley's Annual, 1856–1888.
Pick-Me-Up, 1888–1903.
Pictorial World, 1882–1892.
The Queen, 1861+.
Routledge's Annual Advertiser.
The Sketch: A Journal of Art and Actuality, 1 February–17 June 1959.
The Sphere: An Illustrated Newspaper for the Home, 27 January 1900–27 June 1960.
Truth, 4 January 1877–27 December 1957.
Vanity Fair, 1878–1905.
Weldon's Ladies' Journal of Dress, Fashion, Needlework, Literature and Art, July 1879–
    March 1954.
Women's World, 1887–1890.
World of Dress, April 1898–February 1909.
Young Ladies' Journal, 13 April 1864–February 1920.

Printed Sources Before 1918

"The Arts of Advertising." *The Leisure Hour*. October 6, 1866.
Babbage, Charles. *The Exposition of 1851*. London: John Murray, 1851.
Carlyle, Thomas. *On Heroes, Hero-Worship*. London: Chapman & Hall Ltd., 1897.
Cassell's Household Guide. London: Cassell, Petter & Galpin, 1869–1871.
"Coronation Advertising." *Advertising*. April 1902, pp. 348–350.
Ellis, Mrs. *The Women of England: Their Social Duties and Domestic Habits*. London:
    Fisher & Sons Co., 1839.
Ellis, Mrs. *The Mothers of England: Their Influence and Responsibility*. London: Peter
    Jackson, Late Fisher & Son Co., 1846.
Family Doctor. "The Adulteration of Food: How to Detect or Avoid It." *Cassell's
    Family Magazine*, 1877, pp. 462–465.

Haweis, Mary Eliza. *The Art of Housekeeping*. London: Sampson Low, Marston, Searle and Rivington Ltd., 1889.

"Food and Its Adulterations." *Quarterly Review*. v. 96, 1854–1855, pp. 460–493.

House of Commons. *Report from the Select Committee on Patent Medicines*. London: His Majesty's Stationery Office, August 1914.

Mill, J. S. *On Liberty*. London: Murray & Sons, 1859.

Palmer, H. J. "The March of the Advertiser." *The Nineteenth Century*. January 1897, pp. 135–141.

Praga, Mrs. Alfred. *Appearances: How to Keep Them Up On A Limited Income*. London: J. Lang, 1899.

Quarterly Review, "Advertisements." v. 97, 1855, pp. 183–225.

Ruskin, John. *Sesame and Lilies*. New York: J. Lupton & Co., 1896.

Sampson, Henry. *A History of Advertising From Earliest Times*. London: Chatto & Windus, 1874.

Teignmouth Shore, W. "The Craft of the Advertiser." *Fortnightly Review*. February 1907, pp. 301–310.

Tonnies, Ferdinand. *Gemeinschaft and Gesellschaft*. Ts. Charles Loomis. East Lansing: University of Michigan Press, 1964.

Veblen, Thorstein. *The Theory of the Leisure Class*. New York: Macmillan, 1908.

Walsh, John Henry. *A Manual of Domestic Economy*. London: G. Routledge & Co., 1857.

Warren. Eliza. *How I Managed My House on Two Hundred Pounds a Year*. London: Houlston & Wright, 1864.

Victorian Ephemera

The John Johnson Collection of Printed Ephemera, Bodleian Library
Advertisement Blanks, Boxes 1–2.
Advertisers, Boxes 1–29.
Bazaars and Sales, Box 1.
Beauty Parlour, Boxes 1–4.
Blotters, Box 1.
Bookmarkers, Boxes 5–7.
Boots and Shoes, Boxes 1–2.
Calico, Box 1.
Clocks, Boxes 1–2.
Clothing, Boxes 1–15.
Cookery and Household, Boxes 1–2.
Dentistry, Box 1.
Domestic Pets, Boxes 1–2.
Fashion, Boxes 1–24.
Electrical Advertisements, Box 1.
Electricity and Electrical Appliances, Boxes 1–3.
Fancy Work, Boxes 1–5.
Fire Fighting Applainces, Box 1.
Fire Grates, Cooking Ranges etc., Box 1.
Food, Boxes 1–9.
Fuel, Box 1.
Funerary, Boxes 1–5.
Furniture, Boxes 1–5.

Gas and Gas Appliances, Boxes 1–2.
Gramophones, Boxes 1–3.
Hats, Box 1.
Houses, Boxes 1–9.
Indoor Games, Boxes 4–9.
Iron Foundries and Machinery, Box 1.
Ironmongery, Box 1–6.
Men's Clothing, Boxes 1–6.
Moveables, Box 1.
Musical Instruments, Boxes 1–3.
Office Equipment, Boxes 1–3.
Oil Lamps and Candles, Boxes 1–2.
Oil Lamps and Stoves, Box 1.
Paperbags, Boxes 1–3.
Patent Medicine, Box 1–14.
Scientific Instruments, Boxes 1–2.
Sewing Cottons and Machines, Box 1.
Shops and Shopping, Boxes 1–2.
Silver, Jewellery, Box 1.
Silver Jewellery, Plate Cutlery, Pewter and Commemorative Pieces, Boxes 1–2.
Soap, Box 1–8.
Soft Drinks, Box 1.
Tea and Coffee, Boxes 1–4.
Tea and Grocery Papers, Boxes 1–3.
Tobacco, Boxes 1–4.
Toys/Games, Folder 1.
Umbrellas and Trunks, Box 1.
Watches and Clocks, Boxes 1–2.
Window Bills and Advertisements, Boxes 1–4.
Wines and Spirits, Boxes 1–6.
Women's Clothes and Millinery, Boxes 1–9.

Unpublished Theses

Berridge, Virginia S. "Popular Journalism and Working Class Attitudes, 1854–1886: A Study of Reynolds Newspaper and Lloyd's Weekly Newspaper." Ph.D. Thesis, University of London, 1976.

Fox, Frank. "Advertising and the Second World War." Ph.D. Dissertation, Stanford University, 1973.

Nevett, T. R. "The Development of Commercial Advertising in Britain 1800–1914." Ph.D. Thesis, University of London, 1979.

Pope, Daniel Andrew. "The Development of National Advertising 1865–1920." Ph.D. Dissertation, Columbia University, 1973.

Storer, Louis Kennison. "Military and Nationalistic Themes in War-Time American Consumer Advertising." Ph.D. Dissertation, New York University, 1971.

Printed Sources Published After 1918

Aaker, David, and George S. Day. *Consumerism: Search for the Consumer*. New York: The Free Press, 1971.

Alexander, David. *Retailing in the Industrial Revolution*. London: Atholone Press, 1970.

Altick, Richard. *The English Common Reader*. Chicago: University of Chicago Press, 1967.

Anderson, Gregory. *Victorian Clerks*. Manchester: Manchester University Press, 1976.

Anderson, Michael. *Approaches to the History of the Western Family*. London: MacMillan Press, 1980.

Andren, Gunnar et al. *Rhetoric and Ideology in Advertising: A Content Analytical Study of American Advertising*. Stockholm: LiberForlag, 1978.

Aspinall, Arthur. *Politics and the Press*. London: Home & Van Thal, 1959.

Attar, Dena. *A Bibliography of Household Books Published in Britain 1800–1914*. v. I. London: Prospect Books, 1987.

Bailey, Peter. *Leisure and Class in Victorian England: Rational Recreation and the Contest for Control 1830–1885*. London: Routledge & Kegan Paul, 1987.

Baker, Michael. *The Rise of the Victorian Actor*. London: Croom Helm, 1978.

Banks, J. A. *Prosperity and Parenthood*. London: Routledge & Kegan Paul, 1954.

Banks, J. A. and Olive. *Feminism and Family Planning*. Liverpool: Liverpool University Press, 1964.

Banks, J. A. *Victorian Values: Secularism and the Size of Families*. London: Routledge & Kegan Paul, 1981.

Barker, T. C., J. C. McKenzie, and J. Yudkin. *Our Changing Fare*. London: MacGibbon & Kee, 1966.

Barish, Jonas. *The Antitheatrical Prejudice*. Berkley: University of California Press, 1981.

Barthel, Diane. *Putting on Appearances: Gender & Advertising*. Philadelphia: Temple University Press, 1988.

Basch, Francoise. *Relative Creatures: Victorian Women in Society and the Novel*. New York: Schocken Books, 1974.

Bebbington, D. W. *Evangelicalism in Modern Britain*. London: Unwin Hyman, 1989.

Belk, Russell W. and Richard Pollay. "Images of Ourselves: The Good Life in Twentieth Century Magazine Advertisements," *Journal of Consumer Research*, March 1985, vol. 11, no. 4, pp. 887–897.

Belkaoui, Ahmed and Janice. "A Comparative Analysis of the Roles Portrayed by Women in Print Advertisements, 1958, 1970, 1972," *Journal of Marketing Research*, May 1976, vol. 13, pp. 168–172.

Bensman, Joseph and Robert Lilienfeld. *Between Public and Private: The Lost Boundaries of the Self*. London: MacMillan, 1979.

Benson, Susan P. *Counter Cultures: Saleswomen, Managers and Customers in American Department Stores 1890–1914*. Urbana: University of Illionis Press, 1986.

Berelson, Bernard. *Content Analysis in Communication Research*. New York: Hafner Publishing Co., 1952.

Berman, Ronald. *Advertising and Social Change*. Beverly Hills: Sage Publications, 1981.

Berridge, Virginia and Griffith Edwards. *Opium and the People*. London: St. Martin's Press, 1981.

Bloom, Paul N./Ruth Belk Smith. *The Future of Consumerism*. Toronto: Lexington Books, 1986.

Bradley, Ian. *The English Middle Classes Are Alive and Kicking*. London: Collins, 1982.

Branca, Patricia. "Image and Reality: the Myth of the Idle Victorian Woman" in Hurtman, Mary and Lois W. Banner (eds.), *Clio's Consciousness Raised*. New York: Harper, 1974, pp. 179–191.

Branca, Patricia. *Silent Sisterhood: Middle Class Women in the Victorian Home*. London: Croom Helm, 1975.

Branca, Patricia. *Women in Europe Since 1750*. London: Croom Helm, 1978.

Braudy, Leo. *The Frenzy of Renown: Fame and Its History*. New York: Oxford University Press, 1986.

Braun, John. *Advertisements in Court*. London: David Fanning, 1965.

Briggs, Asa. *Friends of the People*. London: B.T. Batsford, 1956.

Briggs, Asa. "Middle Class Consciousness in English Politics," *Past and Present*. 1956.

Briggs, Asa. *Victorian Things*. London: B.T. Batsford, 1988.

Briggs, Asa. *Victorian Wine and the Liquor Trade 1860–1984*. London: B.T. Batsford, 1985.

Brown, Lucy. *Victorian News and Newspapers*. Oxford: Clarendon Press, 1985.

Buccellati, Graziella. *Biscuits*. Milano: Franco Maria Ricci, 1982.

Buckley, Jerome Hamilton. *Tennyson: The Growth of a Poet*. Cambridge: Harvard University Press, 1960.

Buckley, Jerome Hamilton. *The Triumph of Time: A Study of Victorian Concepts of Time, History, Progress and Decadence*. Cambridge: Harvard University Press, 1966.

Burman, Sandra (ed.) *Fit Work for Women*. New York: St. Martin's Press, 1979.

Burnett, John. *A History of the Cost of Living*. Harmondsworth: Penguin Books, 1969.

Burnett, John. *Plenty and Want: A Social History of Diet in England from 1815 to Present Day*. London: Methuen, 1966.

Burton, Elizabeth. *The Early Victorians at Home 1831–1861*. London: Arrow Books Ltd., 1972.

Bury, John Bagnall. *The Idea of Progress*. London: MacMillan & Co. 1928.

Calder, Jenni, *The Victorian and Edwardian Home from Old Photographs*. London: Batsford, 1979.

Calder, Jenni. *The Victorian Home*. London: Batsford, 1977.

Campbell, Colin. *The Romantic Ethic and the Spirit of Modern Consumerism*. London: Basil Blackwell, 1987.

Cannadine, David. "The Context, Performance and Meaning of Ritual" in E. Hobsbawm (ed.), *The Invention of Tradition*. Cambridge: Cambridge University Press, 1983.

Cannadine, David. *The Decline and Fall of the British Aristocracy*. New Haven: Yale University Press, 1990.

Carney, Thomas F. *Content Analysis: A Technique of Systematic Inference from Communications*. Winnipeg: University of Manitoba Press, 1972.

Cartwright, D. P. "Analysis of Qualitiative Material" in L. Festinger and D. Katz (eds.), *Research Methods in the Behavioural Sciences*. New York: Holt, Rinehart & Winston, 1953.

Casteras, Susan. *Images of Victorian Womanhood in English Art*. Cranbury, New Jersey: Associated University Press, 1987.

Casteras, Susan. *The Substance or the Shadow: Images of Victorian Womanhood.* New Haven: Yale Center for British Art, 1982.

Chadwick, Owen. *The Victorian Church.* London: SCM Press Ltd., 1966.

Chapman, Stanley. *Jesse Boot of Boots the Chemist.* London: Hodder & Stoughton, 1973.

Clair, Colin. *A History of Printing in Britain.* London: Cassell, 1956.

Clark, Eric. *The Want Makers: The World of Advertising. How They Make You Buy.* New York: Viking, 1988.

Collier, J. and M. *Visual Anthropology: Photography as a Research Method.* Alburquerque: University of New Mexico, 1986.

Colls, Robert and Phillip Dodd. *Englishness: Politics and Culture 1880–1920.* London: Croom Helm, 1986.

Colman, J. & J. Ltd. *The Advertising of J. & J. Colman.* London: J. & J. Colman Ltd., 1977.

Cominos, Peter. "Late Victorian Sexual Respectability and the Social System." *International Review of Social History.* v. 8, 1963, pp. 18–48, 216–250.

Cooper, Nicholas. *The Opulent Eye: Late Victorian and Edwardian Taste.* London: Architectural Press, 1977.

Corina, Maurice. *Fine Silks and Oak Counters: Debenham's 1778–1978.* London: Hutchinson Benham, 1978.

Corley, T. A. *Quaker Enterprise in Biscuits: Huntley & Palmer of Reading 1822–1972.* London: Hutchinson, 1972.

Cornforth, John. *English Interiors 1770–1848.* London: Barrie & Jenkins, 1978.

Cott, Nancy. "Passionless: An Interpretation of Victorian Sexual Ideology, 1790–1850." *Signs.* v. 4, 1978.

Courtney, Alice and Sara Wernier Lockertz. "A Woman's Place: An Analysis of the Roles Portrayed by Women in Magazine Advertisements." *Journal of Marketing Research.* v. 8, February 1971, pp. 92–95.

Courtney, Alice E. and Thomas W. Whipple. *Sex-Stereotyping in Advertising.* Toronto: Lexington Books, 1983.

Cowan, Ruth Schwartz. *More Work for Mother.* New York: Basic Books, 1983.

Crow, Duncan. *The Edwardian Woman.* London: George Allen & Unwin, 1978.

Crow, Duncan. *The Victorian Woman.* London: George, Allen & Unwin, 1971.

Csikszentimihaly, Mihaly and Eugene Rochberg-Halton. *The Meaning of Things: Domestic Symbols and the Self.* Cambridge: Cambridge University Press, 1981.

Cullin, M. J. *The Statistical Movement in Early Victorian Britain.* London: Harvester Press, 1975.

Curl, James Stevens. *The Victorian Celebration of Death.* London: David & Charles, 1972.

Daedalus. "The Family." Spring 1977.

Davenport-Hines, Richard. *Sex, Death and Punishment: Attitudes to Sex and Sexuality in Britian Since the Renaissance.* London: Collins, 1990.

Davidoff, Leonore and Catherine Hall. *The Best Circles.* London: Croom Helm, 1973.

Davidoff, Leonore. *Family Fortunes: Men and Women of the English Middle Classes 1780–1850.* Chicago: University of Chicago Press, 1987.

Davidson, C. *A Woman's Work Is Never Done.* London: Chatto & Windus, 1982.

Davin, Anna. "Imperialism and Motherhood," *History Workshop Journal.* v. 5, Spring 1978, pp. 9–65.

Davis, Dorothy. *A History of Shopping*. Toronto: University of Toronto Press, 1966.

Davis, Kathy. "Critical Sociology and Gender Relations," *The Gender of Power*. London: Sage Publications, 1991.

Delamont, Sara and Lorna Duffin (eds.). *The Nineteenth Century Woman*. London: Croom Helm, 1978.

De Vries, Leonard. *Victorian Advertisements*. London: John Murray, 1968.

Dempsey, Mike and Tim Schackleton, Tim. *Pipe Dreams: Early Advertisement Art from the Imperial Tobacco Co.* London: Pavillion Books, 1982.

Dempsey, Mike (ed.). *Early Advertisement Art from A. and F. Pears' Ltd.* London: William Collins & Co., 1978.

Dijkstra, Bram. *Idols of Perversity: Fantasies of Feminine Evil in Fin-de-Siècle Culture*. Oxford: Oxford University Press, 1986.

Dispenza, Joseph. *Advertising the American Woman*. Dayton: Pflaum Publications, 1975.

Dondis, Donis. *A Primer of Visual Literacy*. Cambridge, Massachussetts: M.I.T. Press, 1973.

Dornbusch, S. and L.C. Hickman. "Other Directedness in Consumer Goods Advertising." *Social Forces*. v. 38, December 1959, pp. 98–101.

Douglas, Mary Tew. *World of Goods*. London: Penguin Books, 1983.

Drummond, J. C. and William Graham. *The Englishman's Food*. London: Jonathan Cape, 1939.

Dyhouse, Carol. *Girls Growing Up in Late Victorian and Edwardian England*. London: Routledge & Kegan Paul, 1981.

Dyhouse, Carol. "Mothers and Daughters in the Middle Class Home c. 1870–1914" in Jane Lewis (ed.), *Labour and Love: Women's Experience of Home and Family 1850–1914*. Oxford: Basil Blackwell, 1986.

Earle, Peter. *The Making of the English Middle Class*. London: Methuen, 1989.

Edelstein, T. J. "Augustus Egg's Triptych: A Narrative of Victorian Adultery." *The Burlington Magazine*. v. 125, April 1983, pp. 202–210.

Egoff, Shiela A. *Children's Periodicals of the Nineteenth Century: A Survey and Bibliography*. Library Association Pamphlet #8. London: Library Association, 1951.

Ehrenreich, Barbara and Deirdre English. *For Her Own Good: 150 Years of the Experts' Advice to Women*. Garden City: Anchor Press, 1978.

Ellegard, Alvar. *The Readership of the Periodical Press in Mid Victorian Britain*. Stockholm: Goteberg, 1957.

Elliott, Blanche E. *A History of English Advertising*. London: B.T. Batsford, 1962.

Errington, Lindsay. *Social and Religious Themes in English Art 1840–1860*. New York: Garland, 1984.

Ewen, Stuart. *Captains of Consciousness: Advertising and the Social Roots of Consumer Culture*. New York: McGraw-Hill, 1976.

Ewen, Stuart and Elizabeth. *Channels of Desire: Mass Images and the Shaping of American Consciousness*. New York: McGraw-Hill, 1982.

Fletcher, T. W. "The Great Depression 1873–1896." *Economic History Review*, 2nd series, v. 13, April 1961, pp. 417–439.

Flower, Margaret. *Victorian Jewellery*. London: Cassell, 1967.

Flugel, John Carl. *The Psychology of Clothes*. New York: IUP Paperbacks, 1969.

Foster, Vanda. *A Visual History of Costume in the Nineteenth Century*. London: Batsford, 1984.

Fowles, Jib. *Mass Advertising as Social Forecast*. Westport, Conn.: Greenwood, 1976.

Fox, Frank. *Madison Ave. Goes to War: The Strange Military Career of American Advertising*. Provo, Utah: Brigham Young University, 1975.

Fox, Richard Wightman and T. Jackson Lears. *Culture of Consumption*. New York: Pantheon Books, 1983.

Fox, Stephen. *Mirror Makers: A History of American Advertising and Its Creators*. New York: William Morrow & Co., 1984.

Fraser, Antonia. *A History of Toys*. London: Weidenfeld & Nicholson, 1967.

Freeman, Sarah. *Isabella & Sam: The Story of Mrs. Beeton*. London: Victor Gollancz Ltd., 1977.

Furst, Lilian. *Contours of European Romanticism*. London: MacMillan, 1979.

Gay, Peter. *The Bourgeois Experience, Victoria to Freud: Education of the Senses*. v. 1. New York: Oxford University Press, 1984.

Gay, Peter. *The Bourgeois Experience, Victoria to Freud: The Tender Passion*. v. 2. New York: Oxford University Press, 1986.

Gay, Peter. *Freud for Historians*. New York: Oxford University Press, 1985.

Gernsheim, Alison. *Fashion and Reality 1840–1914*. London: Faber & Faber, 1974.

Gilbert, Alan. *The Making of Post-Christian Britain*. London: Longman, 1980.

Gillis, John R. *For Better for Worse: British Marriages 1600 to the Present*. London: Oxford Unviersity Press, 1985.

Gillis, John R. *Youth and History: Tradition and Change in European Age Relations 1770–Present*. New York: Academic Press, 1974.

Ginsburg, M. *Victorian Dress in Photographs*. London: Batsford, 1982.

Girouard, Mark. *The Victorian Country House*. New Haven: Yale University Press, 1979.

Gittins, Diana. *Fair Sex: Family Size and Structure 1900–1939*. London: Hutchinson, 1982.

Gloag, John. *The Englishman's Chair*. London: Allen & Unwin, 1964.

Gloag, John. *Victorian Comfort*. London: A. C. Black, 1961.

Gold, Philip. *Advertising, Politics and American Culture: From Salesmanship to Therapy*. New York: Paragon, 1987.

Goldthorpe, John. *The Affluent Worker in the Class Structure*. London: Cambridge University Press, 1969.

Gorham, Deborah. *The Victorian Girl and the Feminine Ideal*. Bloomington: Inidian University Press, 1982.

Graham, Irvin. *Encyclopedia of Advertising*. New York: Fairchild Publications, 1952.

Grant, Michael/John Hazel. *Who's Who in Classical Mythology*. London: Weidenfeld & Nicholson, 1973.

Hadley, Peter. *The History of Bovril Advertising*. London: Alabaster Passmore & Son, n.d.

Haley, Bruce. *The Healthy Body and Victorian Culture*. Cambridge: Harvard University Press, 1978.

Halsted, John B. *Romanticism*. New York: Walker & Co., 1969.

Hamish Fraser, W. *The Coming of the Mass Market 1850–1914*. London: Archon Books, 1981.

Harrison, Fraser. *The Dark Angel: Aspects of Victorian Sexuality*. London: Sheldon Press, 1977.

Harrison, J.F.C. *Early Victorian Britain 1832–1851*. London: Collines, 1971.

Harrison, J.F.C. "The Victorian Gospel of Success," *Victorian Studies*. v. 1, December 1957, pp. 155–164.

Haug, Wolfgang. *Critique of Commodity Aesthetics*. London: Polity Press, 1986.

Hays, H. R. *The Dangerous Sex: The Myth of Feminine Evil*. New York: G. P. Putnam's Sons, 1964.

Heald, Tim. *By Appointment: 150 Hears of Royal Warrant and Its Holders*. London: Queen Anne Press, 1989.

Hewitt, M. *Wives and Mothers in Victorian Industry*. London: Greenwood Press, 1958.

Hichberger, Joan W. M. *Images of the Army: The Military in British Art*. Manchester: Manchester University Press, 1988.

Hindley, Diana and Geoffrey. *Advertising in Victorian England 1837–1901*. London: Wayland, 1972.

Hobsbawm, E. J. *The Age of Empire 1875–1914*. New York: Pantheon Books, 1987.

Hobsbawm, E. J. *Industry and Empire*. Harmondsworth: Penguin Books, 1968.

Holbrook, Stewart. *The Golden Age of Quakery*. New York: Macmillan Co., 1959.

Hollander, Anne. *Seeing Through Clothes*. New York: Viking Press, 1978.

Holme, Brian. *Advertising: Reflections of a Century*. London: Heinemann, 1982.

Holsti, Ole. *Content Analysis for the Social Sciences and Humanities*. Reading, Massachussetts: Addison-Wesley Publishing, 1969.

Honeycombe, Gordon. *Selfridges: Seventy-Five Years. The Story of the Store 1909–1984*. London: Park Lane, 1984.

Houghton, Walter. *The Victorian Frame of Mind*. New Haven: Yale University Press, 1957.

Howe, Ellic. *Newspaper Printing in the Nineteenth Century*. London: Private printing, 1943.

Jarrett, Derek. *The Sleep of Reason: Fantasy and Reality from the Victorian Age to the First World War*. London Weidenfeld & Nicolson, 1988.

Jeffrey, J.B. *Retail Trading in Britain 1850–1950*. Cambridge: Cambridge University Press, 1954.

Jenkyns, Richard. *Dignity and Decadence: Victorian Art and the Classical Inheritance*. London; Harper Collins, 1991.

Jenkyns, Richard. *The Victorians and Ancient Greece*. Oxford: Basil Blackwell, 1980.

Jervis, Simon. *Victorian Furniture*. London: Ward Lock, 1968.

Jordan, Thomas E. *Victorian Childhood*. Albany: University of New York Press, 1987.

Jones, David. *Crime, Protest, Community & Police in Nineteenth Century Britain*. London: Routledge & Kegan Paul, 1982.

Jubb, Michael. *Cocoa & Corsets*. London: Her Majesty's Stationery Office, 1984.

Kassarjian, Harold. "Content Analysis in Consumer Research," *Journal of Consumer Research*. v. 4, June 1977, pp. 8–18.

Kent, Christopher. "Image and Reality: The Actress and Society," in Martha Vicinus (ed.), *A Widening Sphere*. Bloomington: Indiana Unversity Press, 1977, pp. 94-116.

Kern, Stephen. "Explosive Intimacy: Psychodynamics of the Victorian Family." *History of Childhood Quarterly*. v. 1, Winter 1974, pp. 437–462.

Key, Wilson Bryan. *Subliminal Seduction: Advertising Media's Manipulation of a Not So Innocent America*. New York: Signet Books, 1973.

Key, Wilson Bryan. *Media Sexploitation*. Englewood Cliffs, N.J.: Prentice-Hall, 1976.

King, Roger and John Raynor. *The Middle Class*. London: Longman, 1981.

Kitson Clark, George. *The Making of Victorian England*. New York: Atheneum, 1976.

Kitson Clark, George. "The Romantic Element 1830–1850" in *Studies in Social History: A Tribute to G. M. Trevelyan.* London: Longmans, Green & Co., 1955, pp. 209–239.

Klein, Viola. *The Feminine Character: History of an Ideology.* London: Routledge & Kegan Paul, 1946.

Komisar, Lucy. "The Image of Women in Advertising" in Gornich, Vivian and Barbara Morgan (eds.), *Women in Sexist Society.* New York: Basic Books, 1972.

Krippendorff, Klaus. *Content Analysis: An Introduction to its Methodology.* Beverly Hills: Sage Publications, 1980.

Kunzle, David. "Dress Reform as Antifeminism," *Signs.* v. 2, Spring 1977, pp. 570–579.

Lambert, Richard S. *The Universal Provider: A Study of William Whitely and the Rise of the London Department Store.* London: George C. Harrop & Co., 1938.

Landen, Dinsdale and Jennifer Daniel. *The True Story of H.P. Sauce.* London: Metheun, 1985.

Landes, D. S. *Unbound Prometheus: Technological Change and Development in Western Europe 1750–1914.* Cambridge: Cambridge Unviersity Press, 1965.

Lasch, Christopher. *The True and Only Heaven: Progress and Its Critics.* New York: W.W. Norton & Co., 1991.

Laski, Margharita. "Advertising—Sacred and Profane." *The Twentieth Century.* v. 165, 1959, pp. 118–159.

Laslett, Peter. *The World We Have Lost.* London: Methuen & Co. Ltd., 1965.

Lauterbach, Edward, "Victorian Advertising and Magazine Stripping," *Victorian Studies,* v. 10, June 1967, pp. 431–434.

Leech, G. N. *English in Advertising.* London: Longmans, 1966.

Lehman, B. H. *Carlyle's Theory of the Hero.* New York: AMS Press Inc., 1966.

Leiss, William, Stephen Klein, and Sut Jhally. *Communication in Advertising.* Toronto: Nelson Canada Ltd., 1990.

Levenstein, Harvey A. *Revolution at the Table.* London: Oxford University Press, 1988.

Levitt, Sarah. *Victorians Unbuttoned: Registered Designs for Clothing, Their Makers and Wearers 1839–1900.* London: George Allen & Unwin, 1986.

Lewis, Jane (ed.). *Labour and Love: Women's Experience of Home and Family 1850–1914.* London: Basil Blackwell, 1988.

Lewis, Roy and Angus Maude. *The English Middle Classes.* London: Penguin, 1949.

Lister, Raymond. *Victorian Narrative Paintings.* London: Museum Press, 1966.

Lockwood, David. *The Black-Coated Worker.* London: Allen & Unwin, 1958.

Lurie, Alison. *The Language of Clothes.* New York: Random House, 1981.

Maas, Jeremy. *Victorian Painters.* London: Barrie & Jenkins, 1969.

Magnus, Philip. *King Edward the Seventh.* London: John Murray, 1964.

Mangan, J. A. and James Walvin (eds.). *Manliness and Morality: Middle Class Masculinity in Britain and America 1800–1940.* Manchester: Manchester University Press, 1987.

Marchand, Roland. *Advertising the American Dream 1920–1940.* Berkeley: University of California Press, 1985.

Marcus, S. *The Other Victorians.* London: Basic Books, 1964.

Masse, Michelle A. and Karen Rosenhaum. "Male and Female They Created Them: The Depiction of Gender in the Advertising of Traditional Women's and Men's Magazines." *Women's Studies International Forum.* v. 11, 1988, pp. 127–144.

Mathias, Peter. *Retailing Revolution.* London: Longman's, 1967.

Mayfield, Frank M. *The Department Store.* New York: Fairchild Publishing, 1949.

McBride, Theresa. *The Domestic Revolution.* New York: Holmes & Meier Inc., 1976.

McGregor, O. R. *Divorce in England.* London: William Heinemann Ltd., 1957.

McKendrick, Neil and J. H. Plumb. *Birth of a Consumer Society.* London: Europa Publications, 1982.

McPherson, Bruce. *Between Two Worlds: Victorian Ambivalence About Progress.* Washington: University Press of America Inc., 1983.

Mechling, Jay. "Advice to Historians on Advice to Mothers." *Journal of Social History.* v. 9, 1975, pp. 44–63.

Meisel, Martin. *Realizations: Narrative, Pictorial and Theatrical Arts.* Princeton: Princeton University Press, 1983.

Meyers, William. *The Image Makers.* New York: Times Books, 1984.

Middlemas, Keith. *Pursuit of Pleasure: High Society in the 1900s.* London: Gordon & Cremonesi, 1977.

Millet, Kate. *Sexual Politics.* New York: Doubleday, 1970.

Millum, Trevor. *Images of Women: Advertising in Women's Magazines.* London: Chatto & Windus, 1975.

Mintz, Steven. *A Prison of Expectations: The Family in Victorian Culture.* New York: University Press, 1983.

Mitchell, Juliet. *Woman's Estate.* New York: Random House, 1973.

Mitterauer, Michael and Reinhard Sieder. *The European Family: Patriarchy to Partnership.* 1982.

Moers, Ellen. *Dandyism.* London: Secker & Warberg, 1960.

Moog, Carol. *"Are They Selling Her Lips?" Advertising and Identity.* New York: William Morrow, 1990.

Moore, Katherine. *Victorian Wives.* London: Allison & Busby, 1974.

Musgrove, Frank. *Youth and Social Order.* London: Routledge & Kegan Paul, 1964.

Nead, Lynda. *Myths of Sexuality: Representations of Women in Victorian Britain.* Oxford: Basil Blackwell, 1988.

Nevett, T. R. *Advertising in Britain.* London Heinemann, 1982.

Nevett, T. R. "London's Early Advertising Agents." *Journal of Advertising History.* December 1977, pp. 15–17.

Nisbet, Robert. *History of the Idea of Progress.* New York: Basic Books, 1980.

Norris, James D. *Advertising and the Transformation of American Society 1865–1920.* New York: Greenwood Press, 1990.

Opie, Robert. *Rule Britannia: Trading on the British Image.* London: Viking Books, 1985.

Opie, Robert. *The Art of the Label.* London: Simon & Schuster, 1987.

Oram, Hugh. *The Advertising Book: The History of Advertising in Ireland.* Dublin: M.O. Books, 1986.

Palmer, Arnold. *Movable Feasts.* Oxford: Oxford University Press, 1984.

Palmer, Bryan. *Descent into Discourse.* Philadelphia: Temple University Press, 1982.

Parssinen, Terry. *Secret Passions, Secret Remedies.* London: Institute for the Study of Human Issues, 1983.

Pearsall, Ronald. *Public Purity, Private Shame.* London: Weidenfeld & Nicolson, 1976.

Pearsall, Ronald. *The Worm in the Bud*. London: Weidenfeld & Nicolson, 1969.

Pemble, John. *The Mediterranean Passion*. Oxford: Clarendon Press, 1987.

Perkin, Harold. *Origins of Modern English Society 1780–1880*. London: Routledge & Kegan Paul Ltd., 1969.

Perkin, Harold. "The Origins of the Popular Press." *History Today*. 1957, pp. 425–435.

Perkin, Harold. *The Rise of Professional Society*. London: Routledge, 1989.

Peterson, M. Jeanne. "No Angels in the House: The Victorian Myth and the Paget Women." *American Historical Review*. v. 89, 1984, pp. 677–708.

Pevsner, Nikolaus. *High Victorian Design: A Study of the Exhibits of 1851*. London: Architectural Press, 1951.

Philips, David. *Crime and Authority in Victorian England*. London: Croom Helm, 1972.

Pigott, Stanley. *OBM (Ogilvy, Benson & Mather) A Celebration: 125 Years in Advertising*. London: OBM, 1975.

Pimlott, J.A.R. *The Englishman's Holiday*. London: Faber & Faber, 1947.

Pollay, Richard. *Information Sources in Advertising History*. Westport: Greenwood Press, 1979.

Pollay, Richard. "The Importance and the Problems of Writing the History of Advertising." *Journal of Advertising History*. v. 1, 1977, pp. 3–5.

Pollay, Richard. "The Subsiding Sizzle: A Descriptive History of Print Advertising 1900–1980." *Journal of Marketing*. v. 49, 1985, pp. 24–37.

Pollay, Richard. "Wanted: A History of Advertising." *Journal of Advertising Research*. v. 18, 1987, pp. 63–68.

Poe, Alison. "Active Women in Advertisements." *Journal of Communication*. v. 26, 1976, pp. 185–192.

Pope, Barbara C. "Angels in the Devil's Workshop: Leisured and Charitable Women in Nineteenth Century England and France" in Bridenthal, Renata, Koonz, *Becoming Visible: Women in European History*. Boston: Houghton Mifflin Co., 1977, pp. 296–324.

Pope, Daniel. *The Making of Modern Advertising*. New York: Basic Books, 1983.

Potter, David. *People of Plenty*. Chicago: University of Chicago Press, 1954.

Presbrey, Frank. *The History and Development of Advertising*. Garden City: Doubleday, 1929.

Rattray Taylor, Gordon. *The Angel-Makers: A Study in the Psychological Origins of Historical Change 1750–1850*. London: Secker & Warburg, 1958.

Raynor, John. *The Middle Class*. London: Longmans, 1969.

Reed, John R. *Decadent Style*. Athens: Ohio University Press, 1985.

Reed, Walter. *Meditations on the Hero: A Study of the Romantic Hero in Nineteenth Century Fiction*. New Haven: Yale University Press, 1974.

Rees, Barbara. *The Victorian Lady*. London: Gordon & Cremonesi, 1977.

Rees, Goronwy. *St. Michael: A History of Marks and Spencer*. London: Weidenfeld & Nicolson, 1969.

Richards, Thomas. *The Commodity Culture of Victorian England*. Stanford: Stanford University Press, 1990.

Richards, Thomas. "The Image of Victoria in the Year of the Jubilee." *Victorian Studies*. v. 31, 1987, pp. 7–32.

Roberts, Helene E. "The Exquisite Slave: The Role of Clothes in the Making of the Victorian Woman." *Signs*. v. 2, 1977, pp. 554–569.

Robertson, Priscilla. *An Experience of Women: Patterns and Change in Nineteenth Century Europe*. Philadelphia: Temple Unversity Press, 1982.

Rubinstein, W. D. *Elites and the Wealthy in Modern Britain*. New York: St. Martin's Press, 1987.

Rubinstein, W. D. *Men of Property: The Very Wealthy in Britain Since the Industrial Revolution*. London: Croom Helm, 1981.

Rybczynski, Witold. *Home: A Short History of an Idea*. New York: Viking, 1986.

Saul, S. B. *The Myth of the Great Depression*. London: MacMillan, 1972.

Schlereth, Thomas. *Material Culture: A Research Guide*. Lawrence: University of Kansas, 1968.

Scott, Joan. *Gender and the Politics of History*. New York: Columbia University Press, 1991.

Searle, G.R. *The Quest for National Efficiency*. Oxford: Basil Blackwell, 1978.

Semmel, Bernard. *Imperialism and Social Reform*. New York: Doubleday, 1960.

Sender, John. *Images Incorporated: Advertising as Industry and Ideology*. London: Croom Helm, 1987.

Sennett, Richard. *The Fall of Public Man*. New York: Alfred A. Knopf, 1977.

Sexton, Donald and Phyllis Haberman. "Women in Magazine Advertisements." *Journal of Advertising Research*. v. 14, 1974, pp. 41–46.

Sharp, Len. *The Lintas Story: Impressions and Recollections*. London: Lintas Ltd., 1964.

Shaw, Christopher and Malcolm Chase. *The Imagined Past: History and Nostalgia*. Manchester: Manchester University Press, 1989.

Shil, Edward, Trans. *Max Weber on Law in Economics and Society*. New York: Simon & Schuster, 1967.

Shorter, Edward. *The Making of the Modern Family*. New York: Basic Books, 1975.

Simmons, Douglas A. *Schweppes: The First 200 Years*. London: Springwood Books, 1983.

Sinclair, John. *Images Incorporated: Advertising as Industry and Ideology*. London: Croom Helm, 1987.

Smelser, Neil. *Social Change and the Industrial Revolution*. London: Routledge & Kegan Paul, 1959.

Smith, F. Barry. "Sexuality in Britain 1800–1900: Some Suggested Revisions" in Martha Vicinus, *A Widening Sphere*. Bloomington: Indiana University Press, 1977.

Smith, F. B. *The People's Health*. London: Croom Helm, 1979.

Sombart, Werner. *Luxury and Capitalism*. East Lansing: University of Michigan Press, 1967.

Spitzer, Leo. "American Advertising Explained as Popular Art" in *A Method for Interpreting Literature*. Northampton, Massachussetts: Smith College Press, 1949.

Springhall, John. *Coming of Age: Adolescence in Britain 1860–1960*. London: Gill & MacMillan, 1986.

Springhall, John. *Youth, Empire and Society 1883–1940*. London: Croom Helm, 1977.

Stearns, Peter N. *Be a Man! Males in Modern Society*. New York: Holmes & Meier Publishing 1979.

Stone, Lawrence. *Road to Divorce: England 1530–1987*. Oxford: Oxford Unversity Press, 1990.

Strasser, Susan. *Satisfaction Guaranteed: the Making of the American Mass Market*. New York: Pantheon Books, 1989.

Sussman, Herbert. *Victorians and the Machine*. Cambridge: Harvard University Press, 1968.

Taylor, Jane. *Regency and Victorian Crafts or the Genteel Female, Her Arts and Pursuits*. London: Ward Lock, 1969.

Thompson, Dorothy. *Queen Victoria: Gender & Power*. London: Virago, 1990.

Thompson, E. P. *The Poverty of Theory*. New York: Monthly Review Press, 1979.

Thompson, F.M.L. *Rise of Respectable Society*. London: Fontana, 1988.

Thompson, F.M.L. *English Society in the Nineteenth Century*. Toronto: University of Toronto Press, 1963.

Thompson, Paul. *The Edwardians*. St. Albans: Paladian, 1975.

Thornton, R.K.R. *The Decadent Dilemma*. London: Edward Arnold, 1983.

Thorslev, Peter. *The Byronic Hero*. Minneapolis: University of Minnesota, 1962.

Tilly, Louise A. and Joan Scott. *Women, Work and Family*. London: Holt, Rinehart, & Winston, 1978.

Tinter, Adeline L. "The Sleeping Woman: A Victorian Fantasy." *Pre-Raphaelite Review*. v. 2, 1978, pp. 12–26.

Travers, Tim. *Samuel Smiles and the Victorian Work Ethic*. New York: Garland Publishing Inc., 1987.

Trudgill, Eric. *Madonnas & Magdalens*. London: Heinemann, 1976.

Tse, K.K. *Marks & Spencer*. Oxford: Pergamon Press, 1985.

Tuan, Yi-Fu. *The Good Life*. Madison: University of Wisconsin Press, 1986.

Tuchman, Gaye, Arlene Daniels, and J. Benet. *Hearth and Home: Images of Women in the Mass Media*. New York: Oxford University Press, 1978.

Turner, E. S. *The Shocking History of Advertising*. London: Michael Joseph, 1965.

Turner, Frank Miller. *Between Science and Religion: The Reaction to Scientific Naturalism in Late Victorian England*. New Haven: Yale University Press, 1974.

Unilever. *The History of Unilever: A Study in Economic Growth and Social Change*. London: Cassell & Co., 1954.

Vance, Norman. *The Sinews of the Spirit*. Cambridge: Cambridge University Press, 1985.

Venkatesan, M. and Jean Lasco. "Women in Magazine Advertisements." *Journal of Advertising Review*. v. 15, 1975, pp. 49–54.

Vestergaard, Torben and Kim Schroder. *The Language of Advertising*. Oxford: Basil Blackwell, 1985.

Vicinus, Martha (ed.). *Suffer and Be Still*. Bloomington: Indiana University Press, 1972.

Vicinus, Martha (ed.). *A Widening Sphere*. Bloomington: Indiana University Press, 1977.

Vincenzi, Penny. *Taking Stock: Over 75 Years of the Oxo Cube*. London: Brooke Bond Oxo Ltd., 1985.

Von Arx, Jeffrey Paul. *Progress and Pessimism*. Cambridge: Harvard University Press, 1985.

Wadsworth, A. P. *Newspaper Circulations 1800–1954*. Manchester: Manchester Statistical Society, 1954–1955.

Wagar, W. Warren. *The Idea of Progress Since the Renaissance*. New York: John Wiley & Sons Inc., 1969.

Wagner, Louise and Janis Banos. "A Woman's Place: A Follow-Up Analysis of the Roles Portrayed by Women in Magazine Advertisements." *Journal of Marketing Research*. v. 10, 1973, pp. 213–214.

Walkowitz, Judith. *Prostitution and Victorian Society: Women, Class and the State*. Cambridge: Cambridge Unversity Press, 1980.

Waugh, A. *The Lipton Story*. London: Cassell & Co., 1951.

Weeks, Jeffrey. *Sex, Politics & Society: The Regulation of Sexuality Since 1800*. New York: Longman, 1981.

Weibel, Kathryn. *Mirror, Mirror: Images of Women Reflected in Popular Culture*. New York: Anchor Books, 1977.

Weintraub, Stanley. *Victoria: An Intimate Biography*. New York: E.P. Dutton, 1987.

White, Cynthia. *Women's Magazines 1693–1968*. London: Michael Joseph, 1969.

Wiener, Martin J. *English Culture and the Decline of the Industrial Spirit 1850–1980*. Cambridge: Cambridge University Press, 1981.

Williams, Edmund. *The Story of Sunlight 1884–1984*. London: Unilever, 1984.

Williams, F. *Dangerous Estate*. London: Longmans, Green & Co., 1957.

Williamson, Judith. *Decoding Advertisements: Ideology and Meaning in Advertising*. London: Calder & Boyers Ltd., 1978.

Williams, Raymond. "The Magic System." *The New Left Review*. v. 4, 1960, pp. 27–32.

Wills, Geoffrey. *Victorian Glass*. London: G. Bell, 1976.

Wilson, Adrian. "The Infancy of the History of Childhood: An Appraisal of Philllipe Aries," *History and Theory*. v. 19, pp. 132–154.

Wilson, C. H. *The History of Unilever*. London: Cassell & Co., 1954.

Wohl, A. *The Victorian Family*. London: Croom Helm, 1978.

Wohl, A. *Endangered Lives*. London: Dent, 1983.

Wolff, Janet and John Seed (eds.). *Culture of Capital: Art, Power and the Nineteenth Century Middle Class*. Manchester: Manchester University Press, 1988.

Wood, Christopher. *Victorian Panorama: Paintings of Victorian Life*. London: Faber, 1976.

Young, Harvey. *Toadstool Millionaires*. Princeton: Princeton University Press, 1961.

Young, Robert A. "The Impact of Darwin on Conventional Thought," *The Victorian Crisis of Faith*. Anthony Symondson (ed.). London: SPCK, 1970.

Index